THE LOW SKY
Understanding the Dutch

If you ask for traditional Dutch dishes, there is a good chance this will be one of them: boerenkool met worst. *The* worst *is smoked pork sausage and the* boerenkool *is curly kale mixed with mashed potatoes. Thick gravy makes the whole dish really appetizing.* Boerenkool met worst *is only eaten in the winter, and then by no means every day.*

HAN VAN DER HORST

The Low Sky

The book that makes the Netherlands familiar

Understanding the Dutch

SCRIPTUM/NUFFIC

Contents

Every cloud has a silver lining.

Prologue

The first edition of 'The Low Sky' was published in 1995. Each time the book was reprinted, I updated it. At first, that was not so difficult. I added a prologue which gradually expanded as I described the most recent events and developments in the lives of the Dutch people. From the beginning, the prologue expressed the increasing concern and unrest at the heart of Dutch society. That feeling has now become acute, especially after the murders of politician Pim Fortuyn and film-maker Theo van Gogh. The Netherlands of the twenty-first century is no longer just a variant of that of 1995. It is a society undergoing radical change.

Of course much from the earlier editions is still fresh, lasting and topical. I had to keep that. Yet 'The Low Sky' too has undergone radical change. Different times call for a different book.

Han van der Horst
Schiedam, Autumn 2006

Introduction

When the Dutch think of their country, there is a very good chance that the image in their minds will contain a few clouds. They can hardly imagine the sky above their heads without them. In the Golden Age of the seventeenth century, Rembrandt and his colleagues rarely painted a blue and cloudless sky. And here, when they want to spirit themselves, they will say: *Achter de wolken schijnt de zon,* behind the clouds, the sun is shining, the equivalent of the English expression 'Every cloud has a silver lining.' In earlier times – and perhaps for some people still today – cloudy skies, rainstorms and gales made them think of their fierce *Heere God,* the Lord God, striking out and punishing them for their worldliness and lack of faith.

The people of the Netherlands live under a low sky. They are accustomed to looking out across endless, flat countryside. Their view of the horizon is, at the most, obstructed by a distant dyke, or perhaps a few high-rise buildings in the next town. Yet above them, they rarely see the endless firmament. Those who live in the urban west of the country will see at most one or two stars, even on the clearest of nights. The rest simply cannot compete with the artificial light radiating from the cities, the factories and the glasshouses. This light covers such a large area and is so bright that it can be seen by astronauts orbiting in the International Space Station. So even at night, the Dutch sleep under a low sky.

A book like this could be seen as a kind of 'survival guide' for those living under the low sky of the Netherlands, perhaps a set of instructions for understanding the Dutch. The Dutch themselves are cautious about offering a helping hand. They think that everyone should be allowed to decide and find things out for themselves. They do not impose, wishing to be left in peace themselves unless they have given clear indications to the contrary. And a book sits on a shelf in a bookshop – you can take it or leave it.

The question is, then, what is 'Dutch'? Clogs, tulips, St. Nicholas, the canals in Amsterdam, the Delta Project, a damp southwest wind in your face as you walk on the dyke, the flat expanse of the polders with their pedigree Frisian cattle. They are all part of the overall picture, but for 90% of Dutch people they mean little or nothing at all. Anyone who lives here for an extended period of time becomes acquainted with a completely different reality. These things are all typical but not representative.

The *'Oude Maasweg'* in Rotterdam is far more representative.

> *Ik zit hier op de snelweg met een lege tank.*
> *Regen klettert op het dak.*
> *Ik zal nu wel naar huis toe moeten liften,*
> *'k denk aan jou bij elke stap.*
> *In de verte blijft de Transit staan.*
> *Ik kom nooit meer van je los.*
> *Ik zie de Caltex in een nevel,*
> *olievlekken op de Maas.*
> *Ik loop maar door,*
> *maar ik kan nergens heen.*
> *Het regent nog steeds*
> *en ik voel mij zo alleen,*
> *nu ik je nooit meer zie.*
> *Oude Maasweg, kwart voor drie.*

> I'm sitting on the highway, with an empty tank
> The rain beating down on the roof.
> Now I'll have to hitchhike home,
> And with every step I'll be thinking of you.
> The Transit gets smaller as I move away.
> I'll never be able to forget you.
> I can see the Caltex through the haze,
> Oil flecks floating on the Maas.
> I walk on,
> I've nowhere to run.
> It's still raining
> And I feel so alone
> Since you went away.
> Oude Maasweg, a quarter to three.

This is a rough translation of the first hit for the Amazing Stroopwafels, well-known in the Netherlands and world-famous in the Rotterdam area. We, the fans, never let them get away without playing this song. The lyrics of *'Oude Maasweg'* have become a part of the spiritual baggage of a whole generation from that part of the country. The song is based on Leon Russel's 'Manhattan Island Serenade'. The Stroopwafels acknowledge that debt by printing their own lyrics side by side with those of the original, which goes as follows:

Sitting on a highway
In a broken van
Thinking of you again.
Guess I'll have to hitchhike
To the station.
With every step I see your face
Like a mirror looking back at me,
Saying you are the only one
Making me feel
I could survive
And so glad to be alive.
Nowhere to run and
Not a guitar to play
Messed up inside,
And it's been raining all day
Since you went away,
Manhattan Island Serenade.

In the Dutch version, the rain is heavier and more tangible. There is an implicit reference to environmental degradation. The geographical information is a lot more detailed and the pain is expressed in shorter – in my view, less poetic – words and phrases. Yet the two have a great deal in common. Large cities tend to be similar and New York undoubtedly has an *Oude Maasweg* of its own. Countries and peoples have their own characters, but these cannot be captured in a superficial glance at their folklore. A global culture has also grown up, with its own image and its own symbols. It is a part of modern industrial society and is expressed in popular culture, fashion, new inventions and lifestyles. In the final paragraph of his essay *De stad als kunststuk*, The city as a work of art, published in 1987, the Amsterdam cultural sociologist Abram de Swaan explains why this is:

'This is the city which can straddle an ocean and set the tone for the cultural life of this continent, which – as a genuine global metropolis – not only dominates the culture of its own nation, but is also the centre of everything that goes on throughout the continent and, ultimately, between the cultures of all the other continents. This is New York, the focal point of Atlantis, the cultural capital of Europe.'

In another article, *Perron Nederland*, Platform Netherlands, De Swaan defines this influence, with New York at its centre (but explicitly not as the centre of cultural imperialism), as the internationalization of culture. He also uses the term 'global culture'. He writes:

'The internationalization of the Netherlands is taking place at two levels. Firstly, there is an increasing actual interdependence between the Netherlands and the

The pleasures of bathing and widely differing ideas on modesty. Many Dutch people suspect Muslims of wanting to ban all the good things of life.

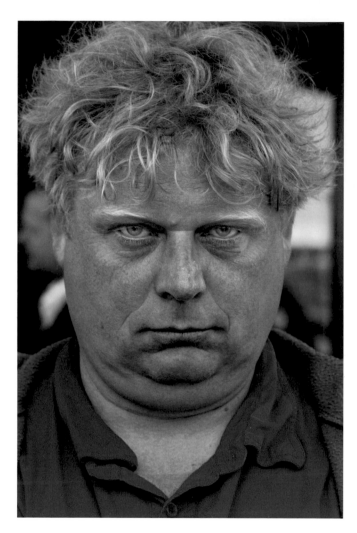

Theo van Gogh, director of the film Submission, *who was killed in 2004.*

rest of the world, particularly the countries around the Atlantic. Secondly, Dutch culture – and Dutch mass culture in particular – is increasingly taking its lead from global culture, and from American culture in particular.'

Previously, in *Verdriet en lied van de kosmopoliet*, The sorrow of the cosmopolitan, (1985), De Swaan welcomed this new global culture:

'Every week the dance halls are sold out because there is an African band playing. Twenty-five years ago, African musical groups also came to the Netherlands. The women danced bare-breasted while a man beat a drum. Everyone thought it was very interesting and authentic but that was as far as it went. The music played by the African groups who come here now is "bastardized", a shameless mixture

In 2002 Pim Fortuyn suddenly emerged from the wings with a nationalist message, in which fear of Islamic domination played a major role.

of tribal folklore, Islamic chanting, Caribbean carnival and pure American commercial sounds. More a mishmash than a synthesis, it is lively and loud and it never stops. This is the cosmopolitan culture, it has broken loose from its tribal roots, thrown off the shackles that bound it to the village.'

De Swaan concludes: 'The Netherlands is a station on that worldwide circuit. The function and value of the Dutch language and culture is that it allows you to step in and out of that world. A nation is but a platform for the outside world.'

There is a certain optimism in De Swaan's observations. He sees cultural inter-nationalization – epitomized by New York, as the world's cultural broker – as a positive trend. He wrote his essays long before two aircraft were deliberately flown into the Twin Towers. 9/11, as this fateful day is now known with no further elaboration necessary, meant an attack on the cultural brokerage and the meeting place of global cultures that New York City stands for. It was an assault of closed minds against openness, against the *Umwertung aller Werte*, against the spirit of curiosity and doubt that arises when dogmas crumble and wide horizons are opened up, as once – according to Vondel's poem – the Amstel and the Ij did for the Amsterdam of Rembrandt.

Since 9/11, the city and globalized society are no longer seen as a meeting place, or – as the old American cliché would have it – a melting pot. Many observers see rather a 'clash of cultures'. This was the title of the controversial book by American researcher Samuel Huntington, which caused such a furore in the 1990s. Huntington predicted a conflict between closed and open cultures for world domination in the near future. For many people, the attack on the Twin Towers, Islamic fundamentalism and movements like Al-Qaeda can be understood in these terms. As a result of globalization, countries are no longer the carriers of specific cultures, but population groups who live in close proximity to each other and who pass on their own characteristics from generation to generation. Mass migration does not result in a melting pot, but leads to groups of people living close to and yet separately from each other.

In recent years, many opinion leaders in the Netherlands seem to have adopted these views. They feel that the Dutch way of life, as it has evolved throughout the ages, is under threat from the inside by a migrant culture which isolates itself from the wide range of lifestyles, religions and faiths in its immediate surroundings. In the views of these militants, the murders of politician Pim Fortuyn and film-maker Theo van Gogh – whose thinking was strongly influenced by Huntington's theories – simply prove what they already suspect.

Does this undermine De Swaan's observations? The fact that there have been serious clashes does not mean that the process of cultural internationalization can be checked. It is even possible that terrorism is a manifestation of that process. The message terrorists hope to convey through their actions is, after all, aimed at the whole world. They make demands of all humanity. And they use the technology of globalization to increase the impact of their deeds. It may be more accurate to say that the process De Swaan identifies has lost its innocence, that it has shown its less attractive side.

That is what this book will do, too. And that is why it is not about tulips, clogs and St. Nicholas. There are already plenty of books available for non-Dutch readers who want to know more about these. The same goes for cycling. The bicycle is an excellent means of transport as long as you don't have to go uphill. And there are few hills in the Netherlands. Other than that there is little to say about it. This book takes another path, looking not so much at the way the Dutch look but at how they behave. It tries to give the reader an insight into the mentality that determines the way they live.

How can we understand this mentality better? The Royal Tropical Institute in Amsterdam has been conducting research into other cultures for over a hundred years. The institute has put this experience to practical use in a rather unusual way by offering courses to introduce foreigners to the Dutch way of life. The course identifies five traits that are characteristic of Dutch society: egalitarian, utilitarian, organized, trade-oriented and privacy-minded. Practically all the phenomena which a foreigner who comes to live here for any length of time will be confronted with – and which may at first lead to amazement, shock, anger or despair – are dealt with under one or more of these five categories. This book devotes a chapter to each of the epithetic traits which the Royal Tropical Institute attributes to the Dutch.

Supporters of the Dutch football team, known as Oranje *because it always plays in the colours of the Royal Family. In recent years, the fans have dressed themselves increasingly in carnival style. 'Act normally, that's crazy enough?' This is, of course, an example of group behaviour. Among all the other supporters this fan of the Dutch national team is not conspicuous. But he would never go shopping dressed like this. After all, no one wants to stand out in the crowd.*

1

Egalitarian

Let those who have abundance remember that they are surrounded with thorns

Act normally, that's crazy enough. Real wealth keeps a low profile. No one should dominate. The principle of consensus. The 'normal' image of the monarchy. Calvinist hard doctrine and soft practice. Sovereignty in one's own domain. The embarrassment of riches. The avoidance of risks. The welfare society. The new primacy of the individual.

Few people in the Netherlands have heard of Carel Nolet, but his 'Ketel 1' *jenever* is to be found on the shelves of any liquor store. Nolet's success is based on a clever marketing strategy. He lays heavy emphasis on the fact that his family company has been in business since 1695, leading the consumer to believe that what he is drinking is the product of three centuries of craftsmanship and experience. This strategy is successful – and is reflected in the price of the product – as can be seen from the large number of requests received from people wishing to come and visit what is apparently a traditional company. The visitors find themselves in a highly efficient, computerized distillery, which produces not only Ketel 1, but also a whole range of other drinks.

Ketel 1 vodka – specially developed for discerning drinkers in the United States – was once promoted by means of a prize-winning film for wholesalers in the United States. The film could, however, not be shown in the Netherlands without explanation. Carel Nolet appears in the film once only, driving in his Daimler. It is explained to Dutch viewers that the Daimler was rented especially for the film. The boss does not, of course, really drive around in a car like that. Toonder Studios, the makers of the film, had insisted that the Daimler was necessary for the American market. If the director did not drive a luxury car – and a European one at that – the US wholesalers might have their doubts about the company's solidity.

To Dutch eyes, the effect is exactly the opposite. The Daimler is proof that the director wants to show what an important man he is. He obviously has no loyalties towards the company. You can see from the car where the profits go to. With such an arrogant man at the helm, Ketel 1 won't last long. And above all, Ketel 1 is not cheap – why should we pay for the boss's car?

Minister of Justice Piet Hein Donner gets onto his bicycle in front of Huis ten Bosch palace. He has just presented Queen Beatrix with his recommendations for the formation of a new government. Note the lackey on the right, who has just brought the minister's bicycle from the bike shelter.

The Dutch viewers of the Ketel 1 film are easily convinced by the Daimler story. A clever idea, renting a limousine for a day to impress foreign customers. They are thinking to themselves: luckily we're not like that, here in the Netherlands. *Doe maar gewoon, dan doe je al gek genoeg.* Just act normally, that's crazy enough. But if we have to do something crazy to earn a few pennies abroad, so what? *Je moet iedereen in zijn waarde laten.* To each his own.

Early in 2006 Hans Anders, a chain of opticians, brought out a very Dutch television commercial. A man who was supposed to be Hans Anders arrived home at his humble flat in the 'company car', a Fiat 600. What looked like a flat-screen TV on the wall proved to be a big old model that had been set into the brickwork. And that was how Hans Anders could be so cheap. As all Dutch people know, *zuinigheid met vlijt bouwt huizen als kastelen.* With thrift and hard work you can build a castle.

No hovels, but no palaces either

The phrases in italics in the previous section are well-known Dutch sayings. At first sight they appear contradictory. The first is an appeal to conformist behaviour, while the second gives everyone the right to choose their own lifestyle, even though it may be a little strange. The third advocates a diligent and thrifty life – prosperity does not just fall into your lap, you have to earn it. But this is no excuse for extravagance. There are few castles in the Netherlands. There are no hovels but no palaces, either. Even the 'palaces' inhabited by the Royal Family are actually oversized villas and are in no way comparable with Versailles, Sans Souci, Buckingham Palace or Windsor Castle.

The popular press regularly publishes pictures of the goings-on at eccentric and fetishist gatherings like the notorious Wasteland parties and what they show would certainly cause the average family man to raise an eyebrow. But there is one thing missing – jewellery. In the Netherlands, eccentric party-goers do not decorate their slave belts with gold or diamonds – even though their bank accounts might justify such extravagance. This would provoke an aggressive response from the wider public. As it is, the proceedings at such get-togethers are followed with a kind of bemused interest, but not with anger or revulsion. *Ze zoeken het maar uit*. What they do is their business.

'Probably the wildest party on earth,' Wasteland boasts on its website. Yet in the daytime many regular customers are barely distinguishable from the rest of the

Since the last quarter of the twentieth century, Dutch architects have returned to more traditional ways of building. This brand-new estate is reminiscent of the building styles of the 1920s and 1930s. The little boy is growing up in an environment that is similar to the one his grandparents knew as children.

crowd, going about their business in their nondescript outfits. This puts into proportion the apparent contradiction between the conformist motto *Doe maar gewoon, dan doe je al gek genoeg* and the more liberal *Laat iedereen in zijn waarde*, to each his own.

For the genuinely rich, a low profile is practically a commandment

The number of millionaires in the Netherlands has been growing for several decades, and reached 102,600 in 2004. Their combined worth was 253 billion euros. Per capita annual income in the country has risen above 30,000 dollars, more than six times higher than half a century ago. Multinationals like Shell and Philips are largely based on Dutch soil. Financial consortia such as ABN AMRO and RABO are among the top twenty international banks, but the super-rich, are not so easy to recognize. For the genuinely rich, a low profile is practically a commandment. In the thirties, many a minister still took the tram to the ministry. Although their modern counterparts may now have a chauffeur-driven car, this is by no means taken for granted. Piet Hein Donner, Minister of Justice in the Balkenende governments, goes to work every day on a classic black enamelled bicycle, undoubtedly made in the Netherlands. He sits straight up as he cycles, a posture that has become the trademark of this intellectual descendant of a Calvinist family that has produced leading scholars and politicians for more than a century. But Donner, too, has an official car with a chauffeur for longer journeys. High-ranking politicians and members of the business community justify this luxury by referring to their overfull schedules and saying how easy it is to work in the back of a limousine. Captains of industry follow their example. They protect their privacy by living in large country houses, often in places like Wassenaar or Aardenhout, favoured by millionaires but still modest by international standards. They exercise their influence through the boardroom and avoid the glare of publicity. The average company director – and the same is true of politicians and top civil servants – will not often attribute his successes to his own talents. At least, not in public. He will insist to the contrary that it was a team effort, that it would never have been achieved without the dedication and hard work of those around him. This he – and it is almost always a 'he'; women may be gaining ground in middle management, but have not as yet penetrated the very top, especially in the world of big business – this he will do, at least if he is sensible, otherwise he will bear the brunt of contemptuous public opinion.

The families of these great men remain firmly in the background. Not that the partners of the Dutch elite are content to spend their time flower arranging. They often try to build careers for themselves, but then in a way that has nothing to do with their partners. Respect for the privacy of others prevents the kind of curiosity which, only an hour's flight away to the west, ruins many a politician's career in London. This never happens in the Netherlands. During the election campaign in 2002, a gossip magazine published the rumour that Ad Melkert, the leader of the PVDA (the Dutch Labour Party) was a regular visitor to S&M-clubs. Melkert did not respond the allegations and the party's spokesperson announced that it made no comments on the candidates' private lives. That put an end to the affair. Melkert's great rival, the very successful political newcomer Pim Fortuyn, took a different tack. He was not ashamed of his extravagant homosexual lifestyle, discussed the taste of sperm on the radio, and responded in the press to an imam who had accused him of xenophobia by saying: 'I know a lot of Moroccan men – I go to bed with them.' The general reaction from the public was that that was his business. Public persons should be judged by their public acts and not by what they choose to do in their private lives. The conviction that this is not as interesting as it might seem is illustrated by the fact that so many Dutch people leave their curtains open at night, giving a clear view of their conventional, well-made furniture and their tidy, dust-free living rooms. Despite his extravagant personality and lifestyle, Pim Fortuyn missed the good old days, when young people would give up their seats in the tram to the elderly. He called for a return to the old norms and values. His main – and genuine – concern was how people behaved in public, not in their living rooms or bedrooms. Yet the open curtains still seem to be a sign that so many Dutch people wish to show that, unlike the otherwise very popular Pim Fortuyn, they also act 'normally' in their private lives. This provides much food for thought. The Dutch word *kamertjeszonde*, for example, is a good starting point. The word,

Pim Fortuyn greets opponents who compare him with Jörg Haider, the extreme-right leader from Austria ('Stop Holland's Haider'). Disarming behaviour on all sides!

[23]

which has no English equivalent, is defined in the Dutch dictionary, as 'vice, with a hint of small-mindedness, of being commonplace'. The suggestion is of petit-bourgeois suburbia, with small-scale lasciviousness going on behind closed doors. Yet those who place too much credence in such ideas are on the same thin ice as protohistorians who attempt to reconstruct an 'original society'. The fact of the matter is, the curtains are open and they reveal an overwhelming homogeneity.

Throughout the centuries, many travellers have been struck by these aspects of Dutch society. The way they have interpreted or commented on what they have seen depends to a certain extent on their own tastes. We find in their works enthusiastic descriptions of the Dutch sense of tolerance and democracy, evoking images of a multi-facetted and multicoloured society. But also of dull paintings of a conformist, colourless mass of people. More than a century ago, the Portuguese writer Ramalho Ortigão held the Netherlands up to his fellow countrymen as an example, for its openness and its progressive outlook. In the 1980s, his compatriot Rentes de Carvalho entitled a similar treatise 'Where the other God lives'. This was a cold-weather God, keeping watch over a puritan society which confuses its indifference with tolerance. *Adieu, canards, canaux, canaille,* Voltaire is supposed to have said, after a brief visit to the Netherlands. And German social researcher Ernst Zahn, a professor for many years at the University of Amsterdam, complains about an academic climate which reduces everything to the predictable. This is a long way from the magical attraction that gave Amsterdam a reputation, in the 1960s, almost equal to that of swinging London or San Francisco, where you went with flowers in your hair. At that time, the Netherlands was seen as the focus of international renewal, where people experimented with new lifestyles, a first encounter with what was later to be called the 'post-industrial society'. The keyword for the time was *ludiek*, playful – in other words, the very opposite of 'normal'.

Yet, even in those years, the open curtains revealed a conventional three-piece suite and the grey glow of a television set (colour had not yet arrived). And Piet de Jong, the prime minister throughout that period, watched all the 'fun' with a bemused smile on his face. He was a conservative Catholic and an ex-submarine captain. His position was never under threat – not for one minute.

And yet – it must be said again – this conventional Dutch society demands a far lower price for unconventional behaviour than many others do. This mentality has developed over many generations and is closely related to the history of the Dutch state.

The idea of the Netherlands as an entity in itself is only a couple of hundred years old. In the Middle Ages, in the delta where the Rhine, Maas and Scheldt reach the sea – the area now covered by the Netherlands and Belgium – there was no single uniting monarchy. The area was divided into a large number of counties and duchies which were to all intents and purposes independent. Most present-day provinces have their origins in these small states and their borders are still often recognizable.

They were feudal states. Social relations were based on personal dependence, where the weak pledged their loyalty to the strong in exchange for protection and other privileges. These relations became increasingly hereditary in nature and could become incredibly complicated, not least because the counts and dukes – the 'great nobles' – seldom possessed the military power to actually enforce loyalty. They therefore found themselves increasingly forced to buy off their positions by granting new privileges to their subjects.

This situation became even more acute with the emergence of a new class of merchants, whose only aim was to accumulate money, something which the nobles, traditional landowners with a loathing for business, were chronically short of. Anywhere where the minimum requirements for a safe existence could be guaranteed, settlements grew up of the kind that, these days, we would call 'towns'. Shortage of money and the pursuit of power forced the nobles to grant these settlements all kinds of rights, to the extent of allowing them a certain degree of self-rule in exchange for their loyalty or their cash. The oldest document in which the name Amsterdam appears, contains a privilege granted by Floris v, the Count of Holland, in 1275. He exempted the inhabitants of the city from paying tolls within his area of jurisdiction, undoubtedly with the ulterior motive of wooing them away from his competitors, the Lords of Aemstel.

It is tempting to see this development as an early form of democracy, as a whole array of 'historical' ideologies later did with great enthusiasm, but this is a misconception. In the final analysis, it was a very complex system of special privileges and – even though the documents concerned referred to a specific region, village or castle – agreements between families. In the cities, too, power was concentrated in the hands of a small number of families.

Eventually, all the counties and duchies came into the hands of the Habsburgs, the family that also wore the crown of the Holy Roman Empire. It was a complicated process that took more than a century of strategic marriages and inheritances, which often had to be claimed by force of arms. The upshot was that by 1540, the area around the estuaries of the Maas, Rhine and Scheldt had a single sovereign lord, the emperor Charles v, who referred to these possessions as the lowlands or Netherlands. He, too, had inherited a whole complex of rights and privileges, which in effect restricted his power to the extent that he reaped small benefit from his position.

Charles v attempted to impose order and unity on this chaotic situation. He appointed a regent for the whole region, who resided in Brussels. He also appointed in each county or duchy a lieutenant or stadholder, who was authorized to use the royal seal and who – with lines of communication being so slow and difficult – enjoyed considerable freedom to make his own decisions. Generally speaking, the emperor chose important nobles for these positions who had a personal connection with the region. One of these was William of Nassau-Dillenburg, Prince of Orange, who had grown up at court in Brussels. He was chosen because his family owned large estates in the Duchy of Brabant, of which Brussels was the capital at that time.

*William of Orange,
father of the Fatherland
(aka William the Silent),
in middle age.*

Anyone studying the European history of the sixteenth and seventeenth centuries will come across countless disputes between centralized monarchs and subjects claiming rights dating back to the Middle Ages. Generally speaking, the monarchs won these disputes. France and Spain are the most striking examples of such victories. In the Netherlands, however, the reverse happened. The outcome of what the Dutch proudly refer to as the 'Eighty-Years' War' (1568–1648) was that these medieval rights and privileges continued to be the basis of their polity.

After Charles v had abdicated, the Netherlands passed into the hands of his son Philip, better known as Philip ii of Spain. The Spanish crown had succeeded in depriving most of its subjects of their *fueros*, their privileges. Philip ii, a consistent man, instigated a similar process in the Netherlands. He also attacked Protestantism with far greater vigour than his father, enforcing a long-existent law under which the practice of religious beliefs other than Roman Catholicism (heresy) was punishable with death by fire.

In the Netherlands there was a certain amount of sympathy for the reformist tendencies in the church that were springing up throughout Europe after Luther's protest in 1517. Not that there was a any real schism to speak of, but the new ways of thinking were finding support in leading circles in the city and in the countryside, and even within the church itself. It was a little like the 1960s when, without actually being a communist yourself, you could summon up a certain appreciation for 'Uncle Ho', Chairman Mao and Che Guevara.

Erasmus, the internationally renowned thinker, was in some ways a typical example of this tendency. For many years, people did not know whether he should be considered a reformer or a trusty Catholic. These elites therefore tended not to make too great an effort to persecute genuine Protestants, travelling preachers and manifest heretics, in spite of pressure to do so from far-off Spain. This even applied to the followers of John Calvin.

Calvinists were subject to a very strict code of behaviour

Most of them live in the country, but anyone who is sufficiently acquainted with them, can recognize them in the larger towns and cities, too. They are the followers of the 'black-stocking' church. On Sundays, you can see whole families hurrying along the street, the women in long dresses with their heads covered, the men in overwhelmingly dark suits, with perhaps a slightly more cheerful grey here and there. The traditional black stockings may have been replaced by slightly more colourful designs, but the general feeling is one of humility and a sense of guilt.

They are on their way to the first of the two hour-long church services they always attend on this, the Lord's Day. There they sing His praises in long drawn-out tones, but the focal point of the service is the sermon. The minister rebukes them all without mercy, his talent for oration, the fruits of centuries of development, reducing him to tears. 'Let but one be saved!' the preacher calls out in desperation, for their God is above all a wrathful judge who ruthlessly separates the chosen from the great mass of sinners who shall be cast into the fires of hell.

The believers avoid all that 'conforms to the world', since this surely leads to eternal damnation. By this they mean all that gives life its colour – fashionable clothing, going out, films and – although this is shunned to a lesser extent these days – the television. This strict faith has as many as 600,000 followers in the Netherlands, largely concentrated in a wide band stretching from Zeeland in the southwest to Overijssel in the northeast, where they sometimes impress their heavy stamp on entire rural communities. They consider themselves the true descendants of Calvin. They believe that, unlike the large Protestant communities, they have not prostituted his legacy to the world and its sinful temptations.

Next to Martin Luther, Calvin was the most influential reformer in the history of Christendom. Not only for his theological teaching but for the new form of organization he developed for the church. His spirit and his beliefs had far-reaching effects in the Netherlands.

Man, said Calvin, is by nature bad. Through the mercy of God alone can a chosen

John (Jean) Calvin, the French reformer who is the inspiration for almost all the Protestant churches in the Netherlands. Here he is depicted in a contemporary portrayal of the beeldenstorm *of 1566, when his followers destroyed the interiors of churches because the statues of the saints were considered a form of idolatry.*

few be saved. But this is not a reward for their merits. Calvin believed that God determined in advance which fortunates would inherit the kingdom of heaven and who would be cast down into hell. And yet, each of us is responsible for his own fate and his relationship with the Almighty. All of this is laid down in the Bible, the only source of knowledge of the divine.

This led to a strict code of beliefs and behaviour which left no room for Catholic pomp and circumstance. Calvinists had to lead their lives according to this code. Most of life's small pleasures, such as playing cards or dice, dancing or going to the theatre were seen as cardinal sins. And, in imitation of the Sabbath of the Orthodox Jews, Sunday was a day of complete rest.

Diligence and the exercise of one's duty, on the other hand, were virtues, as were simplicity in clothing and behaviour. Most Protestant churches in the Netherlands consider themselves Calvinist, but it is only the smaller and more radical communities that still embrace it in its purest form. Calvin designed a model for the church in which preachers were appointed by elected church councils of true Calvinists. These councils were empowered to place all of the members of the church under their supervision. This meant that they could impose a wide variety of punishments on those who did not adhere to the code of behaviour or who held deviant opinions. It was a typical model of leadership by a disciplined vanguard and bore close resemblance to the organization devised three centuries later by Lenin to bring about the victory of Bolshevism. And it was a perfect breeding ground for conspiracies.

The effectiveness of this form of organization became clear when events became far too complex and began to move too fast for a simple book such as this. In outline what happened was that in 1566 – a year of crisis and famine – the dissatisfied populace, led by Calvinists, began to destroy the interiors of churches because the statues of the saints were considered a form of idolatry. In response to this unrest, which was particularly fierce in Flanders, Philip II appointed a new regent in Brussels, the Duke of Alva. Alva is still considered one of the great villains of Dutch history. During the German occupation, many made the comparison – and not without reason – to Adolf Hitler. He arrived with an army of occupation, introduced a special court for religious offences and forced the local elites – who had petitioned the king to be tolerant – to make a clear choice, for or against. Just to show he meant business, he had two prominent figures who had signed the petition beheaded. A third, William of Orange, escaped to Germany just in time.

And drive the plague that try us and tyranny away

Alva the Tyrant's foulest deed, however, was the 'tenth penny' tax on commercial transactions, which he imposed on the orders of Philip II. The tax ignored all existing rights and privileges and is better remembered by later generations than Alva's religious persecution. There is another Dutch expression that expresses this indignation: *het in je portemonnee voelen*, to suffer in your pocket. Intervention of this kind invokes great emotions among the Dutch.

The Calvinist vanguard now came into its own, part of it transforming itself into a guerrilla movement with little difficulty. They were known as the *geuzen*. *Geus* is a bastardization of the French word *gueux*, meaning beggar. This was a reference to those who had signed the petition asking for tolerance. There were *Bosgeuzen*, who operated from the safety of the forests, and *Watergeuzen* who attacked from the sea. William of Orange and his brothers used their wealth to assemble armies of mercenaries which they used to make unsuccessful attacks against Alva's troops. It was finally the *Watergeuzen* who gained a foothold in a number of towns in the County of Holland from 1572 onwards. This led to a series of disconnected revolts

throughout the Netherlands which were not initially directed against Philip II but against his unjust servants. William of Orange more or less declared himself leader of the whole movement. Around this time, an anonymous bard wrote the battle hymn *Wilhelmus* which, in 15 verses, encapsulates the ideology of the revolt. It is now the official national anthem of the Netherlands and every Dutch man, woman and child knows the first few lines:

> *Wilhelmus van Nassauwe
> ben ik van Duitsen bloed
> den vaderlande getrouwe,
> blijf ik tot in den dood.
> Een prince van Oranje,
> ben ik vrij onverveerd,
> de koning van Hispanje
> heb ik altijd geëerd.*

> William of Nassau,
> Scion of a Dutch and ancient line,
> I dedicate undying faith
> To this land of mine
> A prince I am, undaunted,
> Of Orange, ever free,
> To the King of Spain
> I've granted a lifelong loyalty.

The part about the king is sung out in long, sustained tones and is little understood by current generations. This is, however, not true of the sixth verse, the only part of the rest of the anthem with which many people are familiar:

Mijn schild ende betrouwen
zijt gij, o God, mijn heer,
op U, zo wil ik bouwen,
verlaat mij nimmermeer.
Op dat ik vroom mag blijven,
Uw dienaar, t' aller tijd,
De tyrannie verdrijven,
die mij het hart doorwondt.

A shield and my reliance,
O God, thou ever wert.
I'll trust unto Thy guidance
O leave me not ungirt.
That I may stay a pious
Servant of Thine for aye
And drive the plagues that try us
And tyranny away.

These two verses contain three crucial elements: the central role of William of Orange as the leader of the movement, the appeal to God for help and the desire to drive out tyranny.

Revolt always leads to radicalization. If the opposing party then becomes more acceptable to the more moderate elements by adopting a conciliatory approach, a new situation arises. Philip II created such a situation through a rather clever combination of force and concessions. In 1579, those provinces which still refused to be reconciled signed the Union of Utrecht in the city of that name. Two years later, they solemnly released themselves from their Oath of Allegiance to the king. They based this act on a revolutionary ideology – that monarchs did not receive their authority from God, but from a contract with the lower levels of government, who were entitled to displace the sovereign if he (or she) should resort to tyranny.

The signatories to the Union of Utrecht repudiated Philip ii. It would also have been logical to abolish the office of stadholder, the king's representative in each of the provinces, but this did not occur. After all, William of Orange, the unofficial leader of the revolt was a stadholder. The office remained intact until the end of the Republic in 1795. And the position was always filled by a member of the family of Orange, so that it gradually acquired the characteristics of a monarchy. In practice, sons succeeded their fathers, although there were occasional long periods during which the Province of Holland had no stadholder because many regents were afraid of the power of Orange. The family also enjoyed considerable support among the common people who, in their turn, saw the successors of William the liberator as their protectors against the urban patricians who sat on the Council.

Philip ii wrongly saw William of Orange as the evil genius behind all this. He declared the prince an outlaw and then sent secret service hitman after him.

In 1584, they succeeded. The prince was the first of a long line of politicians throughout the world to die by the gun. The bullet hole in the wall can still be seen in Delft. The Union of Utrecht, an alliance between a number of former counties and duchies, lasted until 1795.

As time passed the Union began to function as a kind of constitution, eventually forming the administrative foundation of the 'Republic of the United Provinces', as the country was known in the seventeenth and eighteenth centuries. It was, however, a rather unstable foundation, based as it was on the preservation of rights, privileges and exceptional provisions that dated back to the Middle Ages.

The same was true of the constitutions of the individual provinces, whose extremely complex structure more or less gave them the form of feudal states. And, to complicate the situation even more, they also acquired territories that were subject to their authority. There was no central rule to speak of. The provincial governments, known as States, sent representatives to The Hague, where they formed what was known as the States General. But they were only able to take decisions on which there was unanimous agreement.

In a system of this kind, there was little to be achieved by hauteur

In a system of this kind – if it can even be described as a system – there was little to be achieved by *hauteur*. It was better to adopt a cautious, conciliatory approach accompanied by a discreet shake of the purse when required. The fact that this actually resulted in cooperation was due to two factors: firstly, the existence of a common enemy (there was usually one of some kind) and secondly that, in spite of the king's authority being repudiated, the system of stadholders had been maintained. The position was always held by a member of the family of Orange, who successfully managed to increase their power from generation to generation. To achieve this, however, they had to strike up alliances, since they were never able to break down the complex structures of authority. It was also to their advantage that Orange could generally count on the support of the mass of the people. If necessary, they would not hesitate to use the threat of popular uprising as a political factor. The popularity of the royal family today has its roots in this tradition.

Yet none of this provided sufficient cohesion to prevent the eventual disintegration of the Republic. There was a third factor – the Province of Holland. Holland was by far the richest of the seven provinces and bore a good 70% of the joint costs of the Republic. This gave it a dominant voice in affairs of state. The radical Calvinists had succeeded in setting the tone of the revolt. But as the situation stabilized more and more on the side of the Union of Utrecht, they began to lose their grip on the local elites. As with their grandparents in the time of Charles v and Philip ii, the members of the elite largely agreed with Calvin's views but many of them were not prepared to subject themselves to his theocratic model, to allow their lives to be run at a distance by the church councils and the strict preachers, who denounced them as 'libertines'. The Calvinist preachers were unable to achieve the 'mullah-like' power they sought and the administrative elite continued in practice to be libertines. They gradually acquired a dominant influence on the church and ultimately relegated the stricter preachers to the sidelines.

Current generations of Dutch people recognize many of the traits of such intolerant preachers of the past in present-day Islamic fundamentalism. That goes a long way to explaining the great mistrust that Islam invokes in many people. The threat of a state dominated by the church is an old Dutch nightmare: the veiled girls on the street remind them too much of Staphorst and other black-stocking villages. And you don't see these girls in the villages, but in the centres of the large cities, which are so proud of their libertine principles. They walk around the Albert Cuypmarkt in Amsterdam, the city that prefers to take pride in its gay parade.

In the seventeenth century, power was concentrated in the hands of the urban elites, who had built their wealth on fisheries, trade and, to a lesser extent, industry. Today, Rotterdam is the largest port of Europe, but then the Province of Holland – and Amsterdam in particular – played a similar role. It was a European distribution centre, not only for bulk goods like timber, grain, fish, sugar and tobacco, but also for luxury articles including East Indian spices, Chinese silk and muslin from India. This gave Holland the highest standard of living in the whole of Europe, a position it managed to maintain well into the eighteenth century.

The role that Amsterdam had at that time in Europe was similar to the position enjoyed by present-day Shanghai with respect to China. It was a glittering metropolis, bulging with wealth, where the economic strings of the whole continent came together, an emporium stacked full of products from throughout the world, a city that earned a living from trade, services and processing raw materials.

The city's elites depended on trade for their wealth. To use a modern term, they had to assure for themselves the right business climate. This meant that people had to be certain of their money under all circumstances. The Amsterdam bank issued coins with a guaranteed precious metal content. There was a whole complex of laws and regulations which, as far as was possible given the constraints of the period, protected businessmen against fraud. Crimes of violence, theft, robbery and other offences against property were subject to draconic punishments, although the chances of being caught were relatively small. Property was sacred and inviolable.

On the other hand, the city's government showed great tolerance, particularly where it might promote prosperity. The rapidly growing province of Holland attracted large numbers of immigrants from throughout Europe. As long as they brought money with them, they were welcome. At the beginning of the seventeenth century, Portuguese Jewish merchants who had been driven from their own country had no trouble in settling in Amsterdam. They were even given a form of internal self-rule. Their synagogues are still among the most splendid buildings in the centre of the city. Destitute refugees from war-torn Germany, however, did not fare so well. The *schutterij*, a kind of citizens' militia (who were immortalized in Rembrandt's painting 'The Night Watch') would descend on them from time to time and force them out of the city or press-gang them into serving with the war fleet.

The government in Holland interfered as little as possible with people's private lives – at least, in as much as it only affected them personally. There was a fairly large Catholic minority throughout the Republic, whose freedom of movement was limited by discriminatory regulations. This was due to the efforts of the Calvinists during the early years of the revolt. The Catholics had lost their churches and were not even permitted to practice their religious beliefs, at least not officially. But as long as Catholic churches were not recognizable as such from the outside, the government generally turned a blind eye. In practice, in spite of clear legislation to the contrary, tolerance had become second nature for political leaders in the Netherlands. And just as a Catholic church was tolerated at that time as long as it looked like a barn or a house, small-scale entrepreneurs may sell soft drugs today, as long as the outlet looks like a coffee shop.

But, as it should be, the government always has the law to fall back on. Catholics who were too outspoken in the Golden Age found this out to their regret. As have modern hash dealers whose coffee machines have, in the eyes of the authorities,

Rembrandt's Night Watch

become a little too symbolic. In recent years, the authorities have become less tolerant. The mayor of Venlo, on the German border, closed coffee shops on the road to the east of the town, because they were too accessible for German customers. More and more local councils have also forced coffee shops close to schools to relocate. This decreasing tolerance also applies to the cultivation of marijuana in glasshouses, attics and garden sheds. Almost daily, there are media reports of the police rounding up yet another batch of illegal weed plantations in some residential district or another. The culprits are usually small producers, but twenty years of experience and refining the plants have resulted in a high-quality product that really blows the mind. The authorities turned a blind eye to this 'cottage industry' for many years, but it has become so widespread and so lucrative that they now see it as a threat to society. Furthermore, they defend the clamp-down with the practical argument that growing marijuana – which has to grow under heavy, hot lamps – is a fire hazard and generates an offensive smell. At the same time, more and more people are calling for the cultivation of marijuana to be legalized, so that growers can become part of the formal economy.

The policy on xtc pills took a similar tack. Revellers at large house parties could get their pills checked to see if they contained dangerous cocktails. Simultaneously the authories tried resolutely, but with little success, to restrict the production of what was rightly seen as a threat to public health. Again, this was inconsistent, but it saved lives, in the same way that clean needles were distributed to drug addicts from an early stage to combat the spread of HIV, in spite of the strict ban on the use of hard drugs.

Regent: today the word has negative connotations

Since the seventeenth century, the word *regent* has been used in Dutch to describe local and provincial administrators. Today, the word has negative connotations. A common definition is: 'A regent is someone who thinks that the people do not know what is good for them. The regent knows better.' This is a direct reference to the Republic of the United Provinces. In the account given above, I deliberately avoided using the word 'democracy'. Administrators were appointed over-whelmingly by co-optation. This ensured that political power remained essentially concentrated in the hands of a small number of leading families. To the outside world, the regents were the *hoogmogende heren*, their 'high mightinesses', their official title. They always acted jointly, expressing their power collectively. This not only gave an impression of power being imposed from above, but also that it was being exercised by a single entity. Michiel de Ruyter, the admiral of the fleet and the bearer of many foreign titles and distinctions, was permitted to sit while reporting to the *hoogmogende heren* rather than stand. This was considered a greater honour than the title of duke, bestowed upon him by a foreign admirer of royal blood.

Rulers from the Golden Age: a group of regents.

As a group the regents gave an impression of great arrogance, but they could not allow themselves to stand out too much as individuals because to do so would endanger the good relations and the culture of compromise in the group. Overly ambitious regents, particularly those who did not try to hide their intentions, were promptly put in their places by their fellows.

We can see the result of this system if we look at the many portraits of regents hanging in the country's museums. They appear self-confident, but not threatening. They are well-dressed, but not conspicuously so. The paraphernalia is modest. Here, too, the order of the day is *doe maar gewoon dan doe je al gek genoeg*. Yet the paintings also capture the aura of excellence that surrounds these high and mighty gentlemen; they feel that they are better than the rest of humanity. They are in control, they know the rules of the game as no other. They have earned the right to take themselves seriously and they clearly do just that. They may be humble, but they are the *hoogmogende heren*. And it would be wise not to forget.

The regents' houses have the same aura. They are always imposing buildings with three of four storeys, but they stand neatly in line alongside the canals of the city. This gives them a certain feeling of equality. Great attention has been devoted to the façades. There are steps up to the front door and decoration on the outer walls. But it would be wrong to call them ornate. Even in the bend of the Herengracht in Amsterdam, roughly between the Leidsestraat and Wolvestraat, which was the richest part of the whole country until deep into the nineteenth century, there is no extravagance. The regents had houses, not palaces, even though they were often financially better off than the average European noble, who would commission a 'Versailles' all of his own. The German scholar Max Weber, one of the founding fathers of sociology, linked all this to Protestantism. In his *Die protestantische Ethik und der Geist des Kapitalismus,* The Protestant Ethic and the Spirit of Capitalism, he explained how the cult of simplicity preached by Calvin not only created the mentality to invest in new and profitable activities but also the money, which was saved rather than squandered on 'wine, women and song' and other examples of Roman Catholic frivolity – such as buying a Daimler. It is an attractive theory, especially for self-aware Calvinists, although it has lost some of its power over the course of time. But Weber's vision – if it is not adopted exclusively and fanatically – continues to be illuminating. The Protestant ideal of self-control was certainly very suited to the calm consultation, the unflappable manner, the cautious step-by-step approach that was required to obtain a share of power in the Republic.

In time this attitude developed into a kind of gentility

In time this attitude, as adopted by the members of the elite, developed into a kind of gentility. The word itself summons up not only good breeding and respectability but the affectedness that can accompany it. It also means the elite itself, those 'of noble birth'. It is very close to what is called in Dutch *uit de hoogte*, roughly the equivalent of the English word 'haughty'. It is possible to identify people with a 'snooty' accent. It usually goes together with certain formal gestures, a controlled manner of speaking and expensive-looking, but never flamboyant, clothes which are in no way the height of fashion – more probably they are hopelessly outdated.

This gentility concealed much social decay and corruption, which manifested itself only when, in the eighteenth century, with the entire world economy losing momentum, the Republic went through a period of economic stagnation and began to fall behind later economic starters elsewhere on the continent, sharing a similar fate to England, once the motor of the industrial revolution. In the same century, the arrival of the 'patriot movement' presented a clear opposition to the regent system and, later, the stadholdership held by the family of Orange, which depended for its support on the petit-bourgeoisie and groups that felt excluded from power, such as rich Catholics. After the storming of the Bastille in 1789, the patriot movement identified closely with the ideals of the French Revolution. When French troops occupied the Republic in 1795, the patriots took power and the stadholder, William v of Orange, fled to England.

The eighteen years that the Netherlands was under French influence, initially as a vassal state and later as part of Napoleon's empire, did bring about a revolution.

A single body of legislation was created – which simply entailed the wholesale adoption of Napoleon's civil and criminal codes. The confederation made way for a single state with provinces and municipalities. The state and the government acquired the basic structures they still have today. It is due to the patriots that every Dutch citizen is equal before the law. It not only put Jews and Catholics on the same footing as Calvinists, it also abolished all the old rights and privileges with one stroke of the pen.

When, in 1813, it was clear that Napoleon's days were numbered, a small group from the Hague elite decided that it would be advisable to commit a kind of *coup d'état* before Prussian or Russian troops moved in to occupy the country. They put all their cards on what they hoped was the still strong loyalty felt by the mass of the population for the House of Orange. Their true feelings about the common people are suitably expressed in one sentence from their proclamation: 'The people shall be given a day of festivity at the expense of the treasury.' In those days, this meant free drink for all. The people were not intended to take any initiative themselves. William Frederick, the son of the last stadholder, returned to the Netherlands and found himself proclaimed sovereign prince and then King of the Netherlands. For the first fifteen years, this also included what is now Belgium. The union was not

King William I consolidated the unified state that had been created during the period of French domination from 1795 to 1813.

successful and in 1830, the Belgians instigated a revolution of their own and cut themselves loose from the new kingdom.

William I – for this is how he has gone down in history – did not wish to return to the dark days of the old republic any more than the 'gentility' among his supporters wanted to. He preserved the system introduced by Napoleon almost intact, including the existing structure of government. In his residence in The Hague, the new king tried to surround himself with the trappings of a real monarchy, as recent dynasties are wont to do. The centre of The Hague still has a whole collection of statues of people largely forgotten by history – such as the Prince of Wied, who commanded William's army – which bear witness to this failed attempt to create a sense of grandeur. Even Noordeinde – William's palace, now used as an 'office' by Queen Beatrix – is too small and far too modest, standing as it does in a narrow street, to be an adequate symbol of the monarchy.

Orange cannot and shall not rule a nation of slaves

During the German occupation, the illegal newspaper *Oranje Bode* described the difference between Wilhelmina, the Dutch queen in exile in London, and Adolf Hitler. 'She is – and wants nothing other than to be – our Queen, the royal mentor of an independent people. This healthy relationship between the monarch and her subjects is the source of an indestructible strength. Orange cannot and shall not rule a nation of slaves, that bows to a repressive tyrant only under protest. The German people may allow themselves to be browbeaten and oppressed, they may groan as they feel the weight of the despot's foot on their neck, but such a position does not suit the people of the Netherlands.'

The House of Orange has never derived its reputation from a spectacular Royal Court or from any other form of grand spectacle. Those that did take steps in that direction soon felt the pressure of disapproval and clearly it was not really in their blood. The message from the *Oranje Bode* – particularly what it says about the Germans – obviously has to be seen in the context in which it was written, but it does hit the nail on the head. The reputation of the Orange dynasty is based on the fact that it protects freedom. It is associated not with power but with justice. Orange stands above all other parties and guarantees the freedom of each individual to be himself.

The real national day of celebration in the Netherlands is *Koninginnedag*, the Queen's official birthday. Queen Beatrix was born on 31 January 1938, in the middle of winter. It was therefore decided that *Koninginnedag* should continue to be held on the previous Queen's birthday. Juliana, Beatrix's mother, was Queen from 1948 until she abdicated in 1980. Her birthday is in spring, on 30 April, when there is a better chance of good weather. This is crucial, because *Koninginnedag* is celebrated out of doors. There is a carnival atmosphere, and street markets are held in many towns and villages. Amsterdam in particular celebrates on a grand scale. For this

Crown Princes Máxima, née Zorreguieta.

one day, anyone can sell whatever they like without a licence, and the whole city turns into one gigantic open-air market. It attracts enormous crowds, which regularly exceed a million people.

Of the celebrations organized in every community in the country, the Queen selects two which she visits personally, accompanied by her whole family. This is broadcast live on television and tops the viewing list year after year. The Queen arrives in the middle of a public celebration that has all the trappings of a funfair, and the whole family spontaneously joins in with the activities. The princes test their strength against the members of the local sports clubs, while the Queen speaks graciously to the children. Crown Princess Máxima is a favourite, with her effusive personality and dazzling smile, but it is the Queen who plays the main role. The whole circus leads the onlooker to conclude with surprise that the people and the Royal Family are one. Yet everything, even the 'spontaneity', is planned to the last detail. This is not to say that it is mere playacting. Everything is sincere, the entire community displays its support for the monarchy and the Royal Family feels the closeness of its ties with the people. All barriers between ruler and ruled have been removed.

In spite of this, however, there is still something a little 'sacred' about each and every member of the House of Orange. Dutch Calvinists of the old school undoubtedly believe that God has made a special covenant with the people of the Netherlands, in the same way that Jehovah did with the Jews, and that the House of Orange is an expression of that pledge. This inevitably puts a distance between monarch and people and, in their presence, nothing must go wrong.

Local administrators and leaders of industry always get into an advanced state of panic if the Queen accepts an invitation for a working visit or to join in the *Koninginnedag* celebrations. They will treat Her Majesty as a normal person and, in doing so, will leave nothing to chance. And that is what makes the whole thing so special. The stories of companies that have new toilets installed just in case Her Majesty feels the call of nature during her visit are legion. Speeches and guided tours are planned in the minutest detail. Extensive instructions are drawn up to indicate who will be introduced to the Queen at what particular moment and the exact words that will be used. When a sudden shower threatened to put a damper on the royal visit to the village of Zeewolde on *Koninginnedag* in 2006, the mayor addressed the assembled mass of enthusiastic Orange supporters, saying: 'The Royal Family are aware that it is raining and understand that it can happen.'

My mother still remembers the day that Queen Juliana looked me directly in the face – I was then a four-year-old child – as she passed in a limousine on her way to launch a new ship at a nearby shipyard. My mother and I were part of an enthusiastic crowd lining the route. *Juliaantje* – the Queen was often referred to by this affectionate name – was wearing a small black hat and she waved as she passed. Our eyes met for a moment, perhaps three seconds, but my family still speak of it now and then. My brother long ago surpassed me, however. My family owns a colour photograph in which he is explaining a piece of electronic research to none other than Queen Beatrix.

All this makes membership of the Royal Family an extraordinarily difficult task. It is the only position in the Netherlands that is not earned by merit or ambition. It is inherited – and the psychological pressure this brings must be overwhelming. Now and then, commentators may be heard to say that it is inhuman to demand such a price of any family. They are denied a normal life not only in appearance, but also in reality.

The only advantage of this extraordinary position is that the House of Orange has protected its privacy from the glare of the gossip magazines with greater success than other European royal families. Not that Dutch paparazzi have more integrity than their international colleagues, it is simply that their readers would not tolerate such malignant gossip. Anyone who speaks ill of the Royal Family is met with an effective rebuff from massed public opinion. 'The Queen cannot defend herself' is a common response. Gossip and other forms of criticism of the Royal Family are therefore seen as cowardly attacks on defenceless people. The Queen stands above all parties and is therefore above criticism. But this does not mean that the Royals can get away with anything. The father of Crown Princess

Crown Prince Willem Alexander, Crown Princess Máxima (who is not officially permitted to be addressed as a Crown Princess, but no one takes any notice), their two daughters and grandmother Queen Beatrix. The eldest, Amalia, will remain heir to the throne even if she has younger brothers, as Article 1 of the Constitution forbids discrimination on the grounds of gender.

Máxima Zorreguieta from Argentina was not welcome at her wedding. In the 1970s, as a junior minister for agriculture, he had been a member of the notorious Videla regime. Prince Floris, one of Crown Prince Alexander's younger brothers, had to give up his rights to the throne because he had failed to mention that his fiancée, Mabel Wisse-Smit, had been a close associate of the gangster Klaas Bruinsma. The relationship had been over a decade earlier and Bruinsma had since become the victim of a gangland murder. Yet, as long as such 'work related accidents' can be prevented at an early stage and in a subtle manner, most Dutch people feel that an attack on the Royal Family is an attack on the society they are a part of and the 'unity in diversity' which is its main distinguishing characteristic.

Furthermore, the Queen is still seen as the protector of the weak. Simple citizens who lose their way in the maze of bureaucracy and feel that – intentionally or unintentionally – they have been badly treated, frequently threaten to write to the Queen. The royal household does not encourage this but always ensures that complaints are forwarded to the correct address.

William I accepted the throne in 1813 only on the condition that a 'wise constitution' would be introduced. The new constitution created a governmental structure, based on the English system, with a *Tweede Kamer* as a 'House of Commons' and an *Eerste Kamer* as a 'House of Lords' for the nobility so enthusiastically created by William I from among the descendants of the leading regent families. The entire system depended on indirect elections, so that only the very rich had any influence on the government and even this extended little further than a limited share in decision-making. William's kingdom was in a state of crisis. The old money was still there, but it was often invested abroad. William I, familiar with the industrial revolution that had swept England, tried to introduce modernization here and there but it did not really take hold. He called in technical experts from England to introduce technological change in very much the same way that 'development workers' do today in the Third World. And largely with just as little success. Modern historians estimate that, in 1850, only 4% of all machinery in the Netherlands was powered by steam. In England, this had long been around 50%. The elites were happy with the status quo. It was only after William had long gone to join his forefathers that they were confronted *en masse* with the backwardness of their country. The cause of this was Thomas Cook, founder of the famous travel agency.

They were shocked, and they were embarrassed

In 1851, Cook organized group trips to Crystal Palace in London, where the first World Exhibition was being held. It was the Dutch elite's first acquaintance with organized tourism and they were unable to resist the temptation. A large number of them therefore made the trip to Crystal Palace, the temple of steam power, miracles and progress. The Dutch stand, with its traditional trades and products, was a pale contrast to all the latest technical achievements they saw around them. They were shocked, and they were embarrassed. Those who had not gone to London were able to read all about the exhibition in detailed series of reports in the *Algemeen Handelsblad*, the largest liberal newspaper of the time, whose tradition survives today in the quality daily NRC *Handelsblad*. They observed, for example, that, whereas the British presented their products as 'new' or 'improved', Dutch companies preferred mottos like 'tried and trusted'.

In 1851, the Netherlands had a liberal government. The most outspoken advocate of liberal ideology was Leiden University professor Johan Rudolf Thorbecke. His theories provided the foundation of the new constitution drawn up in 1848 and

An attendant carefully polishes the bust of Johan Rudolf Thorbecke, the statesman who gave the Netherlands its parliamentary government and civil freedoms.

1849 when King William II, alarmed by the revolutions in Naples and Paris and a small number of demonstrations at home, was – in his own words – 'converted from a conservative to a liberal overnight'. The new constitution preserved the monarchy, but also established the inviolability of the king. All responsibility for government rested on the shoulders of the ministers, who were accountable to a parliament, where the *Tweede Kamer* was directly elected. Not by the 'people', but by men who paid a specified minimum of taxes. In practice this was the richest 100,000 in a country with a population of approximately three million. It was no democracy. It was a kind of oligarchy, but it was a first step on the road to universal suffrage.

Shocked by what they had seen in London, the elites began to work on modernization of the infrastructure, the basis for which had already been laid by William I. In the twenty years following 1848, the country acquired a complex network of railways. New canals were dug, legislation was updated and telegraph poles sprung up across the country. An efficient and fast postal system was set up, complete with postage stamps. Mass education, introduced during the French occupation, expanded enormously. The tax on newspapers and periodicals, introduced to ensure that political comment remained the prerogative of those with money, was abolished. The country became one of the last in Europe to abolish corporal punishment and simultaneously the first to do away with capital punishment. The guiding principle of the government's economic policy was – and has remained – free trade, and as much of it as possible.

It prepared the country for its own industrial revolution, which started about 1870. During the last thirty years of the nineteenth century the country went through a period of phenomenal economic growth, very similar to that being experienced by China and the 'tigers' of South East Asia.

Accustomed to two centuries of stagnation, the major cities – The Hague, Rotterdam, Amsterdam and Utrecht – saw their population increase two to fivefold in a period of twenty-five years. The population of the entire country grew phenomenally, but the economy grew even faster. The general state of public health – around 1870 the average age was still about thirty – improved quickly. This was due not so much to better medical care, but to improved sanitation as a result of new water supplies and sewers. Almost all children now had the opportunity to at least attend primary school, where they learned to read, write and do arithmetic. Without the crippling taxes, daily and weekly newspapers became accessible to the mass of the people. Papers aimed at this new market thrived alongside elite newspapers like the *Algemeen Handelsblad*. Among these was *De Echo*, famed for its exciting stories, published in a series of separate episodes. There were also hundreds of local papers which – primitive and fragmentary as they would appear to us today – brought the world into people's homes.

And in the cities, the steam engines pounded, the chimneys belched smoke, the machines rattled and the riveting hammers battered away. In 1879 a new weekly newspaper appeared in Amsterdam. It was called *Recht voor Allen*, 'Justice for All', and it was published by a Lutheran preacher who had lost his faith in God, Ferdinand Domela Nieuwenhuis. The whole socialist movement in the Netherlands – from the most moderate to the most radical – considers Domela Nieuwenhuis as its founder. In the same year another preacher, whose faith had been re-kindled with a vengeance, founded the first modern political party in the Netherlands. The preacher's name was Abraham Kuyper and he called his creation the *Anti-*

In 1879, Abraham Kuyper founded the first modern Dutch political party. He drew up a Calvinistic political programme, the traces of which are still to be seen in the policies of the current *Christen Democratisch Appèl (CDA). Christian Democratic leaders like Jan Peter Balkenende or Piet Hein Donner are still inspired by Kuyper's ideas.*

Revolutionaire Partij. Abraham Kuyper was what we might today call a fundamentalist. Like most people living in the Netherlands at the time, Kuyper had to survive during a period of sweeping social change, when many fled the growing unemployment in their villages to seek what work they could find and live in squalid little rooms in a large, anonymous city. There they would read papers like the *Geïllustreerd Politienieuws*, with its exaggerated tales of crime and decadence – accompanied by the goriest of illustrations – which would destroy any sense of security they might have retained. In the big city, God and his commandments no longer had a secure footing; traditional guidelines for behaviour no longer seemed to work, or at least were certainly not applied by the rich and successful, who would pass you by on their way to the stock exchange or a fancy restaurant, or stroll by with a beautiful fiancée on their arm dressed in the height of fashion. From a small world, you had been thrown into a very large one. And that makes you feel insecure.

Sovereignty in one's own domain

Kuyper knew instinctively where that security was to be found – in the Bible, in the words of Calvin. Old as they were, Kuyper felt that they still provided the answers. It was not this orthodox belief that made Kuyper's thought new, it was his ability to combine it seamlessly with the new technology born of modernization and the industrial revolution. Kuyper placed his simple, straightforward faith at the centre of the modern age. It provided a solid basis which allowed people to function in those unsettled times. He had a daily newspaper and a weekly magazine which he used to distribute his views among the people. He took advantage of the rail network and the daily postal service to set up mass organizations across the country. He founded the Free University to further education with the blessing of God. Kuyper was, in all senses, a modern man and a child of the nineteenth century.

An extremely wide choice of schools

Anyone looking for a school for their children will still be confronted with Kuyper's life's work. In addition to the schools run by the state or the local authority, there is a whole range of others, the majority of which have a religious background of some sort. And this is just as true in small rural communities as in the big cities. Protestant, Catholic and, these days, a growing number of Islamic or Hindu schools are entirely funded by the state. They must comply with government quality standards and receive regular visits from the Education Inspectorate. But they are free to choose their own spiritual direction, or rather this is decided by the school board, known in official texts as the 'competent authority'. Parents in the Netherlands may therefore choose a school which reflects their own beliefs. If they have no strong religious convictions, or if they wish their children to grow up with friends from all kinds of backgrounds, they can send them to the state or municipal school, which has no religious basis. The law contains a whole range of provisions to ensure that the ministry of education does not give preferential treatment to these public schools. If anything, they guarantee the contrary. The heads of schools in the public sector frequently complain that they have less elbow room than their colleagues at the 'religious' schools.

Parents who cannot find a school that suits their religious tastes are free to set one up themselves. The law specifies all kinds of quantitative requirements that have to be met and the lessons must be given by qualified teachers. If these requirements – which are not overly strict – are complied with, the government is bound to provide the funds for the new school. And that is exactly what Abraham Kuyper had in mind.

As a Calvinist, Kuyper was condemned to constant opposition to the liberal state, dominated as it was by a free-thinking elite. He accused them of imposing an a-religious neutrality on the population. Their main instrument was an increasingly mass-oriented system of education which, as the law demanded, brought children up to believe in 'generally accepted social and Christian virtues'. As an alternative to this, Kuyper presented his political ideology of 'sovereignty in one's own domain'. Education was emphatically and primarily the responsibility of one's own immediate circle. Parents should be given the opportunity to set up schools in which they would determine the nature of the education to be given, but which would be funded by the government. His Calvinist Anti-Revolutionaire Partij, named to express its resistance to consequences of the French Revolution, adopted this as the centrepiece of its political programme. But Kuyper's teaching went further. Sovereignty in one's own domain meant not only the church, education and politics, but a whole range of social relations, such as trade organizations, interest groups, and cultural and recreational societies.

Kuyper directed himself not so much at the elite as at the social groups below them. He called them the *kleyne luyden*, the 'little people', a term from the Eighty-Years' War. Much of his inspiration was drawn from this period, when the struggle against the Spanish produced much revolutionary rhetoric. To achieve his goals, Kuyper needed the votes of the *kleyne luyden*. He therefore actively promoted extension of the right to vote. This set in motion a process which in 1922 resulted in universal suffrage for women. Only then could the Netherlands rightly call itself a democracy.

Abraham Kuyper's teaching proved to be a suitable model for the Catholics – then about 30% of the population – who replaced their converted barns with proud neo-Gothic cathedrals but who still – rightly – frequently felt themselves to be second-class citizens. In the final quarter of the nineteenth century and the first ten years of the twentieth, they set up a similar network of political, religious and social organizations – but then with a relatively strict Catholicism as the guiding principle. They found their own Kuyper in the person of politician-journalist-priest Hermanus

Schaepman. In the *Tweede Kamer*, the Calvinists and the Catholics formed a tactical alliance which was primarily intended to achieve their common educational objectives. They were successful in 1917.

This was all essentially an offensive against the forces of revolution, with the liberals as the main victims. A rowdy socialist movement grew up around *Recht voor Allen* and Domela Nieuwenhuis, which may have caused much fear and consternation but, in the beginning, could in no way equal the organizational talent of the Protestants and the Catholics. It was not until lawyer-poet Pieter Jelles Troelstra set up the *Sociaal-Democratische Arbeiders Partij* (SDAP), based on reformist ideals, that the movement achieved any real form of genuine organization. The socialists rather grudgingly gave in to this growing tradition and formed their own network of similar organizations. They kept their distance, however, from education, although plans were made to set up schools based on social-democratic principles. Circumstances forced them, too, to adopt 'sovereignty in their own domain'. Once democracy finally arrived, there was little left over for the liberals than just under 10% of the electorate.

Great tolerance for other ways of thinking

Sovereignty in one's own domain is connected in a certain way to the old divisions of the Republic, which forced the regents to develop their culture of compromise. There never was one leading 'domain'. There were various 'domains', particularly within the Protestant part of the population, where the different versions of orthodoxy led to division. Abraham Kuyper thought that the Dutch Reformed Church was too pluriform and forced a schism that has only been repaired in the very recent past, with Kuyper's Free Reformed Church re-uniting with a number of other smaller denominations to form the United Protestant Church in the Netherlands. The doctrinal freedom within this mega-merger was, however, absolute and that led to a new schism: the Restored Dutch Reformed Church has now joined the ranks of fundamentalist Protestant church communities in the Netherlands. Because the VPS refused to give up any churches, its members – and there are easily 50,000 of them – meet in school canteens and private function rooms. The schism weakened the reunified church, leaving Christians in the Netherlands as divided as ever.

Dutch society rests on a number of separate 'pillars'

Political scientist Arend Lijphart, who was a professor at Leiden University, made the study of this system his life's work. He gave us the word which has come to describe it: *verzuiling*, 'pillarization'. The symbolism is clear – Dutch society rests on a number of separate 'pillars'.

The word 'pillarization' has taken on negative connotations in current debates on the nature of Dutch society. It implies a segmented community, where large groups of the population allow themselves to be manipulated by front men who, by virtue of their strategic positions in a number of important networks, hold the real power in their hands. The 'Roman Catholic Goat-breeders' Association' is a frequently heard cliché in any discussion on pillarization.

So where do these negative connotations come from? It is because the networks, the foundations for which were laid by people like Kuyper and Schaepman, still exist to a certain extent, while the corresponding structures of belief have been diluted. This process started in the 1960s and is still continuing.

The 1960s were a watershed

The 1960s were a watershed in the cultural history of the Netherlands. This may seem a surprising claim at first, since there is another period that would perhaps better deserve the description – the time of the German occupation between 1940 and 1945. This was without doubt the most traumatic collective experience since the Eighty-Years' War and many Dutch people have made the comparison. The German occupiers were not content with sending in troops and using the country's resources for the war effort, they also tried hard to reorganize Dutch society along National Socialist lines. The ideology of pillarization proved strong enough to resist these attempts. Although the Nazis succeeded in taking over most social organizations, they simply folded; membership fell to practically nothing, only to pick up again after liberation. After the war, a coalition of liberals, social democrats and members of the resistance tried to preserve the unity built up during the Nazi occupation, by setting up a mass organization known as the *Nederlandse Volksbeweging* – the Dutch People's Movement – and a new *Partij van de Arbeid* (PVDA – the Dutch Labour Party), but the attempt failed. The PVDA survived and became the core of the traditional 'red' pillar, but proved to be nothing more than the old SDAP in a new jacket. After the Germans had been defeated, the pillars returned to Dutch society more deeply entrenched than before.

Even so, the system would not last twenty years. The most plausible explanation lies in the development of the national economy. The economy had been growing in fits and starts since 1870, but the population had kept pace. After about 1890, per capita income ceased to grow and stayed that way until the start of the 1950s. It was then between a fifth and sixth of what it is today. Nevertheless, generally speaking, public welfare improved considerably during those fifty or sixty years. Thanks to the arrival of mass production, the prices of a number of consumer goods – such as good quality, ready-to-wear clothing – fell. In addition, national income was distributed more equally. This had a lot to do with the fact that the 'pillars' were in many respects emancipation movements. The most important thing for Kuyper, Schaepman and Troelstra was to improve the lot of their respective mass of supporters. The Catholic and Calvinist leaders did not share the social democrats' belief in the class struggle. But improving the lives of the less fortunate among their congregations was another matter. In this way, they were advocating a kind of 'common interest' philosophy, in which each individual receives his due and the fair distribution of national wealth is a matter of consultation. On the whole, the result was that hunger and misery practically disappeared in the Netherlands in the first three decades of the century, although the standard of living of the majority of the population would be considered very modest in modern terms and probably unacceptable to many Dutch people today.

The pillarized society possessed a wide range of sanctions for eccentric behaviour. Priests and preachers alike would tell their congregations from the pulpit – and this was still common practice in the 1950s – that they should give their custom only to fellow believers. And they would also make it clear that certain people were no longer considered to fall within this category. Socialist literature in particular is full of examples of members of the religious pillars who had been ruined after displaying too great a sympathy with 'red' ideas. In short, for most people, non-conformity was a luxury they could not afford.

They were introduced to life's luxuries of by Donald Duck

Around 1950 the average Dutch family – the father would be a skilled worker, the mother would be a housewife – would have furniture of a reasonable quality. The man's wages would be sufficient for them to afford good food and clothing. They would have a daily newspaper, an illustrated weekly magazine, a comic for the children. In the living room, there would be a bookshelf with a row of books, sensible novels from the publisher associated with the family's 'pillar', which were often distributed through some kind of subscription scheme. And that was about it. The one large and expensive article in the house – for which newly-wed couples would first have to save – was the radio. A refrigerator, a record player or a washing machine were simply out of reach of most of the population. Not to mention a television set to pick up the modest range of programmes that were broadcast from 1951 onwards, largely at the insistence of Philips. The possibility of owning a car was beyond their wildest dreams.

And yet, many children knew of the existence of these luxury articles. They were introduced to them in the pictures of a new comic, the 'Donald Duck', which first appeared in 1952 and reached circulation figures unprecedented for the time. The comic was a colourful confrontation with the American way of life, which had also made its presence increasingly known since the end of the Second World War in films, swing music and popular culture. From an international standpoint this American way of life was the alternative to the tyranny of Stalinist communism, the outer borders of which were only three-hundred kilometres to the east. The entire country – with the exception of the communists themselves, of course, who never

A stylish housewife proudly shows off her new refrigerator, a very expensive built-in model.

had the support of more than 10% of the population – was united in its abhorrence of this godless ideology. But the focus on consumption, the outward display of wealth and the enjoyment of the fruits of welfare that are such an important part of the American way of life were not well suited to Dutch frugality, the compromise culture and the considerably more restrained ways in which the regents traditionally enjoyed their wealth. The people were warned against such excesses in the media and from the pulpit. And at the end of the 1940s, the Ministry of Education, Art and Science started a campaign against the decadent influence of comic magazines. The problem for the established powers was that a consumption-oriented way of life was starting to come within reach of more and more people. The Netherlands shared in the welfare explosion that swept Western Europe in the second half of this century. After being stable for more than half a century, per capita income – as already mentioned above – increased more than fivefold.

A sign of self-confidence and prosperity: the first Dutch family car – the Daf – rolls off the assembly line. It had a unique selling point: 'Variomatic' automatic transmission which the company called Het pientere pookje, *the 'clever little stick'. But many car drivers thought automatics were for wimps and old people, and the Daf did not sell as well as hoped.*

I was born into a typical Dutch working class family, where the radio was the greatest luxury. Between 1958 and 1964, we acquired first a television, then a washing machine, a refrigerator, an electric oven and, lastly, a Daf, the newly introduced Dutch family car. Everything was paid for from my father's regular wage increases. The money left over after the family's basic expenses had been met was saved up to allow us to buy more luxuries, because illness, accidents or unemployment would all be covered by a generous system of social security. This was all the work of the post-war governments, in which Catholics, Calvinists and socialists worked closely together, building up the role of the state.

At first, the social organizations they set up – including hospitals, *kruisverenigingen* (which provided home nursing services), night schools and children's homes – were self-financed. The striking exception to this rule was education which, although pillar-based, had been largely dependent on state subsidies since 1917. The pillars attempted to extend this form of funding to the remainder of their respective networks, since it provided a greater guarantee of continuity. This did mean that the organizations became more distanced from their ordinary members, but few objected. An increasing proportion of the social care system therefore became dependent on state funding. This in turn led to expansion of their tasks. Obligations which in many societies are the responsibility of the family, such as caring for the seriously ill, helping parents or destitute cousins, were rightly taken over by special organizations. A woman who has just given birth would (and still does) receive professional help in the home for ten days or so. Parents who are no longer able to live on their own can move into old-people's accommodation with hotel-like service and a wide range of medical facilities.

The organizations which provided these services gradually became more anonymous and bureaucratic. They were there. You could call on them if necessary. They were generally good at what they did. But in a certain way they were also far removed from the normal people.

This was the paradox of the success of the pillar system

Meanwhile these normal people saw the world every day on their television screen. They could afford a holiday abroad. And as their income increased they became more self-aware. Because the social organizations worked so well, the people of the Netherlands were able to think and act more as individuals, who thought for themselves and were no longer just a part of the group. This was the paradox of the success of the pillars.

For whatever reason, in the 1960s the established powers within the pillars quickly began to lose their grip on the ordinary members. This was first noticeable in the media. The Catholic, Calvinist and socialist press suddenly lost out to non-pillarized rivals. Today there is not a single daily newspaper in the country that calls itself Catholic – in the 1950s there will still more than thirty. The most interesting example of this development is *de Volkskrant*. Today it is a quality newspaper, which competes with the traditionally liberal NRC *Handelsblad*. *De Volkskrant* was originally the paper of the Roman Catholic trade association and was always loyal to the political and religious leaders of the Catholic 'pillar'. The more the faithful ignored the orders of the church, the more *de Volkskrant* went its own way so that it could ensure the continued support of the children of the original subscribers, Catholic craftsmen. These post-war craftsmen were the first generation able to offer their children a better education than they themselves had had. The government introduced a system of study grants but perhaps even more significant was the fact that parents could now afford to give their children a secondary education. They no longer relied on them to work from the age of fourteen, the age at which the Dutch traditionally started work. This development was encouraged on all fronts because the economic growth of the country de-manded a more skilled workforce. The young generation – who had experienced nothing other than progress – took this all for granted. They could even afford to object to the society their parents were part of, without having to forego its benefits.

As part of the struggle for cultural liberation in the 1960s, soldiers – at the time, there was still national service in the Netherlands – won the right to wear beards and long hair.

They let their hair grow

After the Beatles first spectacular visit to Amsterdam, you could clearly recognize these young people – they let their hair grow. And they emphasized the normality of their prosperity by wearing denim jeans in their spare time. Jeans were traditionally the symbol of hard, unrewarding work; in the 1960s, they became a symbol of the new freedom. The younger generation adopted, as a kind of cultural banner, the very clothes their parents had hoped they would escape forever. They mocked traditional norms and values of moderation, particularly where relations between the sexes were concerned. The contraceptive pill – which had been readily available since 1963 and was so popular that the demographic trend towards population increase was reversed – made close physical contact far less risky. All this led to a shift in cultural values and norms. *De Volkskrant* reported these changes in detail and with decreasing antipathy. When it moved to a new building, it celebrated by dropping its sub-header 'the Netherlands' Catholic daily'. Since then, the paper no longer defines its position, but it has become the mouthpiece for many who have left the pillars behind them. It does this in a very special way. It advocates cultural individualism but not personal egoism.

The Calvinist daily *Trouw* experienced a similar development, maintaining a readership of over 100,000 despite remaining more faithful to its religious foundations. The rest of the pillar-based press – including the once enormously strong socialist publications – has disappeared without a trace. *De Volkskrant* won the day by taking its leave of the pillar system at the same time as its readers.

The wet earth of Holland has proved fertile soil for paternalism

At first glance, it appears to be a remarkable combination – extreme liberalism in the private sphere together with almost its complete opposite when it comes to the organization of society as a whole. Yet, through Dutch eyes, this is not so strange. The wet earth of Holland has proved fertile soil for paternalism. The roots of Dutch society lie in the Christian faith and, like the Koran, the Bible devotes considerable attention to the poor. Charity is one of the greatest virtues, as is hospitality to strangers and the protection of widows and orphans. As early as the Middle Ages, we find examples of wealthy citizens wishing to do something for the poor. This was usually rather structured and frequently took the form of an inheritance, since leaving money to the poor was a sure-fire way of entering the kingdom of heaven. A good example of this was the hospice for the poor in the provincial town of Schie-dam, which was mentioned in the town charter in 1275. It was intended, in the words of a later document, for the poor of Christ, the old and decrepit, the sick and others who belonged in such an institution. Its name, the St. Jacob's Hospice, illustrates its religious connotations.

The town council had introduced a primitive sort of tax to support the institution. St. Jacob's therefore not only received the best garments of the wealthy and deceased, but also a small percentage of every piece of peat sold in the town.

The Calvinist victory in the Eighty-Years' War led to the disappearance of the whole official infrastructure of monasteries and Roman Catholic brotherhoods. Generally, their properties fell to the local authorities who allowed the charitable activities to continue under their supervision. The strict Calvinist church organization also had to contend with brothers and sisters who were less well off and unable to fend for themselves. Their support became the special area of expertise of a new kind of church official – the deacon. Care for the poor and sick therefore became the responsibility of church and civic officials. This was in no way a matter of what we would today call social justice. It was Christian duty to provide charity, but it could never be enforced, particularly by those who received it. The general rule was that help was given only to those who really needed it. This did not include people without work, but the infirm, children and old people who were unable to rely on their families because they had, for example, been lost during an epidemic.

Foreign observers were impressed by these activities. Compared with the rest of Europe, they were very extensive although it should not be forgotten that, especially during the Golden Age, the standard of living was so high that there was plenty of surplus wealth to put to good use. Furthermore, those who did charitable works made no secret of it. It was a status symbol to care for the weak and the sick. This was expressed in the size of the buildings built for these purposes. The St. Jacob's Hospice is still a dominant landmark in the centre of Schiedam; its façade, in classical Greek temple style crowned with a bell tower, conceals the chapel. On either side, large courtyards are surrounded by high wings, which formerly housed the elderly (this became the hospice's speciality). The enormous building was erected in 1789, when Schiedam was flourishing and could afford such extravagance. The hospice is now a spacious museum of modern art. Many Dutch cities possess historical buildings of this nature. Amsterdam, for example, has the *Maagdenhuis*, formerly a home for orphan girls and now the administrative centre of the university. Then there are the *hofjes,* the equivalent of an English 'court'. These consist of rows of small houses around a central square, often covered with grass. The court is sealed off from the outside world by a door or gate. They were frequently founded at the bequest of a wealthy citizen who would leave sufficient money in his will to cover the building and running costs. As a rule, the patron would stipulate for whom the houses were intended, perhaps widows of limited means or decrepit couples of a certain religious persuasion. These courts can still be seen in most Dutch cities, where they have been beautifully restored and seldom fulfil their original function. They were – and are – showpieces in the historic centres of the cities.

The splendid façades, however, concealed little luxury. Elderly people who wished to be taken in at St. Jacob's had to exchange all their worldly goods for their bed and board. If they had no possessions, they had go from door to door – as long as they could walk – begging for alms in an attempt to recover at least a part of the costs of their upkeep. This practice was still common until well into the twentieth century. Many of the courts also had a system of 'purchasing', whereby future residents paid a fixed amount to guarantee a place for themselves in later life. They also made regular contributions to the court, the value and nature of which differed from case to case. One might be obliged to donate a certain quantity of peat every winter to fire the stove, while others might be required to turn over all their possessions. The rich therefore paid more than the poor for the same service. And orphans were always recognizable by their clothing – it was necessary that they were seen to be needy and dependent on charity.

The embarrassment of riches

And yet there was more behind this care for the needy. The British historian Simon Schama prefaced his cultural history of the Dutch Golden Age, 'The Embarrassment of Riches', with a quotation from John Calvin: 'Let those who have abundance remember that they are surrounded with thorns, and let them take great care not to be pricked by them'.

Charity, so splendidly displayed in the courtyards and palace-like façades, enabled the rich to allay the sense of guilt that their material success brought with it. For no matter how libertine their lives may have been in practice, the Calvinist threat was constantly in the background – that many were called but few were chosen; that their prosperity and wealth could turn against them.

In Schama's words: 'The profusion and munificence of charitable institutions in the Netherlands as elsewhere in baroque Europe, has been classified by modern historians as an exercise in 'social control.' And there is no doubt that part of its momentum derived from prudential consideration. Where elites governed by persuasion rather than coercion, philanthropic donation on a large and obligatory scale was a small price to pay for cushioning themselves against the threat of popular revolt. But this kind of manipulative explanation omits as much as it explains. In particular it pays little attention to the almost perfervid urge with which the Dutch were commanded to honour their good fortune by sharing some of it with the less well off.' And: 'It was rather a moral balancing act that permitted the retention, not the repudiation, of riches, on condition that they were yielded to communally determined ends.'

Yet there is in this charity an even more important element of social control than Schama will admit to. Anyone who reads the regulations of the charitable institutions will be surprised to notice how strictly life there was regulated and how much attention was devoted to preventing abuse. It is striking that the more money the regents pumped into the institutions, the richer they became, while their residents led an exceptionally sober life. The St. Jacob's Hostel even had a small prison in its cellar for any of its elderly inmates who proved difficult to handle. Another striking example is an appeal to the citizens of Amsterdam – dating from the 1840s – to support schools for the children of the poor. The argument was that there the children would learn obedience and gratitude. About this same time, preacher and man of letters Bernard ter Haar published a poem in which he thanked God that he owned a fur coat after seeing a woman shivering in the cold. There was nothing cynical about this – it was perfectly genuine. It had already been noted in the Middle Ages that the poor had been created by God for a reason – to give the rich the opportunity to love their neighbours. On the other hand it is dangerous to judge situations and customs from the distant past according to twentieth century values. This happens a great deal in the Netherlands because regimes like the one at St. Jacob's with its compulsory begging and its prison cell live on here and there in the collective memory. They are horror stories that people like to tell to contrast that time with the present.

Our comprehensive system of social security may have been set up in the past 50 years or so, but the basis was laid much earlier – during the heyday of pillarization and under the influence of rapidly growing socialism. This latter pillar always rested on the fundamental belief in 'a fair day's pay for a fair day's work' but also that everyone was entitled to protection against the effects of unemployment, illness and age. The Catholic and Calvinist pillars had a slightly different solution to these problems, usually in the form of collective savings or insurance schemes rather than leaving it up to the state, but the result was the same – the less fortunate had to be protected against the vagaries of fate. In practice it was the liberals, followed later by Catholics and Calvinists, who developed the first forms of social security. Unemployment insurance was introduced, which was run by the 'pillarized' trade unions and subsidized by the government. And it did not stop there – the government also provided a meagre benefit for the long-term unemployed who were no longer eligible for support from the insurance schemes.

Most benefits were based on an insurance scheme

The welfare explosion after 1950 gave the still-pillarized government the opportunity to restructure this whole complex system of social support. True to tradition, it decided on a compromise – people were entitled to support, but most benefits were based on an insurance system. The first example of this was the *Algemene Ouderdoms Wet*, known popularly as the AOW, which guarantees every individual over the age of 65 a pension approximately equal to the minimum wage. Individuals contribute to the scheme on a pay-as-you-earn basis. The money is, however, not pooled in a fund and invested to accumulate sufficient capital to pay each person's pension as long as is necessary. The pensions are financed from the compulsory contributions paid into the scheme by younger generations. This is known as an 'apportionment' system – the total contributions from those paying in are divided up among those entitled to the benefit in question. The *Wet Arbeidsongeschiktheid* (Invalidity Insurance Act, known popularly as the WAO) and its successor the *Wet Inkomen en Arbeid* (Work and Income Act, WIA), which provide disability benefits, work on the same principle. Under this system, those who pay contributions do not accumulate any rights. The government is entitled to repeal or amend the legislation, change the levels of benefits, the conditions for eligibility or the period during which benefits are received – and has done so in recent years, acquiring for itself the reputation of a bad insurer. There is little understanding among the general public for the apportionment system; after all, this is not the basis of the normal commercial insurance schemes that most Dutch people are accustomed to.

Negotiations between employers and employees very rarely lead to open conflict. This has its roots in the organization of the Catholic and Calvinist pillars, where trade unions and employers' organizations would share a common ideology of listening to each other and of close collaboration. This mentality was later adopted by liberal employers and the socialist part of the union movement. These negotiations, in which working conditions are usually equally as important as wage levels, are conducted per economic sector and result in Collective Labour Agreements (known in Dutch as CAOs) which apply to the whole sector. In addition to agreements on wages and salaries, the CAOs also contain provisions for training, hiring, dismissal and redundancy. Trade union negotiators are usually prepared to accept moderate wage settlements in exchange for other concessions, such as the preservation of jobs.

These days, nearly every sector has its own pension fund, into which both employers and employees pay high contributions. These funds have become the leading players on the capital markets. They are private enterprises, and those who pay into them accumulate rights based on the number of years they pay their contributions. The pensions are supplementary to the state pension to which everyone is entitled under the AOW; they are, as it were, the jam on the bread. Any holes in this safety net are filled by the government. Anyone who is no longer entitled to an unemployment benefit under the *Werkloosheidswet* (ww) – which is also based on the apportionment system – receives a supplementary benefit funded from tax revenues.

Universal doubts about the Christian faith

Yet it was not only the actions of self-willed citizens that led to the disintegration of the pillars that has taken place since the 1960s. Prominent figures in the pillars no longer believed in the hermetically sealed ideological/religious schools of thought that had traditionally been the guarantee of unity. This was particularly true of

The foundation of Christianity in the Netherlands is Protestant, but the country has a large Catholic minority. In the southern provinces of Noord-Brabant and Limburg, Catholics are even in the majority. You can tell whether a town or region is Catholic by the way they celebrate carnival. The Catholics put their all into it, while Protestants simply don't know how, no matter how hard they try.

the Roman Catholic church, which was thrown into the spiritual fast lane by the Second Vatican Council. The Council was called by Pope John xxiii to modernize the ossified structure of the international church. The message was welcomed in the Netherlands – which, until then, had been known for its loyalty to the Pope and to received church truths and traditions. Catholic leaders themselves called into question traditional cornerstones of the church, such as the celibacy of priests. The bishops called for a 'pastoral council' to make the church more democratic.

In the Calvinist churches, a new generation of preachers arose who subjected Protestant traditions to the same critical review. They had something in common with their Catholic colleagues – they no longer believed in a God whose authority was derived from strict laws and the threat of eternal damnation. They preached about a God of love and, as a direct consequence of this, that love should be the key word in relationships between people. The theological debate – which was publicized through the pages of *de Volkskrant* and *Trouw*, and on radio and television – centred around the idea of justice. This idea gradually acquired a more political slant. It became associated with the enormous gap between the rich industrialized countries and the Third World. At home, it was applied to Dutch society, and it was discovered that much inequality still exists. The Divine Message descended from heaven to earth, and in doing so lost much of its forceful character.

In both Catholic and Calvinist communities, congregations began to diminish and fewer people observed their religious duties. Young people in particular had a waning interest in what the church had to offer. None of this affected the smaller, stricter church communities which held on steadfastly to their orthodox beliefs against the run of the tide. They even experienced a period of renewed growth, although – with a total of around 600,000 followers – they remained a relatively marginal group in a population of fifteen million. They did, however, retain all the paraphernalia of the old pillar system, with two daily newspapers and a new broadcasting company, the *Evangelische Omroep*. They survived because their leaders were able to resist the forces of change that were battering at the door.

Social democracy, too, went through a period of change. A new generation of politicians pushed aside – often rather ruthlessly – leaders who had helped recon-struct a country ravaged by war entirely according to the principles of the pillar system. They did this – as did the Catholics and Calvinists – under the banner of freedom. But these new socialists grasped the old symbolism of the revolutionary struggle to distinguish themselves from the post-war leaders. The latter had distanced themselves from the red flag, the singing of the 'Internationale' and the works of Karl Marx to appease their coalition partners. The new generation wanted all this back. They preferred a 'conflict model' to the harmony model that only played into the hands of the regents.

The term 'regents' had returned to the centre of the political stage. The new opposition compared the current leaders with their seventeenth and eighteenth century predecessors who had kept themselves in power by co-optation, nepotism and behind the scenes wheeling and dealing. They saw current policy as once again being formed by compromises apparently agreed upon behind closed doors. In 1966 a group presented by the media as complete outsiders set up a new political party, *Democraten '66*, with a programme which went entirely against the grain of the Dutch political tradition. It advocated openness and proposed the introduction of a national referendum as a way of settling important issues. In the general elections the following year, the party won 7 of the 150 seats, then an astounding result in Dutch terms.

A period of germinating ideas and revolution

Modern citizens considered themselves *mondig*. This word, which literally means 'vocal', also embraces such qualities as self-awareness, maturity, not being afraid to speak up for oneself, making one's own decisions. They could speak for themselves, they did not need spokesmen. They demanded a say in decisions that affected them personally. This was soon radicalized to a demand for full participation in decision-making. The new democratic party's call for a referendum was a direct result of this development. Taking their lead from developments abroad, the party's leaders also preached the end of ideology, by which they meant that individuals could now form their own personal political-ideological complex and therefore no longer needed the ready-made ones provided by pillars.

This shift was not only illustrated by the demise of the pillarized press, it was reflected in election results. The *Katholieke Volkspartij* in particular suffered heavy losses. The two largest Calvinist parties and the social-democratic PVDA also lost support, but to a lesser extent. The trend, however, was clear – the pillars were collapsing and with them, the old model of group solidarity.

Intellectuals in particular remember the 1960s as a period of germinating ideas and revolution. There were spectacular occupations at the universities. Students and lecturers demanded a say in the decisions made by their professors. These new individuals discovered that, by acting *en masse*, they could attract a great deal of attention, particularly via the television. They took part in mass demonstrations, displaying their messages on large banners, reviving a method that had long before been applied by the founders of the pillars but had fallen into disuse. The idea was that the messages on the banners would be easy to read on the television screen. These demonstrations were aimed at the regents, but usually indirectly. The latter-day regents were faithful allies of the United States, with whom the Netherlands was united in NATO, so people took to the streets in their thousands to demonstrate against US involvement in Vietnam.

In Amsterdam a group of young people rediscovered anarchism, a nineteenth century ideology based on the belief that justice can be achieved only if people are free to cooperate with each other voluntarily and without coercion. They called themselves *provo's*, a term coined by the criminologist Buikhuizen to describe those in the younger generation who rejected social norms in order to provoke a reaction. The *provo's* in Amsterdam discovered that the regents and their power apparatus – the police in particular – were extremely easy to provoke, especially if you made them look ridiculous. In one such notorious case, a girl called Koosje Koster was convicted for handing out raisins to people on the street. The *provo's* introduced ideas which appeared utopian but which were disarmingly practical. With their famous 'white bicycle' plan, they planned to rid the centre of Amsterdam of motorized traffic by providing bicycles that could be used by everyone free of charge. But the main focus of their activity was the weekly 'happening' in the city centre. They would gather around midnight only to be dispersed rather heavy-handedly by the police, under the watchful eyes of a crowd of spectators whose sympathies clearly lay with the *provo's*. These happenings were centred around *Lievertje*, a statue of a street urchin donated to the city by a large tobacco company. Although many of the *provo's* were heavy smokers, the statue was a symbol of hypocrisy – the city should not accept gifts from people who were making money from causing cancer.

An atmosphere of harassment developed in Amsterdam and the position of the mayor, Gijsbert van Hall – who was not only a social-democrat but also a descendant of a grand old regent family – became increasingly impossible. The marriage of Princess Beatrix to German diplomat Claus von Amsberg led to serious riots. The uncompromising response of the police had provoked considerable criticism in the press and on the television. The powers-that-be had lost face. After a year, the *provo's* disbanded – the joke had gone on long enough. But they had attracted international attention with their facetious provocation of the establishment.

The success of the *provo's* and other similar groups was partly due to the fact that sections of the media were vaguely sympathetic to their activities. Here, too, the younger generation was pushing back the frontiers of what was acceptable. Author Jan Cremer caused an uproar with his sexual autobiography, which gave rise to a new term in the Dutch publishing world: *onverbiddelijke bestseller* – the relentless bestseller. Gerard Reve, a highly respected Dutch literary figure, produced a whole series of books focusing on the complete compatibility of the traditional Catholic way of life and homosexuality. His most infamous passage at the time was a description of himself having intercourse with God, who has taken the form of a donkey. The act took place in his attic, of all places. He was taken to court for this scene but was acquitted. The authorities – not unaffected by the spirit of the times and afraid of being made to look ridiculous – no longer knew where they should draw their limits. Within a year or two, the restrictions on pornography – which had, until then, been very strict – had crumbled, as a result of which a thriving market for magazines of that genre soon grew up.

Furthermore, the powers-that-be had something in their tradition that could also be applied to the current situation – the principle of sovereignty in one's own domain. Why should these new citizens not be allowed to do as they pleased as long as they were not causing trouble for others? Municipal leaders began to give the new generation more space, often literally. As a result, all kinds of centres grew up where they could, for example, indulge in their hippie sub-culture, in exactly the same way as the 'St. Cecilia' Roman Catholic brass band, the 'Harp of David' Reformist marching band, or the 'Art through Struggle' socialist choir had once enjoyed government support. The revolutionary youth, the new generation of critical citizens, was therefore incorporated by giving them their own space and making them dependent on the system as a whole. This pacified them and resulted in erosion of the conflict model.

Not that these radical young people enjoyed the mass support of the Dutch population. On the contrary, in the second half of the 1960s, *De Telegraaf*, the country's most conservative newspaper, saw its circulation increase almost fourfold to three-quarters of a million, precisely because it had taken a stand against all forms of political radicalism or anything else that threatened what was considered to be common civil decency. The paper was something of a cuckoo in the nest of the pillared society. It was traditionally the mouthpiece of the minority that had managed to wrest itself free of the restraints of the pillars – the remains of the liberal establishment. In Dutch terms, De Telegraaf was quite sensational and populist. In the 1950s and 1960s, its editors preached law and order and vigorously opposed the expanding system of social security, which they associated with a desire to interfere in others' lives and considered both a waste of money and a reward for idleness. The paper also devoted great attention to the pleasures of wealth and prosperity. It embraced consumerism in a way that the concerned Calvinist would find immoral. De Telegraaf had a feeling for show, for the glitter of the stars and for dreams of riches and happiness. It couldn't care less for Schama's embarrassment of riches. And that was what caused the breakthrough.

The same breakthrough occurred on the television and radio. Air-time in the Netherlands was controlled by the five most pillar-based broadcasting companies. These companies had a monopoly on the issue of programme information and each published their own TV and radio guide. Those who took out a subscription to the guide became members and, in this way, the broadcasting companies accumulated hundreds of thousands of members each. There were no commercials. The programmes were funded from an annual contribution from the government which was financed from a tax levied on everyone who owned a radio or television set.

Private entrepreneurs had long tried to present a united front against the broad-casting companies' monopoly. They wanted at least one commercial network that would make a profit from selling commercials. At first the political representatives of the pillars were able to prevent parliament from granting permission, but businessman Bul Verwey responded by setting up a commercial radio station on a ship outside Dutch territorial waters, beyond the reach of the Dutch authorities. The station, Radio Veronica, broadcast mainly music, with verbal link-ups being provided by a disc jockey – a new phenomenon for the Netherlands. Others imitated Verwey by broadcasting television programmes from drilling platforms in the North

Sea, but the authorities soon clamped down on them – the law apparently permitted the boarding of 'artificial islands'. These measures were, however, extremely unpopular and the government was forced to change the legislation regulating broadcasting. Under the new laws, air-time would be distributed democratically, according to the number of members each broadcasting company had, and new companies would be permitted to join the system. A certain amount of advertizing was also allowed.

The extent to which the pillars had disintegrated became clear when the people who had been broadcasting television programmes from the drilling platform set up the *Televisie en Radio Omroep Stichting* (TROS). Within a year, the new organization had become the country's largest broadcasting company. It later had to give up its leading position to Veronica, which also became an official broadcasting company after a change in the law made offshore radio stations illegal. Veronica decided to leave the public broadcasting system and become a purely commercial company. The strength of TROS and Veronica was a mix of unpretentious amusement programmes, films and soap operas – the latter two largely imported from America. Such programmes had long been taboo for the other broadcasting companies. They saw television and radio as a means of educating the public, making sure they stayed on the straight and narrow, and of providing them with information presented from what they considered to be the correct viewpoint. It had been clear for a long time, however, that the new, *mondig* public no longer felt the same way. The other companies had to follow in the wake of TROS and Veronica if they did not wish to lose a lot of their members, perhaps so many that their broadcasting licences would be withdrawn. The only exceptions to this were the conservative Calvinist *Evangelische Omroep* and the VPRO. The VPRO, short for the *Vrijzinnig Protestantse Radio Omroep*, had abandoned its Protestant principles at the end of the 1960s to concentrate on experimental and innovative programmes of an intellectual nature. It could perhaps be described as the Volkskrant of the airwaves. In the early days of the 'renewal', the VPRO achieved notoriety with a series of provocations and scandals that mocked what others considered sacred. It was, for example, the first to show a full-frontal naked woman, an event which is still engraved on the memories of many people in their forties and fifties. Membership of the EO or the VPRO is a well-considered choice. At the end of the 1980s, the public broadcasting system lost its monopoly, when commercial broadcasters were given the opportunity to set up their own networks. The market leader is RTL, with three national channels. RTL is part of the media-multinational Bertelsmann, which originated in Germany. Another company, SBS, also has three channels and, in 2004, billionaire John de Mol joined this overpopulated market with the media company Talpa.

The changes were even more revolutionary on the radio. The government released a number of national frequencies, which were sold to the highest bidders. This resulted in a profusion of channels aimed at specific target groups. At the same time, the government allowed for the further development of regional and local radio. Practically all cities, towns and even the larger villages now have their own radio station, which are often on air 24 hours a day. In many cases, the programmes are made by amateurs. Local radio in the Netherlands is not very commercial. On the other hand, the programme-makers take their lead from well-known national disc-jockeys.

The national public broadcasting companies have been relatively successful in retaining a substantial percentage of radio and television audiences. But criticism is gathering pace. Right-of-centre politicians in particular express doubts as to whether a public broadcasting system set up to meet the needs of nearly a century ago is still appropriate in the twenty-first century. This makes the public system an easy target for cutbacks.

The network of denominational schools seemed to be set in stone for eternity. But modern parents, free of the constraints of the pillars, proved to be more concerned with finding a good school for their children close to their homes. The schools had also been through the process of renewal and the religious influence on education had become weaker and less exclusive. It became very popular for school boards to adopt an ecumenical approach, with various church communities working together. Generally speaking, the traditional belief in the rightness of one's own particular group disappeared. This was often reflected in the names of the schools – the St. Franciscus College in Rotterdam, for example, changed its name to the City College St. Franciscus. The teachers, of course, had experienced the same process of secularization as the parents. It was exactly the same story in institutions providing social services, such as old people's homes and hospitals. The pillars remained intact, but the differences between them became increasingly obscure.

The 'social midfield'

The reason for this was simple enough – there was no need for the pillarized institutions, which were dependent on government grants and tax revenues, to adapt their structures. They got the money anyway. And they kept their customers, too, as long as they did not dish up an overly large helping of ideology along with whatever service they provided. As for the customers themselves, they did not notice that they were paying for these services. They were never presented with the bill, because they paid indirectly, through taxes or insurance schemes. In the 1980s a new term was invented for this complex of services – *het maatschappelijk middenveld*, literally the 'social midfield'. Critics claimed that, in this social midfield, all kinds of boards and committees ran influential organizations on the basis of obsolete principles, making them enormously powerful and yet accountable to no one.

And indeed, these institutions proved unassailable. Their managers and directors formed close-knit networks in which they worked together like the regents of old. And they still had their allies in the national political arena. Faced with structural election losses, the two Calvinist parties and the *Katholieke Volkspartij* worked more and more closely together until, in 1980, they united to form a new party, the *Christen Democratisch Appèl* (CDA). Until the early 1990s, the CDA could count on the votes of a third of the electorate. This was far less than the 50-55% that its predecessors had always achieved in the heyday of pillarization, but it was sufficient to ensure that the Christian Democrats always dominated coalition governments. The party's leader, Ruud Lubbers, who was to lead successive governments until 1994, introduced a motto with little ideological content: 'no nonsense'. With this approach, he acquired the reputation of a careful and cautious financier, who had little patience with those who threatened to waste taxpayers' money. His pre-decessors in the pillarized society would never have dominated politics with such an approach. Something had clearly changed.

The social developments of the 1960s had made quite a large dent in most individuals' traditional sense of belonging to a group. Their respect for the preacher or priest, and for authority in general, had been delivered a heavy blow, as had many other received values and norms of behaviour. Until the 1960s it was considered scandalous for people to live together without being married. This was something that was only done by bohemians who had fled to the big city – that is, Amsterdam – to escape the bounds of social control. Premarital sex was also severely frowned upon. If loving couples did indulge, they certainly kept it strictly to themselves. The widely available contraceptive pill – which you could get from your doctor without a great fuss being made about it – had taken away much of the risk. In addition, the renewal in the churches had made it possible to question many traditional rules and beliefs. Within a few years, it became acceptable for couples to live together without first having made the customary trip to the registry office and the church. Many of these relationships ended up in marriage after a time, but usually for practical reasons, often because of the desire to have children.

At the beginning of the 1970s, a feminist movement grew up which became very influential. The movement focused on the power relations within relationships. It demanded that men took on an equal share of the housework and bringing up the children, something they had – until then – always been able to escape from with the excuse that they had, after all, done a full day's work. The new feminists also claimed that women were less likely to have a higher education and that they were discriminated against in the workplace. They emphasized the fact that women were economically dependent on men, even after they were married. Women should therefore earn their own living as far as possible and develop their own careers. The feminists even suggested that perhaps, for a change, men could give up their careers to stay at home and look after their families. They demanded a wide variety of measures that would enable both partners to work, such as the widespread introduction of crèches and an employment policy that encouraged employers to take on more women. Their lobbying was successful, particularly in the public sector and in non-profit-making organizations. The law now forbids discrimination against women when taking on employees. All job advertisements now include the qualification M/V (short for *man/vrouw*, man or woman); many also state that women are encouraged to apply or that, if more than one candidate is considered suitable for the position, preference will be given to a woman. This, however, still leaves prospective employers sufficient opportunity to appoint men, and the more radical elements among the feminists consider this practice little more than paying lip service to emancipation, while continuing to pursue a traditional policy. This apart, the movement achieved a great deal. At universities and other institutes of higher education, formerly male strongholds, half of the students are now women. At some institutes, they are even in the majority. In the workplace, too, progress has been made. Yet, when the children arrive, it is still largely the women who stay at home. Women also seem to have a strong preference for courses of study that will prepare them for a career in the care sector. In spite of vigorous promotion campaigns by the government, very few girls still take courses in technical subjects. In recent years, only 2% of girls in secondary education chose the pure science specialisation, which is the best preparation for studying science at university.

Divorced women also seem to have difficulties in finding work, as a result of which they continue to be dependent on maintenance payments or social security benefits. Some feminists characterize this as the 'feminization of poverty'.

The women's movement used methods that had been made popular by the new *mondige* citizens in the 1960s. They held demonstrations and formed 'action committees'. Since the sixties, action committees have become a favoured form of organization for groups of individuals who devote themselves to a specific cause. This might be anything – the preservation of an old community, somewhere for young people to get together and play pop music, banning cars from a town centre, or perhaps demanding greater freedom for motorists. The aim of these committees, as their name suggests, is to take action. This means, generally, undertaking activities to attract the attention of the mass media – demonstrations, occupations, petitions or refusing to pay rent. Because the media are continually looking for something out of the ordinary, it is becoming increasingly difficult to attract attention with a normal mass demonstration. All kinds of tricks are therefore used to make the event unique. Simple banners are being replaced by a wide variety of bizarre and sometimes symbolic activities. Demonstrators dress up. They present the representatives of the particular authority they are protesting against with strange gifts, such as a red card of the kind shown to offending players by referees during football matches.

The besieged leaders of the country learned fast. Confrontations with citizens, using the police to break up demonstrations and ignoring protests generally led only to scandal. So they adapted and began to treat the new opposition as they had their colleagues in the other pillars. In response to the conflict model of the action committees, they showed themselves prepared to enter into peaceful consultation. These days, ministers, mayors or councillors will always meet demonstrators, receive the symbolic gift with conciliatory words and show themselves willing to talk. Since the 1960s there has been an enormous growth in the number of PR and public information departments at every level throughout the country. Leaders declared almost from one day to the next that of course individual citizens had the right to be involved in decisionmaking. New proposals, for example in the field of physical planning, were always submitted for public enquiry. Anyone who wished to could come along to a meeting and the authorities would listen with interest – genuine or feigned – to what they had to say. This right was even laid down in legislation. The leaders of action committees soon found themselves invited to all kinds of consultations. Many of them therefore found themselves involved in reaching compromises in a way that the traditional leaders had long been accustomed to.

In this way, the consultation culture spread from the top of the pillars downwards. From then on the leaders of the new opposition were simply invited to sit around the negotiating table. They quickly learned the ropes, how to behave and how to master the compromise culture. They adopted the tone and style of the traditional leaders, while the latter, in their turn, just as quickly learned the language of the action committees. When, in 2003, Minister of Social Affairs Aart Jan de Geus proposed a whole package of cutbacks in social services, together with a wage freeze, a hundred thousand trade unionists demonstrated against his policy. The minister gave way and reached a compromise with the unions. The question was, however, whether De Geus – whose background lay in the union movement – had foreseen the opposition and had proposed such radical changes to improve his position at the negotiating table. The demonstration was all part of the game. And such a great display of communal displeasure was perhaps a very positive development, giving the grassroots members of the unions the opportunity to let off steam. After all, they too had to sacrifice some of their demands for agreement to be reached.

In the old regent culture, formality was required in word and deed. The Dutch language has two forms for the second person: the familiar *jij*, used between brothers, sisters and good friends, and *u*, which is used between people who are less well acquainted, and implies a certain relationship of authority. Most children traditionally addressed their parents as *u*, while they themselves had to be content with *jij*.

The two forms were also used to indicate differences in social standing. Workers, whether they wore overalls or dust coats, would always be addressed as *jij* by the boss, but would never dream of replying in the same form. Office staff, on the other hand, who came to work in their suits, always fell into the *u* category. In families with a working-class background, there are always anecdotes about, for example, a grandfather or great grandfather who turned up at work wearing a hat, rather than the customary workman's cap. The boss had remarked on it and they had discussed the difference between 'hats' and 'caps'. There is still a vague echo of this distinction today in that office staff often prove to be less militant during labour disputes than their blue-collar colleagues. In relations between university students and their lecturers, the word *jij* simply did not exist.

In the 1960s, the accepted rules of behaviour rapidly became far more relaxed.

U was used less and less, eventually being reserved for strangers. Administrators, wishing to show that they were moving with the times, insisted on being called *jij* and by their first names. This made it difficult to recognize the boss at a glance because he or she seemed no different from the rest of the staff. It all gave a very democratic impression. After centuries in the driving seat, the high and mighty seemed to have disappeared from the scene.

Or had they simply hidden their high-and-mightiness from view?

Had they really disappeared or had they simply hidden their high-and-mightiness from view? It is arguable whether relations in the country had become as democratic as they seemed. A secretary was still in a subordinate position, even if she did call her boss 'Laurens Jan', 'Marco' or 'Piet' and could afford to complain now and then without fear of reprisal. The country's managers quickly learned to explain their decisions in great detail. Keen observers realized, however, that – after all the consultations and 'joint decision making' were out of the way – the original proposals usually remained essentially the same. And, in spite of all the jolly 'Jan'-ing and 'Piet'-ing, it continues to be inadvisable to take a radical stand against the decisions of superiors. Not only can it damage your career, it is incredibly difficult to keep it up in the face of so much reasonableness and willingness to listen from above.

De Telegraaf was scornful of all this. Part of the new public wanted nothing to do with the consultation culture which, in their opinion, led only to inert bureaucracy. Their inspiration was the free entrepreneur, whose livelihood depended on his ability to respond alertly to the market. They saw the state as a dangerous and interfering body that – with all its subsidies and social security provisions – took away people's sense of responsibility for their own lives and was therefore ultimately a threat to their freedom. These people found their ideological home in the *Volkspartij voor Vrijheid en Democratie* (vvd), until then a relatively marginal group with its roots in the old liberal party which, since the 1960s, had been granted a minority share in government by the Catholics and Calvinists. The vvd was dominated by free entrepreneurs with a strong dislike of state intervention. The top levels of the party contained quite a large group of intellectuals. A typical example was Pieter Jacobus Oud, who was the parliamentary leader in the 1950s. Oud was a professor at the University of Rotterdam, whose reputation was largely based on his history of the Dutch parliament, a standard work. The vvd was a civilized and refined party. In the 1970s, however, it was led by a Hans Wiegel, a young man who had flunked university and rejected the ideology of his social democratic background because he found the group mentality too claustrophobic. Wiegel adopted a popular tone, very similar to that of the editors of De Telegraaf. He complained about high taxes, sneered at the over-abundance of government subsidies and suggested that those on social security were lazy. The intellectual-

liberal school of thought, as personified by Oud, was pushed into the background.
Wiegel's favourite bogeyman was Joop den Uyl, the political leader of the PVDA.
Den Uyl had climbed to the top of the social democratic pillar, but had absorbed the
new activists into his circles of consultation. He represented an ideology with the
'redistribution of income, knowledge and power' as its main theme. Wiegel referred
to this as *nivellering*, levelling out, or rather levelling down, 'cutting off the heads
of all flowers that stick out above the rest'. Wiegel's model of individual freedom
directly opposed that of Den Uyl, who frequently spoke of the *maakbaarheid*, the
'moldability', of society. By this he meant creating a society that gave everyone the
opportunity to 'develop themselves' individually. This development was more
spiritual and cultural than material. Both leaders had considerable electoral success.
Den Uyl managed to keep his party intact as the social democratic pillar collapsed
and he was even prime minister for a four-year period in the 1970s. Wiegel was the
eloquent spokesman of the conservative opposition. Both gnawed away at the
traditional support of the Catholic and Calvinist parties. In 1977 the PVDA won more
than a third of the votes. Wiegel succeeded, however, in forming a parliamentary
majority with the decimated Catholics and Calvinists, forcing the social democrats
into opposition where – except for a short *intermezzo* – they would stay until 1989.

The changes in the voting behaviour of the electorate also made it clear that the
pillars were disintegrating. The balance of political power in the Netherlands had
always been exceptionally stable. When the Calvinist prime minister Hendrikus
Colijn won two seats in 1933, it was seen as a shift of great political significance
and a considerable electoral success. Since the 1960s, however, political parties –
particularly the new democratic party D66 – have grown accustomed to far greater
swings of fortune. Opinion polls show that the number of 'floating voters' – those
with no fixed ideological preference, who sometimes vote for one party and sometimes for another – has grown to some 20-30% of the electorate.

The elections of 2002 resulted in unprecedented shifts in the political balance. The party led by newcomer Pim Fortuyn came from nowhere to win 26 seats. Fortuyn's party had its roots in a trend that had gathered pace from the 1980s: declining public confidence in what the government did and how it tried to run their lives.

There are, indeed, trends in current Dutch society that point in this direction. The phenomenal growth experienced in the 1950s and 1960s levelled out and was interspersed with periods of severe economic depression. In the 1970s it was already becoming apparent that the complex system of grants and redistribution of wealth in the Netherlands was becoming too expensive. As a minister in the coalition government of Catholic prime minister Dries van Agt, Hans Wiegel (yes, the same Hans Wiegel!) kept the wolf from the door by allowing the budget deficit to increase. But since the beginning of the 1980s it has been impossible to mobilize a political majority behind this solution. The Christian Democrats found themselves a new leader in the Catholic industrialist Ruud Lubbers, who – in his typical 'no nonsense' style – placed the emphasis more on the personal responsibility of the individual for their own welfare. In this view, the government should not be overly protective in trying to shield individual citizens from personal risk. It is up to each individual to make their own arrangements, for example by taking out personal insurance cover rather than depending on collective schemes. The state should reduce its involvement to its core administrative duties, leaving the provision of other 'services' to the private sector. This is 'privatization'. The Lubbers governments also claimed that, in trying to guarantee social justice, the state had developed a whole array of rules and regulations, many of which were perhaps superfluous. This sounded very much like the message that Wiegel had employed with such success in the 1970s.

They operated under the banner of cost control

The Lubbers governments operated in practice under the banner of cost control. They aimed to reduce government expenditure because the state was simply becoming too expensive. They did this together with the vvd until 1989, when they had a dispute and exchanged the liberals for the social democrats. The fact that the pvda allowed Lubbers to pursue his policies in the same vein cost the party a lot of its traditional support.

Dutch society, however, proved rather unwilling to adapt. The cutbacks were an assault on what the networks of social services and interest groups – still largely organized according to the pillar system – considered to be acquired rights. They organized a very effective resistance, ensuring that the government's often radical plans were amended in countless consultations. Lubbers proved to be an accomplished juggler of formulations and compromises and managed to protect the main outlines of his policy against this onslaught. As a result, the entire system of grants and benefit schemes survived largely intact, while the flow of funds steadily diminished. It was the only possible approach, but it prevented genuinely effective action, as became clear from the confusion surrounding the Invalidity Insurance Act (WAO). The WAO provided employees who are unable to work due to sickness or injury with a generous benefit. The number of people receiving WAO benefits rapidly approached the million mark, because it was seen as a perfect way of getting rid of superfluous or difficult employees. The definition of 'sick' was very broad and could include problems of a psychological nature. Such complaints became increasingly common in sectors of industry that were no longer able to afford large numbers of staff due to economic problems. It was a public secret that the WAO was becoming more and more a place to hide the unemployed. The eligibility requirements for a WAO benefit were tightened up and all those receiving benefits already had to be re-assessed under these new stricter rules, but neither the Act itself nor the way in which it was implemented changed radically until the twenty-first century, when Christian Democrat minister Aart Jan de Geus, during the second Balkenende government, tackled the problem more rigorously by replacing the whole Act with the much stricter Work and Income Act (WIA), which shifted the emphasis from invalidity to work to what people with a disability could do themselves to make a living.

During Lubbers' 'reign' the purchasing power of people on a social security benefit fell, while the standard of living of those in work generally increased – though not significantly. Lubbers preached wage restraint as the only way to keep unemployment down and minimize the loss of jobs due to automation. In this respect, he had the support of the majority, for he was simply expressing the widely held belief that *rijkdom niet beklijft*, riches have wings. In the early years of the twenty-first century, christian-democratic prime minister Jan Peter Balkenende revived this policy to combat the effects of the 'dot-com' recessions. Like Lubbers, he first suffered criticism from all corners of society, but that soon dissipated once the economy began to pick up again.

Wealth is the fruit of hard work, but can be swept away in a storm as easily as the leaves of autumn. A little concern and caution is never amiss. This is apparent, for example, in the Queen's speech at the annual opening of parliament. The speech, drawn up by the government, is basically a statement of its policy. The Queen reads it out at a solemn gathering of both Houses. It is always full of concern, even expressing a certain amount of fear for the future. 'The government is concerned to observe...' – it is as though they are always prepared for the worst. But, at the same time, the impression is created that the government will act in time, just before things go really wrong. This is reassuring. Ruud Lubbers was a master at giving concerned replies to questions in his weekly television interview. His social democratic successor, Wim Kok, always managed to give the impression that the government had everything completely under control and that all problems had been predicted in advance. The public could therefore rest assured that it was being protected against every kind of adversity.

An all-too-common sight on the Dutch motorways: congestion.

In spite of all this, there were 7.3 million cars in the country in January 2005. This creates enormous congestion during the rush hour. The media now only report the longest congestion. A queue less than five kilometres long is not even worth mentioning. More and more drivers feel guilty about using their cars. Yet car ownership continues to increase, because concern for the environment is no reason – any more than the fear of God – to change your behaviour radically in practice. Recently there are more suvs on the roads, but not everyone is equally enthusiastic about these gas-guzzlers. They are known by all kinds of imaginative names: 'PC Hooft tractor' is one of the more complimentary. The PC Hooftstraat is a meeting point for the nouveaux riches in Amsterdam. A little more aggressive is 'Aso-bak', which suggests in no uncertain terms that the vehicles and those who drive them are antisocial. And halfway through the first decade of the new century, it was the turn of diesel car-owners to cough up: it was discovered that they were polluting the environment with carbon soot particles – a completely new concept to most people – and were thereby contributing to the greenhouse effect, which would one day turn the Netherlands into a marsh or – opinions differed widely – a frozen desert, if the warm waters of the gulf stream no longer reached our shores from the Atlantic Ocean.

Yet despite all this, the Dutch relentlessly continue to use their cars. The embarrassment is not sufficient to give up the riches, so to speak. But many of them will be troubled by a guilty conscience. At the back of their minds they will still hear the faint voice of Calvin: 'You are bad and God will find you out'. Let those who have abundance remember that they are surrounded with thorns.

This is as Dutch as it gets: cycling along the dyke. With a strong headwind, it's one of the best free workouts you could imagine. Also recommended for ex-pats who want to stay fit!

2

Utilitarian

'And in every region the voice of the water, telling of endless disaster, is heard and feared'

The fight against the water. Polders, windmills and pumping stations. The need for precise coordination and cooperation. The engineer's mentality. You can manage the water but cannot force it. Social engineering. Society's 'water meadows'. Social management, but without a master plan. The policy of tolerance.

H *et was kil op de dijk.* It was bitterly cold on the dyke. To my knowledge, no novel has ever started in this way, but a more Dutch opening sentence is difficult to imagine. The word 'kil' refers to the biting cold caused by our often unpleasant, windy climate. Dykes, embankments to keep the water – the enemy – at bay, crisscross the Dutch landscape. These days, they are crowned with a strip of tarmac, but they are no more than secondary lines of communication. The real trunk roads are the four-lane motorways that have become an equally familiar feature of the landscape – 120 kilometres an hour, raindrops on the windscreen, grey clouds rushing in from the southwest, middle-range family saloons in front and trucks in the slow lane. And the horizon dotted with the apartment blocks of the next town. That is what I see when I think of Holland.

Holland, not the Netherlands. The area characterized by endless flat country-side, canals and dykes actually covers little more than 30% of the country. It stretches out along the North Sea coast and includes roughly the provinces of Zeeland, Noord-Holland, Zuid-Holland, Friesland and Groningen, with a few inroads into the other provinces here and there. This 30% does, however, contain the large majority of the population and all the major cities. It is the heart of the country's culture and economy. The old province of Holland was the driving force of the Republic in the Golden Age and it is still the powerhouse of the country, even though this conclusion might cause a few indignantly raised eyebrows among the people of the remaining provinces, especially those in and around the largest city in Noord-Brabant, Eindhoven, the home of electronics giant Philips and the place where most new technological innovations are made these days. Outside the *Randstad* – the urban conurbation in the west, dominated by Amsterdam, The

Hague, Rotterdam and Utrecht – foreign visitors soon learn not to refer to the country as Holland, but as 'the Netherlands'. The image of a motorway flanked by flat, green fields is not a truly representative image. In Limburg, it snakes through river valleys and in the *Veluwe*, a nature reserve in the centre of the country, it cuts through endless woodlands.

The whole of the Netherlands is a delta

Yet all of these areas are a part of the Kingdom of the Netherlands. The name means 'low countries'. The whole of the country is actually a delta, fed mostly by the Rhine and the Maas but also, to a lesser extent, by the Scheldt and the Eems. The North Sea is never far off and is largely responsible for the windy and rainy climate.

The rivers have minds of their own. The Rhine – which has now been contained – had the tendency to change course. And the quantity of water transported by the Maas tends to vary enormously, as the people of Limburg discovered in 1993 and 1994 when unprecedented masses of water rushed into their valleys. The whole of the country is actually barely above sea level and there is no clearly defined border between the land and the water. At least, there would not be if the people of the Netherlands had not made the distinction much clearer themselves. Yet, as the floods in Limburg showed, the water is not as easily mastered as foreigners – impressed at the astounding feats of civil engineering the Dutch have achieved – might wish to believe. The foreign visitor is often heard to declare 'God made the world, but the Dutch made the Netherlands'. It is a cliché, it has probably been said for three hundred years or more, and we still like to hear it. But it should be put into context.

The contest is, at best, a draw

In their renowned battle against the water, it is only in this century that the Dutch have abandoned their traditional defensive strategy and gone somewhat on the offensive. And, the contest is, at best, a draw. After more than a thousand years, the water has lost none of its power, if anything it has become even more fearsome. Before the Second World War, there were no motorways or apartment blocks to spoil the view for Hendrik Marsman (1899-1945), one of the greatest Dutch poets of this century:

> *Denkend aan Holland*
> *zie ik brede rivieren*
> *traag door oneindig laagland gaan,*
> *rijen ondenkbaar*

ijle populieren
als hoge pluimen
aan de einder staan,
en in de geweldige
ruimte verzonken
de boerderijen
verspreid door het land,
boomgroepen, dorpen,
geknotte torens,
kerken en olmen
in een groots verband.
De lucht hangt er laag
en de zon wordt er langzaam
in grijze veelkleurige
dampen gesmoord,
en in alle gewesten
wordt de stem van het water
met zijn eeuwige rampen
gevreesd en gehoord.

Thinking of Holland
I see wide rivers
Winding lazily through endless low countryside,
Rows of impossibly slim poplars
Like feathers
Lining the horizon,
And farmhouses,
Low and lost
In the immense open space,
And throughout the land
Clusters of trees, villages,
Truncated towers,
Churches and mighty elms
All merging as one.
The sky is low
And the sun is slowly
Smothered by mists
Grey and many-coloured,
And in every region
The voice of the water,
Telling of endless disaster,
Is heard and feared.

'Thinking of Holland, I see wide rivers winding lazily through endless low countryside, rows of impossibly slim poplars like feathers lining the horizon.' Poet Hendrik Marsman wrote these words in the 1920s.

Because the ice is melting at the North Pole, sea levels are rising. The land, on the other hand, is drying out and subsiding. This weakens Dutch defences. Debates on the possible greenhouse effect, which will accelerate the melting of the ice caps, are therefore followed attentively and with some concern. That is why the Netherlands is a strong supporter of the Kyoto protocols and other measures to control the CO_2 level in the atmosphere. Not that the average Dutch person is afraid of getting their feet wet. They are hardly aware that they live several metres below sea level. Their concern is more of a vague worry about what will happen to their children's children. Yet, even now, they still tend to see the water as a threat. You can drown in water. That is the main reason why all schools organize swimming lessons. The fact that swimming is healthy is a secondary concern.

This all rests on a collective experience reaching back more than a thousand years, in which each generation learned the hard way how you can protect yourself against the *wassende water*, the rising waters. The Netherlands – at least the west of the country as it is today – was originally an area of marshland, similar in many ways to present-day Bangladesh. The rivers flowed into the North Sea, splitting into a number of different arms which periodically changed course, as the Ganges, Brahmaputra and Mississippi still do. Most of the water from the Rhine now enters the sea at the Hook of Holland, near Rotterdam. Its main estuary used to be sixty kilometres to the north at Katwijk, near Leiden. All that remains there is a small stream, known as the *Oude Rijn*, the Old Rhine.

But the North Sea can be very fickle, and wash the dunes away

The North Sea can be very fickle. Storms whip up the water. The currents carry large quantities of sand with them, generally from the south to the north, making the coastline unstable. Shallows and, eventually, sandbanks are created. In this way, in about 5000 BC, an uninterrupted line of sand dunes was created, which were stabilized by plant growth. This row of dunes stretches out along the entire Dutch coast, broken only where the rivers flow into the sea.

But the North Sea, which created the dunes, just as easily washes them away, depositing the sand elsewhere. As the sea level continues to rise, this process becomes even more destructive. The dunes would not have lasted much longer if the Dutch had not taken measures to halt the erosion. Existing dunes can be stabilized by, for example, planting marram grass which prevents the sand from drifting in the wind. The currents can be kept at bay by constructing breakwaters covered in basalt, a very hard volcanic rock. These breakwaters, which extend a few dozen metres into the sea and break the force of the current, can be seen for example between the Hook of Holland and The Hague. Sometimes, however, the wind can whip the water up over the breakwaters and whole sections of dune will be washed away. In the north of the country, the sea continually tries to break through the line of dunes. A sea dyke was built as early as the Middle Ages near Petten, and has since regularly been enlarged and re-inforced. Further to the north, the line of dunes was breached in the distant past, creating what we now know as the Frisian Islands. The most northerly point of Texel, the largest of the islands, is still being eroded in spite of all the efforts of modern technology to halt the process. Just off the southwest coast of Texel, on the other hand, a whole new island, the *Razende Bol*, is appearing above water. For many years, the Razende Bol was the subject of a dispute between Texel and the adjoining municipalities. The former finally won out and the area is now a military training ground.

About a thousand years ago, the North Sea forced its way into the area behind Texel and formed a continually growing bay that later came to be known as the Zuider Zee. The northern region of Friesland was eventually divided into two parts, with a great expanse of water between them. The western half is now part of the province of Noord-Holland and has largely lost its Frisian character, with the exception of its name: West-Friesland.

On the south coast of the Zuider Zee, on the edge of the Veluwe – a large area of woodland that is higher and therefore never threatened by the water – is Elburg, the oldest planned town in the Netherlands. The town is laid out entirely in a chessboard pattern. It was designed by Arent toe Boecop, who ordered the original Elburg to be evacuated at the end of the fourteenth century, because the sea could no longer be held back. The new town was founded on the higher ground further inland. Naarden, another very clearly planned town, is a good example of this retreating movement, away from the aggressive Zuider Zee, where the waters of the North Sea were not easily contained.

Behind the dunes, there was originally an area of marshland, crisscrossed with countless streams, which was still affected by the tides and where the sea water infiltrated the many arms of the river. In the present day, salt water can still be registered as far inland as Schoonhoven, a small town in Zuid-Holland on the border with the province of Utrecht. The influence of the tides can be felt even further, at Culemborg, halfway between the coast and the German border. The area very much resembled a mangrove swamp, although the vegetation consisted, of course, of species more suited to the colder climate, such as willow trees. The organic remains of this vegetation formed a particular kind of soil, peat, in which so much of the plant structure is preserved that, after being dried, it makes an excellent fuel. Stoves have burned this peat, which can be cut loose in slices, for centuries.

In spite of its inhospitable nature, this area was populated even in early times. The Roman historian Tacitus, for example, describes in great detail the uprising of a German tribe, the Batavians, against the Emperor Vespasian in the first century AD. This caused later historians to claim the Batavians as their ancestors. After the French occupation in 1795, the country was even known as the Batavian Republic for a little more than a decade.

Archeological research has discovered that the inhabitants of the area were farmers, who mostly kept cattle. They protected themselves against the water by building artificial hills, known as *terpen*, which provided enough space for the peoples and their animals when the water was at its highest. Many of these hills still survive in the northern province of Friesland. They form the core of old villages and have an ancient church at their centre.

It is then a small step to enclose a larger area with an earthen embankment, a dyke. In this way, you can keep more land dry with the same amount of earth. Remains of such dykes have been found that date back to the eighth and ninth centuries. The question that arises is: why would anyone wish to enclose the land in this way?

Land was private property

The classical cultures of the Greeks and the Romans, on which much of present European culture is still based, had the concept of land ownership. Land was private property. In many parts of Europe this eventually came to include the people living on it. They were – as is described in the statutes of the time – tied to their land.

In that other gigantic river delta where Bangladesh is now situated, there was traditionally no notion of land ownership. There were local lords to whom the farmers in the area paid tribute and taxes, but this was due to their power and the authority invested in them, not to the fact they owned the land. Land was a common resource just like the air they breathed. The people of this wet country never developed the technology to protect it against the fury of the sea and the rivers. If the Ganges changed course and the sea swept away parts of the land, the farmers would simply move to the nearest piece of dry land and put their fences up again. The region was not as densely populated as it is today. It was only when the English colonists introduced land ownership that the local lords began to protect their new property with dykes and other constructions to control the water.

The fact that the people in the Rhine/Maas delta were a thousand years ahead of the Bengalis in this respect was probably due to the fact that the land was in private hands, owned by free farmers, nobles and Catholic monasteries. If the river or the sea took a piece of your land, it was a little more difficult to move somewhere else. Anywhere you went was someone else's land.

The monasteries and nobles started to protect their land by building earthen dykes. Some of these still wind their way through the countryside. It is not always clear how it was all organized because the process started at a time when written records were hardly kept.

The first small dykes were adequate because the sea level was much lower than it is now. They also protected relatively small areas of land. A number of inventions probably date from that time, such as the *duikertje*, which is still in use today. This is a pipe with a loose flap at one end. If the water level rises and the water attempts to flow into the pipe, the current forces the flap shut. If the water comes from the other direction, the flap opens.

The Dutch language has an enormous number of words for 'canal'

Enclosure by a dyke has no effect on the marshy nature of the land itself. Furthermore, it forces the groundwater upwards. The construction of a dyke therefore means that the enclosed land has to be drained. This is done by digging dead straight canals, in which the water collects. The Dutch language has an enormous number of words for the English word 'canal': *sloot, gracht, vaart, vliet, tocht* and many more, all of which say something about the width, depth or function of the canal in question. But whatever kind of canal it is, drainage is always part of its function. This also applies to the ponds and streams that are so popular in the suburbs and housing estates. They are not only there because they look nice; they also keep the water out of the cellars of the houses.

Water from outside the enclosed area seeps under the dyke and is in this way connected with the groundwater inside. As sea levels rose, dykes no longer provided adequate protection. The most primitive way of getting rid of excessive water was to simply bail it out. But in the fourteenth century, a new form of energy harnessed for this purpose – the wind. The early windmills were primitive, little more than a shaft with four sails at one end and a water wheel at the other. Each

Drainage of a canalized river.

generation of mill-builders, however, refined the techniques. The mills got bigger, and the sails were eventually mounted on a cap that could be turned into the wind. In the body of the mill there was a wooden mechanism that, for the time, was very energy-efficient. The mills were perfected with the introduction of the Archimedes' screw, which could raise water to a height of four metres. It is difficult to measure the power of the traditional windmill but it is estimated at between 80 and 100 horsepower. This is comparable to that of the Mitsubishi Colt, the 100-horsepower mini car that for the time being is produced by Nedcar in Born, Limburg.

A piece of land enclosed by dykes and drained is called a polder. Polders require a great deal of organization, not only in their construction but also to maintain them. The water pumped out of one, ends up in another. This has proved a great problem in Bangladesh, where new polders can exacerbate the situation in neighbouring villages. This can lead to conflict and even to the dykes being destroyed. Similar conflicts occurred in Dutch history. It would seem obvious that land reclamation should be a task for a central authority. The famous delta civilizations in ancient history, notably in Egypt and Mesopotamia, were extremely authoritarian with a divine monarch and a ruling caste that played a leading role in the organization of irrigation and drainage. The counties and duchies in the

Middle Ages, however, lacked the power to build up such a system. Not that they did not try. The counts of Holland charged their *baljuws* – local officials very much like the infamous Sheriff of Nottingham – with the management of the polders and dykes. They, in their turn, appointed deputies – generally known as *heemraden*, dyke reeves – from among the local farmers but, because of the limited power of the counts, they were not easy to keep under control and acquired for themselves all manner of powers and privileges, in a similar way to the civic leaders in the towns and cities, who bought off their autonomy.

Dykes were built along the river banks. The polders stood shoulder to shoulder. The many streams that crisscrossed the country were closed off with dams. Boats had to be pulled over these dams with ropes, which provided quite a lot of work. Consequently, settlements frequently sprung up around the dams. Many modern-day place names end in -dam, notably the capital, Amsterdam. The first part of the name usually refers to the stream or river that was dammed off: the Amstel in Amsterdam, the Rotte in Rotterdam and the Ee in Edam. Very often, a square or street in the centre of a town or city will also be known as the Dam. The oldest houses will be found here. The Dam in Amsterdam, where the Royal Palace and the National Monument are located, is the most famous in the Netherlands. Most of these dams were later reopened. The gap was then closed off with enormous sluice doors that could be opened to let out excess water or to allow ships and boats to pass.

The maintenance of the dykes was initially organized very simply. Farmers were responsible for the stretch of dyke adjoining their land. This resulted in some stretches being neglected. It was also unfair, because farmers in the middle of the polder, far from the dyke, escaped this obligation. From around the end of the fifteenth century, it was increasingly decided that maintenance of the dyke was the joint responsibility of all those living under its protection. Either they all worked on the upkeep of the dyke together, or they paid a kind of tax to the reeves, who would then appoint a coordinator known as the *dijkgraaf,* or dyke warden.

It was never completely safe behind the dyke

These wardens were very powerful. They could order people to pay taxes or to work on the dykes. They are still authorized to call on the entire population of the area under their jurisdiction to fight against the onslaught of water. It was never completely safe behind the dyke. Sea currents could erode the dyke foundation to the extent that it would suddenly collapse. Heavy storms – particularly in combination with spring tides – could throw such masses of water against the dykes that they simply could not hold out. Every generation would have to live through one or two serious floods, which would claim many victims.

Although it cannot compete with the typhoons that unleash incredible violence every year on the coast of Bangladesh, or Hong Kong or Manila, the North Sea can still whip up a reasonably fearsome storm. Once or twice a decade, it will produce a storm of typhoon force. This is not very often, but it was often enough. Between Gorinchem and Geertruidenberg, on the border between the provinces of Zuid-Holland and Noord-Brabant, there is an area of natural wetlands known as the *Biesbosch*, that closely resembles what the Netherlands must have been like before the dunes and the dykes. But it is not a remnant of the original 'mangrove swamp'. It used to be agricultural polder-land, but was lost to the sea during the St. Elisabeth flood of 1421 – named after the saint on whose day the water broke through. Most of the flooded land has been reclaimed over the centuries, but the Biesbosch is still as it was left when the water receded. The 'drowned land' in Saaftinge and in Zuid-Beveland is also former farmland lost in the floods. In the latter, old bricks are sometimes still found – the remains of the once thriving town of Reimerswaal, whose inhabitants gave up the fight against the water at the beginning of the seventeenth century.

When the water comes, it comes like a wall

The effects of the floods became more serious as the sea level rose and the land subsided. When the water comes, it comes like a wall. The dyke caves in and the water rushes through, boring a deep hole into the ground immediately behind the dyke. It then spreads out, thundering and boiling, sweeping away everything in its path – trees, cattle, people. It smashes against the walls of the houses. The only way to escape its fury is to hide in the attic or – if there is still time – take refuge on a piece of dyke that can withstand the onslaught. Then it is a question of waiting, until the wind has dropped enough for boats to be sent out. During the last great floods in February 1953 – which affected large areas of Zeeland, Holland and Noord-Brabant – 1,835 people were killed. More than 100,000 people had to evacuated in the days following the disaster. It was touch and go whether the dykes protecting the major cities in the west of the country would hold out. It was the most serious flood in more than a century.

But the landscape still bears the scars of earlier catastrophes. The holes made by the screwing movement of the water as it bores into the ground behind the dyke can be twenty or thirty metres deep and fill up with groundwater. These more or less circular lakes, known in Dutch as *wielen* – are a permanent reminder of days and nights spent in fear of the water.

After the floods have subsided, the holes are usually repaired, and then begins the difficult task of pumping out the water. This takes months, even with the latest in modern technology. In the past, they had to rely on windmills. After the floods in February 1953, it was November before the last hole was repaired. Only then can the pumping start.

In olden days, everyone was therefore continually aware of the threat from the water. It has been suggested that this is why the Dutch felt such an affinity with the

The monumental headquarters of the water authorities are an expression of their power. This is the Schielandhuis, which now houses the Rotterdam historical museum.

sombre message preached by Calvin. They did not need to be told – 'Watch and pray, for thou knowest not the day nor the hour.' The wall of water can sweep way everything that you have built up – even your life – in just a few seconds. And, indeed orthodox Calvinism is still strong in the *Alblasserwaard*, one of the lowest regions in the Netherlands, where a large number of *wielen* bear silent witness to past catastrophes.

On the other hand, this enemy – just as much as Alva and his army – was dangerous enough to force people to work together. The various bodies responsible for the upkeep of the dykes agreed on various forms of cooperation. The magnificent seventeenth century *Schielandhuis* in the centre of Rotterdam is a perfect illustration of the power of these bodies. Today it houses a large historical museum.

The North Sea and the rising rivers were not the only causes of flooding. The people themselves frequently gave a helping hand. Peat-diggers, for example, dug up the fenlands in the west, leaving great ponds behind which the surrounding fields were eroded. This created a threat within the dykes and behind the dunes. People must have realized the danger, but they could not live without the peat which, for many, was the only fuel they could afford. In spite of the mild climate in the Netherlands, it is not easy to survive a winter without a stove to warm the house. And particularly a few centuries ago, when temperatures dropped below freezing more frequently than they do now – as can be seen from the countless paintings from the Golden Age depicting skaters and other wintry scenes. The same process that is causing the sea level to rise, has also increased the average temperature by a few degrees.

Eventually, technology was sufficiently advanced to tackle these expanses of water. The greatest land reclaimer of all was mill-builder Jan Adriaensz Leeghwater (1575-1650). His method consisted of enclosing a lake with a dyke and a canal. He then built enough screw-mills to pump the lake dry, after which a drainage system was built. The mills were left where they were to pump away excess water. Leeghwater worked on commission from Amsterdam financiers, who saw a new polder as a good investment. They tackled the problem on a large scale. Leeghwater started with the *Beemster* lake, which covered 7,189 hectares and was continually eroding away at the surrounding land. It took two years to pump dry, after which a flood wiped out the fruits of the work in a single day. The financiers raised new capital and two years later, in 1612, the polder was once again dry. Their investment was returned many times over. The Beemster is now one of the country's most beautiful polders, with splendid historical farmhouses and elegant villages. Leeghwater repeated this magnificent feat with many other – smaller – lakes. He was, however, unable to achieve his greatest ambition – to drain the *Haarlemmermeer*, between Amsterdam and Leiden. Hundreds of mills would have been needed to tame this gigantic lake, on the site of which Schiphol Airport now stands. Leeghwater wrote a widely read and often reprinted book about the drainage of the lake, which was considered by his contemporaries to be more a work of science fiction.

Now they had steam

It was not until the nineteenth century that anyone dared take up the challenge of the Haarlemmermeer. And this was because they were no longer dependent entirely on windmills. Now they had steam.

In the seventeenth and eighteenth centuries the whole of the western part of the country was covered with windmills. Because of their limited capacity, they had to be linked together in all kinds of ingenious ways. Roughly speaking, the first series of mills would pump the water into a reservoir, known as a *boezem*, a second set of mills would then pump it into another reservoir slightly higher up, and so on until the water could be emptied into a river, where it could be carried down to the sea. Only very few of these mills survived the transition to steam power, electricity and diesel engines. The best preserved system of mills is to be seen at *Kinderdijk*, in a corner of the Alblasserwaard. In spite of their great number, these mills had their work cut out to keep the Alblasserwaard dry right from the start. Some areas were often too boggy to be safe, and the average water level in the ditches was higher than now, because that was the best the mills could do. This is how the first steam engines were introduced into the Netherlands – in dribs and drabs – to help in the fight against the water. They proved their strength and reliability, however, in the draining of the massive Haarlemmermeer. Three pumping stations did the job between 1849 and 1851. One of them was named 'Leeghwater', after the seventeenth century master who thought he would need hundreds of mills.

That effectively sealed the fate of the windmills. And now, thanks to modern pumping stations operating on electricity or diesel – which have long superseded steam – it is possible to regulate the water level inside the dykes very precisely. The new pumps are also powerful enough to have solved the problem of boggy ground which had always plagued engineers in the Alblasserwaard and elsewhere. The Netherlands has never been so dry.

Water management in the Netherlands is now the responsibility of a completely separate layer of government, the *waterschappen* and *hoogheemraadschappen*, which are directly based on their medieval forerunners. They are run by elected boards, but they are not strictly democratic, because representation is biased towards land and property owners. Yet they impose taxes on the entire population. The taxes are to guarantee the quality of the water; today's water boards are also responsible for keeping the water free of chemical pollution. Their work is largely carried out in secret. The taxes are not high enough for this to cause indignation among the general public and, consequently, the boards can go about their business undisturbed by calls for greater democracy. There are, on the other hand, frequent confrontations with environmental groups, who generally resist any proposals to 'modernize' the landscape submitted by the water boards.

The steam pumping stations of the Haarlemmermeer had opened the door to modern technology. Engineers came to the conclusion that the achievements of Leeghwater and his contemporaries could be repeated on a far grander scale, that they no longer had to be content with the small land-reclamation projects that had been conducted until then, such as in Zeeland, where clay deposits formed here and there outside the dykes, or in the north, where the Wadden Sea – the stretch of sea between the coast and the Frisian Islands – was becoming increasingly shallow.

Cornelis Lely (1854-1929) was the prototype of the modern engineer who was not afraid to take on large projects. He devised a plan to put an end to the threat from the Zuider Zee. The plan had two parts. Firstly, a dyke was to be built between Noord-Holland and Friesland to cut off the Zuider Zee from the North Sea. In the newly created lake behind the dyke, Lely envisaged the drainage of a large number of polders, so that half the surface area of the lake could be reclaimed as agricultural land. What remained of the old Zuider Zee would become a freshwater lake, later to be known as the IJsselmeer. Four of the polders Lely originally planned have since been created.

Lely was the first of a generation of great engineers who had a deep influence on the shape of the Netherlands as it is today. A large number of them worked for *Rijkswaterstaat*, the government department responsible for the construction and maintenance of hydraulic and other civil engineering works. Rijkswaterstaat focuses primarily on large-scale projects. It keeps the tradition of Leeghwater very much alive, restricted only by the desire of politicians to limit expenditure. Serious flooding, however, always loosens their purse strings. The *Tweede Kamer* approved Lely's 'Zuider Zee Act' two years after water from the Zuider Zee had flooded large areas of Noord-Holland.

Successful invasions of the land by the hostile water are now more likely to provoke an aggressive response

With the development of modern technology, the Dutch have largely lost their fear of, if not their respect for, the sea. Successful invasions of the land by the hostile water are now more likely to provoke an aggressive response than the traditional mumblings about the fragility of existence. The floods of 1916 cried out for decisive countermeasures, immediate action to tame the Zuider Zee, no matter what the

This is a small part of the Maeslantkering, one of the largest civil engineering projects in the world, which has featured in the Discovery Channel programme 'Extreme Machines'. In extreme bad weather, the sliding sluice gates can close off the Nieuwe Waterweg near Rotterdam. The gates are 210 metres long and 22 metres high.

cost. The disaster in 1953 had the same effect. All of the dykes that had been breached were in the estuaries of the Rhine/Maas delta. This was because the storm – of rare typhoon force – had pushed enormous quantities of water inland. The government appointed a commission of engineers within the first two weeks of the disaster to determine whether the delta could be sealed off, followed immediately – if necessary – by the Wadden Sea. The commission drew up a 'Delta Plan' that would involve sealing off all exits to the sea, with the exception of one for the Scheldt and one for the Rhine, to enable continued access to the ports of Antwerp and Rotterdam. They also introduced a new concept – *deltahoogte*, delta height. All dykes and dams had to be high enough and strong enough to withstand a combination of spring tides and storms of a force that only occurred statistically once every ten thousand years.

It took approximately twenty-five years to complete the Delta Project. The enormous dykes and sluices are now a tourist attraction, which Dutch hosts proudly show visitors from abroad. Now and then there are grumblings in the papers about excessive budgets, because Rijkswaterstaat has a reputation of wanting only the biggest and the best, but the whole gigantic project appears to have given the Dutch a boost to both their national pride and their sense of security. Most people believe that disasters like that of 1953 can never happen again. This is, however, an old and dangerous misconception. Studies have shown that most authorities in areas affected by floods traditionally show not the slightest concern until the wall of water is upon them, when they literally had to be called out of bed. National radio companies – at a time of imminent emergency when there was an obvious need for clear instructions and public information – simply stopped broadcasting.

It is also by no means certain that keeping the dykes at delta height offers as much protection as people think. New data on the possible consequences of the greenhouse effect suggest that additional measures will be necessary to keep the water at bay. There is a real chance that the Delta Project will have to be repeated.

Every Dutch heart therefore still misses a beat when, with a storm on the way, the radio news announces 'limited dyke surveillance'.

Dykes at delta height are not enough on their own

Dykes at delta height may be spectacular, but they are not enough on their own. The Dutch keep their feet dry with a complex system of pumping stations and pumps, *duikertjes* and sluices, ditches and canals, across the whole country. This whole system has to be kept running by people. And that means people who know exactly what they are doing.

Water is multifunctional – ships and boats can sail on it. Until the demand for freight transport took on mass proportions, followed closely by the construction of good public highways, most freight in the Netherlands was carried by water. Even freight trains were unable to challenge this dominant position to any significant extent. You could, after all, get practically anywhere in the country by boat. The country was therefore not only crisscrossed by waterways intended for drainage, but also by a large number of canals used for freight transport. These boat canals still cut across the countryside in dead straight lines. Most date from the Golden Age and form part of a forgotten network of public transport. The canals were used by horse-drawn barges. They were slow, with a maximum speed of three or four kilometres per hour. But they were reliable, they sailed on time, and could accommodate large numbers of passengers in their covered saloons. The only thing that could stop them plying their way up and down the canals was ice. In the time of Prince Maurits, during the Golden Age, whole armies were transported to the front by these barges. The soldiers were amazed at this wonderful and happy land, where you didn't even have to walk to the battlefield. For two centuries, the horse-drawn barges were the most reliable form of transport in the world. And the cheapest. Only in the Netherlands could you really plan a journey and be reasonably certain of the day on which – and even the time at which – you would reach your destination. The barges were an important part of the infrastructure that permitted the economic growth of the Golden Age. Today, they are the symbol of slow-moving conservatism. But they acquired that image only when the Netherlands discovered the steam train and constructed a road network, along which the post coach could race, rushing its passengers – at first only wealthy businessmen with cigars and wallets fat enough to pay the fare – to their destinations. The barges even gave rise to a whole series of political pamphlets, the authors of which had thrashed out their standpoints in discussions held in the saloon during the long, slow voyages.

Good organization and close cooperation

This whole complex of water management depends on good organization and close cooperation. Everything has to be carefully maintained according to fixed standards, sluices have to be opened and closed exactly at the right time, mills – and later, pumping stations – have to operate according to a clearly defined pattern. There must be detailed procedures for emergencies, such as storms or exceptionally high water, and they have to be applied in practice. This, in turn, demands a clear designation of tasks and responsibilities, so that everyone knows exactly what to do and not to do at any particular moment. And cooperation is essential, particularly in emergencies, when everything else has to be put on one side, there is no time for discussion, all disputes must be forgotten and all must pull together to avert the danger.

Perhaps this is why the desire for order and organization, in spite of a well-developed sense of individuality and in spite of 'sovereignty in one's own domain', is so strong.

It gives a completely new dimension to God's command to Adam

In any case, there is a clear tradition of belief in the 'moldability' of the landscape. In the west and north of the country there are no longer any genuine 'natural areas'. Everything is the result of human intervention – even the old lakes were created by peat digging. The landscape is the product of man's toil. This gives a completely new dimension to God's command to Adam to be Lord of creation. In olden times, the Dutch had two terms for the virgin land in the higher areas in the east and south of the country: *woeste gronden* and *onland*. These both have very negative connotations. *Woest*, meaning wild and untamed, is the very opposite of controlled and civilized; it also suggests fury, an irrational anger. The prefix *on-* is a denial, clearly suggesting badness, as in *ongeluk* (which literally means unhappiness, but is also the Dutch word for 'accident'), *onkruid* (literally 'un-plant', the weeds that strangle the corn), or *ongedierte* ('un-animals' – used to describe unwanted creatures, such as bedbugs or cockroaches). This wild 'un-land' was a threat, as hostile as the unpredictable sea. Until well into the last century it was also uncompromisingly resilient to human intervention. Agriculture in the south and the east was traditionally a combination of arable and pastoral. Farmers grew crops and kept cattle. The former was limited by the amount of natural fertilizer produced by the latter. In the impoverished province of Drenthe, the fields – with a village at their centre – lay like islands in the great expanse of heathland. On the heath grew the heather, a tough little plant with purple flowers which is excellent food for sheep. Farmers wanting to cultivate the heath for crops could no longer keep sheep and therefore lost their indispensable supply of manure. It was one thing or the other. *Some catch, that catch 22*. The heath of the 'wild lands' proved to have insufficient natural fertility to support crops without additional nourishment. The farmers were in a zero-sum situation that remained unchanged for centuries. It was not until the nineteenth century that cheap artificial fertilizer and specialist machinery provided them with an opportunity to break the deadlock. They allowed farmers to improve their lot on a grand scale, in the same way that their countrymen were reclaiming land from the sea at low tide in Zeeland and the North.

This also made the farmers much more active

This also made the Dutch farmers much more active. Their representative organizations set up a whole network of agricultural education, with Wageningen Agricultural University as its showpiece. Within the pillars, ministers and priests set up church-based farmers' cooperatives, which included a network of banks to provide credit. These have now been incorporated – Catholic and Protestant – into the Rabobank, one of the twenty largest bank conglomerates in the world. Nowadays, the average Dutch farm is organized to produce as much as possible, and is often very specialized, mechanized and increasingly automated. The farmers have made the Netherlands one of the world's leading food exporters. This has made the average farm very capital-intensive. Farmers have to know everything there is to know about their crops and livestock and have as near total control of their production processes as is possible. They have, after all, extensive commitments to the local Rabobank, which finances all this technology.

This form of agricultural exploitation depends on a continually increasing turnover. Since the end of the Second World War – even with the heavily subsidized prices guaranteed by the influential agricultural lobby in the European Community – small farmers have been increasingly squeezed out of the market. In the 1950s, the social-democratic minister Sicco Mansholt set up a system under which farmers who were unable to keep up with technological changes could be bought out by the state. Their land was then sold or leased to neighbours who did have sufficient capital. This scaling-up process continues today. Since Mansholt's time, production has increased enormously, but the number of people who earn a living in agriculture – in 1900, still more than half the population – is now less than 3%. This does not include those employed in the food processing industry.

The subsidies have led to enormous over-production. Since the 1980s, the European Community and the Dutch government have tried to do something about this. Cattle farmers have been given quotas and receive heavy fines if they exceed them.

They believe that they can regulate the environment

The farmers have acquired enemies among those who wish to preserve the environment. More and more Dutch people believe that our control over the environment has gone too far. What their ancestors called the *onland* is now seen as the natural environment, something crucial to the quality of life and therefore to be protected. Furthermore, we are learning from bitter experience that the earth is less manageable that we thought. Sicco Mansholt, the minister who instigated the modernization and up-scaling of Dutch agriculture, openly regretted this policy in his later days. Even the professors at Wageningen now profile their esteemed institution as an 'environmental university'. They believe that they can regulate the environment. In recent years, fields used for growing crops and grazing cattle have been 'returned to nature'. Having realized the value of the *woeste landen*, the wild and untamed lands, the Dutch have decided to recreate them themselves.

This desire to protect the environment rests on an older tradition. Nineteenth century romanticism had a strong influence on the Dutch elites. They began to admire the beauty of the *woeste gronden* and imitated them in their gardens and the first municipal parks. Ornamental gardens were initially inspired by those at the French royal palace at Versailles. They represented the absolute control of man over nature. They were laid out in geometric patterns, with closely cropped lawns and clipped hedges that were often formed with great artistry into the shapes of human inventions, such as windmills. The landscape that received the greatest admiration was the reclaimed land, such as Leeghwater's polders, because it was tamed and was of use.

Romanticism meant a dramatic reversal of this view. The Versailles lookalikes were all dug up, to be replaced by wild woodlands – the wilder, the better. Dutch landscape gardeners soon learned to disguise fences and walls by the subtle planting of trees to give the impression of the edge of a large forest. Contrived-looking ponds were replaced by more 'natural' streams. The more adventurous among them even created 'ruins' and outcrops of rock. Every self-respecting town and city laid out public gardens and parks in this way. The Park on the Maas in Rotterdam and Amsterdam's Vondelpark are perfect examples. Most parks designed since that time have been largely romantic in character. There are almost no gardens left laid out in Versailles style. Gardening has become a popular hobby. Millions of people in this small, densely populated country live in flats and first-floor maisonettes, but every survey proves over and again that the greatest wish of almost every Dutch man and woman is to have a house with a front and back garden.

On the outskirts of most cities, there are complexes of *volkstuinen*. These 'people's gardens', the equivalent of what are known in English as 'allotments', date from the beginning of the twentieth century. The original idea was to allow

Most Dutch people want a house with a garden, which they will cherish with heart and soul. This is perhaps a very extreme example.

the less well-off to grow their own vegetables, since medical science had proved that they were good for your health. Today, these allotments have almost all become ornamental gardens, which their owners cherish with their hearts and souls.

The Dutch take good care of their gardens. Those who do not mow their lawns often enough or fail to remove the weeds from their flower beds so that the seeds end up in the neighbour's garden will suffer the disapproval of the whole neighbourhood and, if they do not conform, will find themselves embroiled in a genuine conflict with the other residents of the street. Weeds are unsightly. Unless, of course, they are part of a completely controlled romantic 'natural garden'. And everyone can tell the difference between this and a neglected lawn.

And yet, these days, the Dutch do see their gardens as a piece of 'nature' in their own backyard, so to speak. There is general consensus that children should grow up in a 'green' environment. But green or not – and this cannot be said often enough – that environment must be as strictly controlled as possible.

At the same time there is a general romantic appreciation of what the Dutch call *de vrije natuur*, the natural, undeveloped environment. This is a very positive term, which contrasts sharply with the more traditional *woeste gronden* and *onland*. This appreciation began to take concrete form in the last quarter of the nineteenth century, simultaneously with the development of a renewed respect for the architecture of the towns and cities. Dilapidated old buildings were seen as the legacy of a great past that needed to be carefully preserved. Many people believed that their ancestors had supremely better taste than the current generations. What had previously been demolished as obstacles to progress and memories of an earlier, less sophisticated epoch now became eligible for protection as national monuments. The Amsterdam art critic and leading Catholic Josephus Alberdinck Thijm, for example, led a campaign against the city council's plans to fill in the *Nieuwe Zijds Voorburgwal*, a medieval canal, to make way for the building of a road. Although he lost, progressive civic leaders have since had little success in obtaining approval to fill in other canals – the product of the revered Golden Age – in the capital. The Nieuwe Zijds Voorburgwal built up a new reputation as the Dutch version of Fleet Street. The new road made it easy to transport the papers and the stock exchange, the source of news on the economy, was only a stone's throw away. At the same time it preserved the name of a piece of Amsterdam's glorious past that had been erased forever. It was a stab in the heart of the city, a perfect example of how not to do things. The government started to draw up a list of protected buildings, known as the 'monument list'. Their owners were not allowed to demolish or alter them without permission. A set of rules was drawn up by a group of experts whose job it was to preserve the historic character of the buildings. Subsidies were granted for 'restoration'. This expertise was provided by the *Rijksdienst Monumentenzorg*, a government department with the same status as Rijkswaterstaat.

Monumentenzorg now has a complete network of branches throughout the country. It employs a large number of specialized architects, who check restoration work and ensure that owners do not change the character of their buildings by, for example, fitting plastic door or window frames.

These days, certain 'views' in towns and villages are also protected. New buildings may be constructed but they must not disturb the view, or at least not to an excessive degree. With the passage of time, the monument list has become longer and longer. In recent years, it has included an increasing number of nineteenth and twentieth century buildings, including factories from the early years of the Dutch industrial revolution. Plans to demolish exceptional old buildings always attract the attention of the specialized action committees and historical associations that are present these days in every municipality in the country.

Woeste gronden are seen in the same way. It is no accident that the leading organization for the protection of the natural environment in the Netherlands is the *Vereniging tot Behoud van Natuurmonumenten in Nederland*, known popularly as *Natuurmonumenten*. It was founded in 1905 in response to Amsterdam's plans to fill in the Naardermeer – an original peat lake that had never been reclaimed – with refuse from the city. The association was set up by the liberal elite politician Gijsbert van Tienhoven and the populist biologist Jacobus Thijsse, who bought the Naardermeer and declared it a nature reserve. This was the first acquisition of many. Natuurmonumenten manages its reserves with great care, leaving nothing to chance. The members of the association have access to the reserves, as long as they remain on the specially marked out paths.

Another typical example of this approach is the release of otters and beavers in the Biesbosch, the remains of the damage caused by the St. Elisabeth flood in 1421. The Ministry of Agriculture, Fisheries and Nature Management released the animals, imported from Eastern Europe, because historical records show that they used to be common in the area. Another example is the distinction made by Dutch biologists between 'indigenous' plants and those imported later. For a long time, it was believed that the latter detracted from the quality of the natural monuments – in the same way as later additions could ruin a historic building. This radical standpoint has lost much of its force in recent years.

Modern environmental activism has its roots in the big cities

Unlike traditional nature management, modern environmental activism has its roots in the big cities. It is in principle a separate issue, because it was originally concerned with pollution of the natural environment by human activity. This is not to say that this has traditionally been neglected. In centuries past, local administrators introduced regulations to protect the public from what we now call 'environmental nuisance'. Foul-smelling leather tanneries, for example, or mills that beat copper – with the accompanying unavoidable racket – had to be situated well away from built-up areas. But as wealth and welfare became more normal, particularly since the 1960s, the public's expectations increased. 'Not much traffic' was the comment made by foreign minister Joseph Luns when he was allowed to look over the Wall during a visit to West Berlin in the early sixties. And indeed, streets with no cars and full of pedestrians were proof enough of the failure of communism. PVDA leader Joop den Uyl frequently expressed his opinion in public that every Dutch family should have a car. A few years later, with his fine nose for which way the wind was blowing, he held impassioned speeches about the 'quality of life' and how it was threatened by the unbridled growth of industry.

An important turning point came in 1963 when a serious fire broke out in the *Superfosfaat*, an artificial fertilizer factory in Vlaardingen, a town in Zuid-Holland close to Rotterdam. An easterly wind blew the clouds of poison gas between the surrounding villages and out to sea. If the more usual west wind had been blowing, the gas would have drifted over the city and tens of thousands of lives might have been lost. The cabinet held an emergency meeting to prepare for a large-scale evacuation. This proved unnecessary at the last moment, but it was touch and go.

Superfosfaat was part of an enormous complex of chemical plants and refineries that had sprung up between Rotterdam and the sea. It had even been built at the expense of a cherished natural monument. Now the country had been given a clear warning of what impact a serious accident could have.

The critical generation of the 1960s embraced environmental degradation as one of the many sins of the establishment. Ernest Zahn's view that the environment replaced a God who was slowly dissipating into nothingness is certainly worth consideration, but the unpleasant experience of a stinking industry that sometimes went up in flames was equally as important.

Furthermore, as time went on, environmental damage became increasingly visible. Old industrial plants, such as gas works, had contaminated the ground so badly that it was a health hazard to the residents of homes built later on the same sites. This meant that the sites had to be cleaned up at great cost and, in some cases, the houses had to be demolished. Hundreds of these sites were discovered, some of which were centuries old, for example, where our industrious ancestors in the Golden Age had built white lead factories. Most were, however, more recent. It was calculated that it would cost 24 million euro to clean up all of these sites. This had to borne by the taxpayer because the culprit was often long dead and would therefore be unlikely to pay the bill. As is customary, the environmental organizations formed a number of action committees, which mostly directed their efforts at a particular polluter or group of polluters and demanded concrete measures. At first, attention was centred on air pollution. People living near factories and other sources of air contamination were no longer prepared to breathe it in day in, day out. It was not long before surface waters and the contamination of the soil also became hot issues. After that it was the turn of capital-intensive agriculture, which used great quantities of artificial fertilizer and

These pigs are being destroyed to ensure that they do not become infected with swine fever.

pesticides to maximize yields possible. And this, while the enormous number of livestock in the Netherlands – nearly 12 million pigs alone – produced so much natural fertilizer that the manure mountain could no longer be used up and created another environmental problem. Political and administrative leaders treated the action committees as any other – they accepted them as partners in the debate and adopted their terminology and aims almost wholesale. The movement formed provincial and national umbrella organizations that received subsidies and started playing the role of an environmental lobby, encouraged and subsidized by the government. Most of these organizations were set up in the early 1970s.

Radical critics even argued that, in the long term, there would no longer be a place in the Netherlands for intensive agriculture, which survived only because of government subsidies. Farmers, they said, should be re-educated as 'nature managers'. The subsidies could be used in far better ways than on their in-creasingly desperate attempts to keep their heads above water by intervening more and more in natural processes, by increasingly intensive crop cultivation and by the application of biotechnology and expensive machinery. Widespread epidemics of bird flu and swine fever in the early years of the twenty-first century gave new credence to these arguments: the animals had to be destroyed in their millions – the agriculture ministry preferred to call it 'culled' – to contain the spread of the diseases. Vaccination was a possibility, but not an option because the EU had decided at some point that animals raised for slaughtering were no longer to be vaccinated, as it would make the meat less marketable.

People who want to turn Dutch farmers into nature managers are still a minority, but there are trends observable in the Netherlands that suggest a movement in that direction. The last of Lely's great polders in the IJsselmeer are now unlikely to be reclaimed. A number of municipalities in the *Oldambt*, a region in the northern province of Groningen decided to flood several old polders, to create a lake that would attract tourists and provide more local jobs. In the heart of the province of Zuid-Holland, between Rotterdam and Gouda, a romantic 'forest' is being planted in an old cattle farming area so that the million inhabitants of Greater Rotterdam have an extra piece of 'nature' in which to get away from it all. The environmental movement follows the activities of the government with a critical eye, frequently with considerable suspicion, but the two parties share the same basic conviction – that nature and the environment can ultimately be regulated and controlled.

In a certain way, engineers are humble

Lely has become a household name in the Netherlands. He gave his name to Lelystad, the capital of the new province formed by his polders in the former Zuider Zee, and to the railway station, Amsterdam Lelylaan. This fame is based on his vision as a hydraulic engineer. But he had many more strings to his bow. Lely was also the father of the Industrial Injuries Act, which provides compensation for people injured at work. He applied his engineer's mentality – the belief that you could regulate and control a great deal with a good set of basic assumptions, a sound knowledge of your field and practical experiments – to the problems of society. Students in Lely's time were deeply impressed by Professor Hendrik Baltus Pekelharing (1841-1922), who taught economics and political economics at the Technical University in Delft. Pekelharing's lectures and seminars were very influential. He spoke of planning – not of the land, but of society. Many of the professor's pupils were active in politics, and frequently ended up in the *Sociaal Democratische Arbeiders Partij*, the Social Democratic Workers' Party. Nobel Prize winner and founder of econometrics, Professor Jan Tinbergen, said in 1936 that his subject was an 'engineering science'. The development of society was equally as controllable as the course of the rivers through the flat deltalands of Holland.

There is something totalitarian about this way of thinking. Yet totalitarian ideologies, such as communism or national-socialism, never really found a solid basis in the Netherlands, not even in the technical universities. It must be admitted, however, that the Dutch mini-*führer* Anton Mussert – who founded the National Socialist Movement in the Netherlands – was an engineer. Such ideologies are, however, contrary to the engineer's creed. They are based on a number of unshakable convictions about the way society should be organized. Whether these are founded on racial superiority, or the dictatorship of the proletariat, or collective ownership of the means of production is of no importance. What they all boil down to is that everything must be forced to conform to a predetermined pattern.

At the Delft Hydraulics Laboratory, they have a different approach. They do not attempt to subjugate the Rhine completely to their will, but to regulate the current to achieve certain restricted aims. In a certain way, engineers are humble: they respect the laws of nature and the forces they are confronted with never to attempt to tame them completely. They know that that is the road to disaster. They also know that these laws are not purely the product of human logic. That logic has been applied to bring order to the chaos of countless empirical observations. Logic makes the laws clear to us. Socially oriented engineers have rarely come across sufficient natural order in society to be able to establish inviolable laws – with the exception of the odd communist or Anton Mussert, but they were isolated examples. These engineers believed in regulation and control and came up with countless proposals to that effect. But the proposals were partly based on a wide variety of beliefs with their roots in the philosophies of the pillars. They also had great faith in the results of scientific investigation. If medical researchers established that the feared disease tuberculosis was common among people who lived in dark, damp houses, they considered it their social duty to subject new buildings to statutory requirements regarding the quality of the materials used, the minimum size of doors and windows, and ventilation. This concern could sometimes take quite an extreme form. There was a department of construction engineers at Delft that spent a great deal of its time trying to design the perfect 'workers' house'. Until the early years of this century, most Dutch people still slept in a *bedstee*, a kind of cupboard set in the wall, or in the *tussenkamer*, a small, dark room between the parlour at the front of the house – where guests were received – and the back room, where the family ate and lived, except on feast days. Modern architects got rid of the *tussenkamer* and located the light points in the ceiling so that a lamp could be hung above the dining table. This would allow the workers to spend their evenings reading, as the lamp threw its clear light onto the pages.

Socially oriented engineers believed strongly in the idea that knowledge is power

Socially oriented engineers believed strongly in the idea that knowledge is power. This was, after all, the basic tenet of their profession. Enormous publishing houses grew up within the pillars, marketing great quantities of good, cheap books which reflected the beliefs of the pillar concerned. The network of public libraries that now covers the country, complete with mobile *bibliobussen* to reach isolated communities, is also a concrete expression of this conviction.

Clearly this faith in the power of regulation and control is closely related to traditional Dutch paternalism, to the mentality of the regent who knows better than the people themselves what is good for them.

Foreign observers regularly remark that Dutch towns and cities are as neatly planned as the countryside. This has its roots in the same mentality. Architects like Berlage and Oud attempted to design public housing that would, as it were, invite the residents to develop themselves spiritually. And not only that, they wanted to preserve the traditional sense of community. They designed 'garden villages', in which the neat little houses – all with front and back gardens – were grouped around a sort of square. The architects of the Amsterdam School preferred to project this sense of security in castle-like complexes of stone, with gates and ornamental towers. These made the residents feel protected, as though they all lived together in a kind of citadel. Many of these complexes are now on the 'monument list'.

In a deregulated society, where everything is determined by the law of supply and demand, such public housing projects rarely get off the ground. For that reason, almost since their party was founded, the social democrats have been

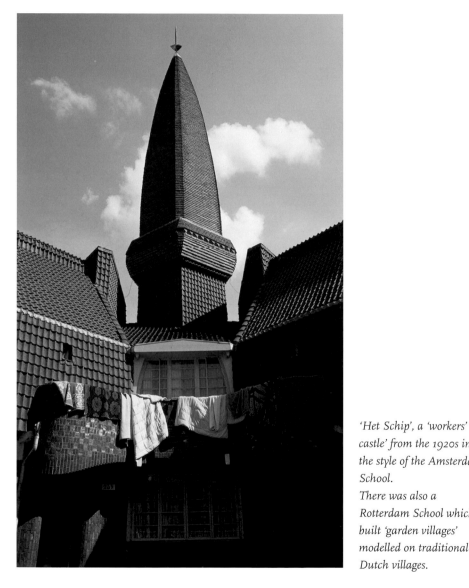

'Het Schip', a 'workers' castle' from the 1920s in the style of the Amsterdam School.
There was also a Rotterdam School which built 'garden villages' modelled on traditional Dutch villages.

demanding that local authorities take responsibility for public housing. Their demands were met, but only after a very long time. Local administrators were generally prepared to support associations that wished to build good quality, cheap housing for their members by, for example, guaranteeing their loans on the capital market. Such associations sprung up everywhere and were soon an integral part of the pillar system. As a result, Catholic, Calvinist and social democratic housing developments were built shoulder-to-shoulder. These associations were largely responsible for the construction of the 'garden villages'.

The government did not take it upon itself to provide public housing on a grand scale until after the Second World War. This was actually an emergency measure demanded by the circumstances. So many houses had been destroyed during the occupation and the fighting that took place in the country, that the solution to the housing shortage could not be left to the free market. A system of distribution was set up so that the shortage could be shared as equally as possible. The rents of the houses built by the government were kept as low as possible through a system of subsidies. The wealthy, after all, had enough money to find their own houses on the free market.

The architects of the time were very enamoured of rationalism and standardized high-rise blocks in the style of Le Courbusier. The advantage of this approach was that standardization kept the price of building down. Large estates sprung up around the larger towns and cities, usually with high-rise apartment blocks surrounded by expansive playing fields and public parks. Their designs promoted a certain lifestyle. Each flat had a shower, something new for people who had been used to washing themselves once a week in a tin tub in front of the fire. To make sure the residents actually used the shower for its intended purpose, most munici-palities also made them rent a small geyser at a very low price, which ensured them hot running water. In the 1970s, architects once again showed a preference for low-rise, 'village garden' style housing, provoking accusations from several quarters of 'neo-frumpiness'. Once again the sense of community was the motivation, but now it appeared to clash with increasing individualism and the disintegration of the pillars. Many Dutch people wanted more privacy and to be bothered as little as possible by those living around them. Countless action committees were set up to deal with problems caused by noisy or otherwise imposing neighbours.

Residents of what local councils considered to be run-down neighbourhoods set up action committees to protest against their demolition – and with some success. Since the 1970s, many municipalities have pursued a policy of renovation, in which the character of the old buildings – particularly the front façades – is pre-served as far as possible. Inside, the visitor finds all the fittings of a modern apartment.

The conviction that all social development can be regulated extended further than physical planning alone. It also gave rise to a comprehensive system of licences that covered an increasing range of social activities. This allowed paternalistic administrators to, for example, limit the number of bars which sold alcoholic drink, which – as everyone knows – is an obstacle to the social and individual development of the people. The government prescribed fixed opening times for shops, not only to protect their personnel from overexploitation, but also to protect small shopkeepers from large chain stores which could easily stay open 24 hours a day by allowing their staff to work in shifts. Shops were not allowed to stay open on Sundays until the 1990s, and then only between 12 and 5. Most municipalities restricted themselves to one Sunday a month, but in the larger cities and a few tourist centres, Sunday shopping was a weekly event. However, when the people of Utrecht – with a population of over 200,000 and the largest shopping mall in the country – were asked during a referendum in 2005 if they wanted Sunday shopping every week, the answer of the great majority was a resolute 'No'.

In the course of the twentieth century, more and more professions and commercial sectors became inaccessible to people without the required qualifications. A strict department of weights and measures ensured that consumer products met the minimum requirements for quality. A system of licences for establishing businesses ensured that not too many companies of the same kind were located in any one area, to avoid cut-throat competition. This administrative mentality gradually acquired a dynamic of its own, with the result that many people occasionally feel that they are suffering under a repressive and tyrannical government. You need a licence, for example, to build an extra fence around your garden. Every building plan, no matter how small, has to be submitted to the planning committee of the local council, whose task it is to ensure that the streets of its town or city continue to be a feast for the eye and are not spoiled by unsightly kitsch. This, in spite of the old Dutch saying, *over smaak valt niet te twisten*, each to his own taste.

Many people and organizations see their tasks as largely a matter of encouraging or facilitating, promoting processes, guiding the activities of others. At some point they will usually introduce the concept of coordination, a characteristic feature of societies where there is little chance of any one individual acquiring sufficient power to become the undisputed leader. Outsiders may get the impression from the type of language used in these organizations that the complicated jargon is a cover-up for doing nothing. This is, however, rarely the case. Encouragement and guidance are very effective ways of exerting influence in a society based on consultation, whose members are accustomed to taking decisions more or less jointly and in which the main aim is a compromise acceptable to all. Encouragement and guidance mean that you are prepared to play a role in these processes, that you are not entering the arena with inflexible premises and unshakable theoretical models. Action is based on observing and interpreting the actual situation. A good illustration of how this works in practice is the role played by the *Centraal Planbureau*, the Central Planning Office, known popularly by its Dutch abbreviation CPB.

The CPB was set up in 1945 at the government's instigation by Jan Tinbergen, the man who said that economics is an engineering science. Tinbergen, a Nobel Prize winner, devoted his life to making economic processes measurable and quantifiable. He believed that sound policy could only be based on hard facts and figures and he developed models to explain economic reality in terms of mathematical formulae. The development of the computer enabled his successors to refine these methods even further.

The CPB is, in fact, not a planning body at all. It measures the economy on the basis of a wide range of indicators and makes prognoses for the future. Its most important task is to calculate the effects of policy proposals on welfare. During negotiations on new coalition governments, the partners increasingly send their compromises to the CPB so that it can 'work out' whether they will achieve the intended goals. Since the 1980s, successive governments have attempted to bring down, or at least contain, unemployment. The politicians involved in the 1994 coalition negotiations discarded many of their own compromises – often the result of hard bargaining – themselves because the CPB's computer models concluded that the effects on unemployment were too small or unfavourable. Since the 1990s all political parties ask the CPB to work out the consequences of their election manifestos. They can then proudly announce that their proposals are both affordable and will produce the best results. In time, the CPB even went so far as to make suggestions for policy itself; such recommendations have now become a feature of the CPB's regular prognoses for the Dutch economy. No matter what you think about this, it illustrates that politicians across the spectrum by far prefer a practical, utilitarian approach to ideological assumptions.

Such devotion to principles is seldom found outside the election campaign. In the final analysis, the belief wins out that the desired aim can be achieved by intervening in the right place at the right time. That belief is still widespread, but no longer has the power it commanded one or two generations ago. In the 1960s, PVDA leader Joop den Uyl introduced the concept of the *maakbare samenleving* (literally, the 'moldable' society) to describe the conviction that society can be moulded to suit some preconceived design. Today, even social democrats admit that the concept is completely outdated and has been overturned by reality. Too many policy measures have not achieved the intended goal, but have resulted in something entirely different or even the complete opposite. Where one lays the emphasis then depends a little on political taste. The regulations controlling dismissal, for example, may make it difficult for employers to sack their employees but, in doing so, may also render it more difficult for the jobless to find work. Or, to take another example, doubling the width of motorways may encourage people to buy cars, thereby increasing rather than decreasing the number of vehicles on the roads – as a result of which congestion only spreads to the urban road networks within the cities.

From the 1980s, belief in the moldable society became increasingly discredited. It was however replaced by an even more radical assumption: that the government could change people. It started with the political newcomer Pim Fortuyn, who put the restoration of traditional norms and values on the political agenda. The Christian Democratic leader Jan Peter Balkenende snapped up this notion, as it complemented another of his favourite ideas: personal responsibility. As a consequence, there has been an increasing appeal from politicians and the public alike for resolute steps to be taken to tackle unacceptable behaviour and those responsible for it. These antisocial groups include smokers, young people hanging about at street corners, recently arrived immigrants who do not speak Dutch well enough and car drivers who cannot keep to speed limits. Even people suffering from obesity were recently added to the list.

In 2006 Rotterdam decided to address the problem of the city's 3,000 homeless by helping them one-by-one to escape from the desperate circumstances in which they lived. Immigration minister Rita Verdonk decreed that all newcomers to the Netherlands had to take a compulsory integration course, which they had to pay for themselves, to learn the language, the history and the norms and values of their new homeland. The course costs thousands of euros and the only support available from the government is a loan. You have to be prepared to invest in your new country, if you are so keen to live in it. Anyone refusing to take part in this form of social engineering at individual level can expect severe fines and other sanctions.

From the debate surrounding all these developments it emerges very clearly that very few of those involved in the debate genuinely wish to return to what they refer to as the 'caretaker state', where the government protects only the life and property of its citizens, and everything else is left to the free play of social forces. The debate is not about the desirability of regulation but about what form it should take. This, again, relates back to the respect for the power of the water which Dutch hydraulic engineers retain in spite of their knowledge and experience. You can redirect the course of a river but you cannot stop it from flowing. Anyone who has been up on the top of a river dyke in the Netherlands will have noticed that they are built quite a way back from the actual banks of the river. The stretches of land between the dyke and the river are known as *uiterwaarden*. These are usually water meadows used by farmers to graze their cattle. Some may be protected by low dykes, but they are largely left to the whims of the water. When the water level is exceptionally high – which is always predicted in time to allow the farmers to remove the cattle – the *uiterwaarden* are generally flooded. If the dykes were built along the river banks, it would be impossible – even with today's technology – to contain the water. The rivers – and the sea, for that matter – must be given room to breathe or they will turn into wild beasts, bursting out of their cages and destroying every-thing in their way. The moral is that much can be regulated and controlled, but if you go too far, you will bring down unheard-of forces upon yourself. A practical and logical approach will always produce acceptable results, as long as you work with, not against, the situation as you find it. And, often enough, in spite of your wishes, intentions and principles, you will find that you have to leave some breathing space, in just the same way as the dykes must never be built too close to the river banks.

Society, too, has its 'uiterwaarden'

Society, too, has its *uiterwaarden*, water meadows beyond the dykes where administrators find it impossible to impose any clear order. This belief is deeply entrenched in the Dutch way of thinking. Those who attempt to steer social processes frequently discover that they are uncontrollable and the most they can hope for is to contain them, to prevent them from getting any worse. And the tradition of enforced tolerance, which the regents of the old Republic had to adopt to survive, makes the idea of restricted control more acceptable, even attractive. In addition to respect for individuality and the recognition of another's sovereignty in their own domain, this mentality is closely related to what foreign observers often see as an exaggerated liberality and lawlessness in the Netherlands.

Rotterdam is by far the largest port in this part of the world. Schiphol is one of Europe's leading airports. The transport of goods to and from other countries is one of the mainstays of the Dutch economy. The slow but unstoppable process of federalization in Europe has led to the gradual phasing out of border controls across the continent. This makes the Netherlands a very open society, and not only in a positive sense. It is not difficult for drug smugglers to conceal a consignment of hashish – or worse – amongst the enormous quantity of goods that pass through the country legally. Using drugs – no matter whether they are hard or soft – is

Since the beginning of the century Rotterdam has no longer been the world's largest port. It had to give up its leading position to Shanghai, but second place is still a very impressive achievement. This shows how they process bulk cargo in Rotterdam.

illegal in the Netherlands. In the past, this never caused any serious problems. A small Chinese minority, which had made its way to Amsterdam and Rotterdam usually via the Dutch East Indies, used opium. The police never succeeded in infiltrating this very closed group. The government, however, believed that there was little harm in opium use as long as it was kept under control and continued to be nothing more than a way of passing the time for old men who had become accustomed to using the drug in their home country. The police therefore tolerated opium dens as long as the owners restricted their clientele to members of the Chinese community.

In this way a grey area developed between the word of the law and how it is practised

In 1911 a Christian-dominated government imposed restrictions on prostitution. Women were not forbidden to sell sexual favours, but all activities relating to it, such as pimping, renting hotel rooms by the hour or running brothels, were illegal. It was clear from the start that this law was impossible to enforce. It was therefore applied only partially. In areas where prostitution traditionally flourished, such as the world-famous *Wallen* in the centre of Amsterdam or *Katendrecht* in Rotterdam, the practitioners of the world's oldest profession were more or less allowed to go about their business. The police were, however, very active in removing young girls below the minimum age from the streets and, where possible, returning them to their parents or finding them places in children's homes.

Prostitution was, however, banned from other neighbourhoods. The authorities believed that this concentrated the problem in an isolated area – Katendrecht was actually a peninsula with only one road connecting it to the outside world. In this way a grey area developed between the word of the law and how it is practised. The authorities defended this approach with the argument that, if the worst came to the worst, they had the situation under control and could stop it getting out of hand. Nevertheless, there was a gradually increasing conviction that the decency laws of 1911 were no longer compatible with the libertine spirit of the times. The laws against homosexuality had already been scrapped. Article 1 of the Constitution forbade discrimination and unequal treatment, and explicitly mentioned sexual preference. Prostitution should therefore be seen as a normal occupation. The time was ripe for the sexual services sector, which generated billions of euros a year, to be legalized. It would make it easier to ensure that brothels and prostitutes paid tax like anyone else. And the government could take protective measures to prevent abuse, like the exploitation of women staying in the country illegally, and to tackle trade in women. And so it happened. Despite opposition from Christian politicians, prostitution in all its forms was legalized.

The consequences were baffling. In the Netherlands, municipal authorities have

Prostitution is one of the trademarks of Amsterdam. The first guide to this ancient profession appeared in the Golden Age.

a 'destination plan' for each district which specifies what activities can take place there. Many local administrators used the plans to make life difficult – or even impossible – for those offering sexual services. Prostitutes and their clients found themselves faced with the kind of detailed rules and regulations which the Dutch bureaucracy is renowned. As a consequence, official legalized prostitution went into decline and, in many places, was driven out completely. An illegal circuit, which made use of the internet and mobile telephones, took over a large part of the clientele. That presented women traffickers and those who exploited women and young girls without official residence status with unlimited opportunities. One circuit that came to light imported under-age girls from Nigeria. Once they arrived in the Netherlands, they reported to a centre for asylumseekers and then disappeared without trace to be put to work as prostitutes. The grey area of the traditional policy of tolerance gave the government more opportunities to keep the problem under control than the new, overly sharp distinction between legal and illegal prostitution.

In the 1960s, hashish and marijuana suddenly became very popular among young people, because the use of illegal substances was a perfect expression of the growing culture of protest. The drugs were of an excellent quality and came into the country through a variety of channels. At first the government's response was very aggressive, as the well-known experimental poet Simon Vinkenoog – the prophet of the young revolution – discovered. He was imprisoned for a few months for the possession of a small quantity of hashish, the use of which he successfully propagated as mind-expanding and inspirational.

Making an example of Vinkenoog had no effect. The use of soft drugs increased sharply. A number of experts declared in the media, without receiving too much criticism, that marijuana and its derivatives were not addictive, or at least less so than alcohol or nicotine. This resulted in a certain amount of tolerance in practice. Some youth centres even appointed their own dealers so that their visitors could be guaranteed a good quality supply of drugs and not run the risk of ending up with a doctored product that contained dangerous chemicals. Gradually this policy led to the tolerance of 'coffee shops' where unsuspecting customers who actually ordered coffee were met with surprise and amusement. The Dutch are great coffee drinkers, but the many cafés and other establishments where they can indulge themselves have not been referred to as coffee shops for twenty years or more. Here, too, the argument is that this allows a practice that cannot be stamped out to be controlled. The authorities, however, act decisively if they discover that hard drugs are also being sold in a coffee shop or if marijuana is sold openly. An illustration of a hemp leaf on the package is permitted, but no more.

One of the arguments for permitting the use of soft drugs was to maintain a clear distinction between the 'hash scene' and the users of heroin and cocaine. The use of hard drugs – in spite of claims to the contrary, particularly from abroad – is not tolerated by the Dutch government and the police devote a great deal of time and manpower to combating it. Nevertheless, since the 1960s, a hard drugs scene has developed in the towns and cities.

Heroin and cocaine are not only extremely addictive but also expensive. Once addicted you need thousands a month to 'score', several times higher than an average salary. Very few people can earn that much from honest work. Hard drug addiction is therefore the cause of a large percentage of the burglaries, muggings, and car and bicycle thefts in the Netherlands. It has also led to an increase in street prostitution. Addicts who earn their shots this way are usually very young women, but not always. And it is a heyday for the pimps, who now use the hypodermic needle to exercise their power. The majority of people in prison in the Netherlands are addicts and the expansion of drugs-related crimes in recent years has necessitated a considerable increase in the number of prison cells. In the hard drugs world, a certain amount of use is tolerated, but the reasoning behind it is slightly different. The authorities concentrate on tracking down the big dealers, the incredibly wealthy leaders of the heroin and cocaine cartels, so that they can 'strangle the evil at its source'. The addict on the street and the small-time dealer generally have little to fear, unless they cause a public nuisance, that is if there are complaints from the neighbours.

At the same time, the police allow all kinds of bodies that provide assistance to addicts all the room they need to operate. Since AIDS has become common among addicts – passed on by the use of dirty needles – there are places where they can get clean hypodermics. An addict without AIDS is always better than one with it. Other organizations help addicts to beat their habit by providing them with methadon, a chemical which removes the withdrawal symptoms but – in typical Calvinist style – does not give the feelings of happiness and contentment that make heroin so tempting. Some of the organizations even have areas where addicts – who are usually on the street and completely down and out – can find shelter for a while and are even allowed to use drugs.

Current practice, with its mixture of tolerance and strict measures has already provoked strong criticism from neighbouring countries. The Netherlands defends itself with the argument that the use of hard drugs in the country is no worse than elsewhere and certainly less of a problem than in large metropolises like New York or Los Angeles. The latter is certainly true. The Netherlands – with a population of over 16 million – has between 22 and 23,000 hard drug addicts, which is not a particularly high percentage. The government, however, is sensitive to the criticism. After the turn of the century, the authorities adopted a harder line. Some politicians on the conservative side of the political spectrum expressed the opinion that the policy of tolerance had gone too far. A thriving underground industry had grown up to supply the coffee shops. Initially it was run by amateur enthusiasts and the first 'nederwiet', as home-grown Dutch weed was called, was of inferior quality. But people can be very creative and inventive. Through careful cross-

Nederwiet, *Dutch weed, fresh from the coffee shop.*

breeding and the development of special lamps, the growers created an optimal cultivation environment, resulting in a product that gave users an unprecedented 'hit'. By the turn of the century, the Netherlands was producing excellent – and very powerful – weed. It was grown in glasshouses and by very many people at home in their attics. Underworld networks controlled the trade between these 'voluntary workers' and the back doors of the coffee shops. It was a lucrative business. Home-growers with 15 to 20 plants could earn thousands of euros on a regular basis. The conservative Balkenende governments insisted that people took responsibility for earning their own incomes, but they found this innovative solution unacceptable. The Christian Democratic minister of justice Piet Hein Donner started a crusade against the weed-growers. Anyone growing weed was not only risking punishment, but would have to bear the costs of destroying their plants and equipment, and would most likely lose their homes too, since the government encouraged housing associations and landlords to evict home-growers. These draconian measures had little effect on the price of the weed, however, showing that those who were caught were just the tip of the iceberg. Donner also announced that he would like to see the coffee shops closed down, and many municipalities tried to rid themselves of these outlets for soft drugs. The minister's plans met with a lot of resistance. D66, the smallest member of the coalition government, continued – as always – to support the policy of tolerance. The ambitious mayor of Maastricht, the capital of Limburg and one of the country's main centres of art and culture, even rapped on a song that defended the policy of tolerance for soft drugs. Donner responded with a rap of his own, praising the police and the courts.

Who is right? Experience in other countries has shown that a hard line, based on repressive laws and criminal prosecution, produces few results. Yet there is equally little evidence to prove that the twin Dutch dykes of help and tolerance have successfully contained the problem to the extent that the people of the Netherlands can feel safe in their social polder.

Where life and death meet

A policy of tolerance, making the best of the situation, regulating the level of the steam as it were, is also pursued in the Netherlands in a much more dangerous area, where life and death meet. In the past twenty years this has led to two fierce debates in the country, first about abortion, and then about euthanasia.

Baas in eigen buik, 'Be the boss of your own belly', was the lighthearted motto of the feminist movement that had grown out of the revolutionary ideals of the 1960s. It was a direct pointer to the possibility of abortion. Another common slogan on their banners was *Vrouw, beslis*, 'Woman, decide for yourself'.

The law was clear – abortion was the equivalent of murder. Yet as early as the 1950s and 1960s it was possible to find doctors who were prepared to terminate

An ideal picture of the multicultural libertine and tolerant society. By the way: these are gays parodying police officers while participating in Amsterdam's renowned (or notorious) gay parade

pregnancies. They justified this by saying that, if they did not do it, it would be done by backstreet abortionists who only too often put their clients' lives in danger. As long as these doctors did not publicize their activities too much, they were left relatively alone. In the sixties, however, the *Nederlandse Vereniging voor Sexuele Hervorming* (NVSH) – the Dutch Association for Sexual Reform – gathered a great deal of support. The association advocated sexual freedom and placed the right to abortion on the agenda. This provoked a great deal of opposition, especially from religious groups, who spoke of the rights of the unborn child and considered the foetus as the 'weakest of the weak' in society, thereby deserving of protection. Non-Christian parties, including the vibrant new D66, pressed for the legalization of abortion, arguing that – particularly in the first few weeks of the pregnancy – the foetus could not be considered a human being. At the same time, clinics started to appear – often set up under the auspices of the NVSH – where abortions could be obtained without problem. Eventually a compromise was reached in the form of a law that allowed abortion up to the third month, subject to a large number of conditions. These were, however, defined in such vague terms that any woman who wishes to can obtain an abortion without problem. This possibility is frequently taken advantage of by women from neighbouring countries, who sometimes arrive in groups in hired buses.

There is still strong opposition to this form of tolerance, but it has little effect. The argument that enforcing the letter of the law would lead to greater problems and the return of the backstreet abortionist has greater public support than the idea that the unborn child is the 'weakest of the weak'.

The *Vereniging voor Vrijwillige Euthanasie*, the Association for Voluntary Euthanasia, defends the right of individuals to put an end themselves to what it calls unbearable suffering. It says that doctors should be able to help patients whose situation offers no hope of recovery to end their lives. This goes against the Hippocratic oath which all medical practitioners in the Netherlands feel bound by. It is their duty to prolong life, not to curtail it. On the other hand, advances in medical science now offer the possibility of prolonging patients' lives even when there is no prospect of successfully treating their illnesses. The most tragic examples are coma patients kept alive for decades, vegetating while machines regulate their vital functions.

People who are seriously ill often end up in a situation where only a heart-lung machine, keeps them on this side of the border between life and death. This places doctors and other medical staff for a terrible dilemma – should they leave the machine on or is it more humane to switch it off? The latter is a form of euthanasia, the 'good death'. And if a cancer patient, suffering indescribably and deteriorating in front of your eyes, says that he or she wishes to die with dignity, who is to refuse? In practice, the machine is disconnected. Many doctors will respect their patients' wishes to die with dignity. Many Dutch people – including myself – know of this happening in their own immediate circle. In my case, it was a married woman under forty who was dying of lung cancer. She had a long talk about it to her Catholic doctor, who gave her enough pills to enable her to end her misery when she thought that the time had come. She did this one afternoon, after giving herself time to take leave of her husband and child. The pills first made her sleepy and, after an hour or so, she died without pain.

This had, and still has, a great effect on me. For everyone who was close to her, including myself, it was a great comfort that a humane doctor had given her the choice. We were grateful for this form of tolerance. The same doctor who had given her the pills certified that she had died a natural death, so there was no need for an autopsy. Otherwise the pathologist would almost certainly have established death by poisoning and the doctor would have been prosecuted. But no one saw any reason to request an autopsy, including the specialists at the Roman Catholic Hospital that had discharged the woman a few weeks before her death in the conviction that, with radiation and chemotherapy, she could live another year. In her case, tolerance allowed her suffering to come to an end.

The activities of the Association for Voluntary Euthanasia were therefore not valued too highly in many medical circles. They focused attention on a practice that in which well considered and responsible decisions were made on a case-by-case basis, but which became more difficult when exposed to the light of day. After all, no matter what euphemism you used, the doctors were intentionally terminating a life. In the eyes of the law, it was murder, manslaughter or negligent homicide. Moreover, the word itself, euthanasia, has negative connotations. It was used by Hitler and the Nazis to describe the extermination of what they considered 'inferior forms of life'. In the 1940s this led to the killing of thousands of mentally and physically handicapped Germans. The opponents of euthanasia compare disconnecting a heart-lung machine to this type of genocide. In their eyes, tolerating euthanasia for incurable patients, which they consider nothing short of murder, is the top of a long and slippery slope.

And, of course, who is to determine at what point suffering becomes 'unbearable'? Sometimes the patient is able to make that decision himself or herself. But what if the decision has to be taken by others – the family, for example? This is a common criticism from opponents in the church. In the 1980s, the husband of a woman who had been in a coma for several years asked the hospital for permission to switch off the life-support machine. The doctors at the hospital, which was a Christian institution, refused to do it and forbade the husband to do so himself. He then sought publicity for his case, hoping in this way to be able to end his wife's suffering. After a heated public debate, his wife was disconnected from the machine and allowed to die. Another aspect of the problem is that of new-born babies who are so severely handicapped that they have little chance of survival are slim and no prospects at all of leading a valuable existence. But who decides what constitutes a 'valuable existence'? Who defines 'little chance of survival'? Does it mean a few months? A few years, perhaps? Never reaching adulthood? In the view of many Dutch people, such questions should never even be asked. That is the top of the slippery slope. Once you start to slide down and you end up thinking like Hitler.

This impassioned debate has resulted in a law which obliges doctors who perform euthanasia to inform the Public Prosecutor, who then decides whether criminal proceedings should be instigated against them. The debate on euthanasia shows up the weak spot in the tolerance approach. It is not so much the room it leaves for subjective judgement, but the fact that the limits tend to be pushed back; or rather – to use a cynical, but in this case justified, analogy – the 'zone of tolerance' gradually spreads, organically, like a spot of black ink on the blotting paper of society.

If only the dykes hold out and our feet stay dry. Marsman's warning is equally applicable to the sometimes stormy waters of social and ethical issues:

> And in every region
> the voice of the water,
> telling of endless disaster,
> is heard and feared

3

Organized

'How I love those gentlemen in black'

The need to be on time. A life regulated by diaries. Appointments for everything. Consultation and the search for consensus. The meeting culture. A feasible compromise as the ultimate aim. Confidence in the government. The primacy of policy.

At every bus and tram stop in the country there is a timetable posted which gives the departure times to the minute – 19.37, 08.57, etc. The timetables in the booklets published by the various transport companies, however, inform passengers that they should allow five minutes either way when planning a trip. They also state categorically that no rights can be derived from the information given. This aside, the aim is clear – the buses should run exactly on time. The same applies to the railways. If a train is delayed, passengers are informed via the public address system and on the departure boards exactly how long the delay will be. They wait on the platforms, angrily cancelling appointments on their cell phones, because they wish that the public transport system would live up to its promises. In practice, it hardly ever does. Buses and trams get stuck in traffic, the rail network continues to be over-burdened – at least until the completion of a large-scale project aimed at doubling many stretches of track from two to four. In 2005 around 85% of the trains ran on time, which most Dutch travellers see as a very bad performance. It leads to angry questions in parliament and discontented commentaries in the newspapers. Arriving late is associated with failure and unreliability.

**Unexpected visitors are treated rather brusquely
and shown the door within ten minutes**

This is evident, too, in making and keeping appointments. Anyone who turns up at a company or other organization without first making an appointment, will be greeted with confusion and, more often than not, irritation. The daily activities of the staff are strictly planned from hour to hour and unexpected visitors interrupt this schedule. They will be treated rather brusquely and shown the door within ten minutes. And they will be lucky if they get this far. More likely they will find themselves confronted with a secretary who will scour the diary of the person they wish to see for a time when he or she is free. This will often be a week or so later and the appointment will be specified to the nearest quarter of an hour. It is then crucial to get there on time, or the whole procedure will start again. The person concerned will, after all, already be busy with their next appointment. They cannot interrupt their schedule or they will also be thought unreliable.

There are exceptions to this rule. Government departments in particular often have information desks where you can ask questions without first making an appointment. You just take a number and wait your turn. But even these departments tend to fall back on the appointment system, especially if you have a question that cannot be answered in a minute or two. Even most hairdressers have adopted the system. Barbers where you can still just walk in and have your hair cut are an exception these days and usually announce this added service with a large sign outside. Often they will be run by immigrants who have not yet succombed to the need of their Dutch colleagues to have every moment of the day planned out in advance.

The appointment system has penetrated deeply into everyday life in the Netherlands. Practically everyone has a diary with them at all times, which is produced immediately someone wants to contact them. Even for a lunch or dinner date, presumably a pleasurable occasion, they will look at their dairies with knitted brow until they can find a time when they have no business or family commitments.

Particularly people whose jobs include considerable organizational responsibilities, or who have to attend a lot of meetings – and that is not uncommon in a society held together by consultation and consensus – tend to have overfull diaries. Automated diaries, like the one available in Microsoft Outlook, are a godsend to the people of the Netherlands. Email and mobile telephones on the other hand have been received with mixed feelings. Not that these innovations are avoided, on the contrary. Dutch society was one of the first to embrace broadband internet *en masse*. There are now more mobile telephones in use than people living in the country. But being available at all times has one disadvantage: it makes it more difficult to plan your day, because you can always be reached. Many Dutch people solve this problem by building an electronic dyke: they hide behind their voicemail and they only check their messages at set times of the day. This is how they respond to the chaos of the twenty-first century and being on-line all day long. The question is, however, how long they will be to keep this up, and whether, in time, Dutch society will lose out to more competitive nations which can more easily adapt to the demands of modern day chaos and seek their strength in brilliant improvisation.

Dutch children receive their first diaries at primary school

Foreigners sometimes complain about the horror of a life controlled by a diary and Dutch people – before taking their leave because they have an appointment somewhere else a quarter of an hour later – eagerly agree with them. The diary culture is very deeply entrenched. Dutch children receive their first diaries at primary school when, after the first few years of playing around, things get serious and they are given their first homework. The teachers dictate the exercises and make sure that they are noted down. A school diary is therefore an indispensable attribute for any self-respecting school child. Once they have passed their final exams and gone out into the world, school children and students can no longer live without their diaries. Shops, banks, companies and government departments start distributing pocket diaries on a grand scale from the middle of November, their name discreetly printed in silver letters on the front cover.

This explains the irritation that arises if the train or bus is too late, or if the traffic going into the city is at a standstill. The system works only if everyone keeps their appointments. Surprises and exceptional circumstances demand improvisation and the subservience to the dictates of the diary have destroyed the ability to find a spontaneous solution to an unexpected situation. Hence the irritation. Anyone who arrives late knows that they will be accused of the kind of *mañana* mentality considered typical of Spaniards and Latin Americans. They cannot keep their appointments and – as a well-known Dutch saying goes – they don't do today what they can do tomorrow. The cause of the problem is often the overburdened infrastructure, but most Dutch people still blame themselves.

As in other parts of the world, the diary culture grew out of the industrial revolution, which started in the Netherlands about 150 years ago and created the practical preconditions for the culture to develop. Farmers traditionally live by the rhythm of the seasons. They have few obligations that need to be fulfilled at certain times of the day. The same applies to towns dominated by trade and craft workshops. Most church towers have had clocks since the Middle Ages, but they were largely symbols of prestige. They became reliable only when Christiaan Huygens, a physicist from The Hague, discovered the secrets of the pendulum and used his new knowledge to build an accurate timepiece. This remained the basic principle of all clocks until electronics offered a digital alternative.

The people rarely looked at the clocks in the church towers. They knew the time of day from the sound of the church bells. They were originally intended to call the faithful to prayer and made different sounds for different occasions. For a Mass, they played long, loud notes; for a wedding they were joyful and for a funeral mournful. Softer tones were used to call people to the Angelus every morning and Vespers in the evenings. Local authorities also used the bells to inform the populace of more worldly events. They were rung, for example, a quarter of an hour before the city gates were closed for the night. In many cities, a special bell was rung to inform craft masters that their apprentices had to go home for their evening meal. Every community had a number of signals of this kind to inform the people that it was time for a certain activity to be performed. The different sounds were achieved by using bells of different sizes. As the range of bells grew, they automatically evolved into a musical instrument. Examples of this instrument, known as a carillon, can still be found in practically every town and city. They have been status symbols for many centuries. Carillon bells are not tolled in the way that conventional bells are. They are struck on the outside by hammers operated by a kind of keyboard, which the carillonneur plays by striking the 'keys' with his fists.

This is why, in many Dutch towns, you can still hear the bells ringing at unusual times of the day. They may be calling long-dead apprentices for their dinner or warning the people that the city gates, dismantled long before, are about to close. These traditions are frequently continued without local residents – with the exception of a small group of initiates – knowing why the bells are ringing. It may even simply be because their ancestors had built the signal into the Huygens clock mechanism two or three centuries previously.

The carillon music that tinkles across many a market square is often mechanical. The hammers are activated by a gigantic – often very old – music box. Most churches with a carillon do, however, have a carillonneur, who they share with the other churches in the area, and who is called in to give a concert at certain times, perhaps on market day or on feast days. This is their chance to really show what they can do. Bent over the keyboard, they alternate traditional Dutch tunes and Bach with ragtime, the latest hits from the pop charts or songs about the merits of the national football team. It is background music for the people on the street, but most concerts are announced in the local press, sometimes with a list of the numbers to be played.

The rhythm of the machine and mass production

These are sweet memories of distant, less hectic times. Most towns also have relics dating from the era when the foundations of modern society, with its obsession with time, were laid. These are the street clocks, mounted on poles for all to see. Many of them are still there, but there used to be far more. They enabled people without watches to arrive where they were going on time. They were a public service in the same vein as street lighting. This is because the rhythm to which the Dutch live, according to their diaries, is the rhythm of the machine and mass production.

A craftsman works at his own pace and with his own tools. He takes the raw material and turns it into an end product. That is no longer possible once production is organized differently. If you take the work of the craftsman, divide it up into separate tasks and ensure that every worker contributes a small part of the end product, then all those involved have to work at the same speed, starting and stopping at exactly the same moment. Production then progresses far more quickly and efficiently, as Adam Smith, the prophet of capitalism, illustrated in the 'Wealth of Nations' with his example of a pin factory. If one link in this chain fails, however, none of the others can produce anything. That is why assembly line production demands greater control and discipline.

This becomes even more important when the pace of the work is no longer determined by the people themselves but by machines. Once a steam engine has worked up enough pressure to set all the wheels turning, everyone has to be ready. And then there is no mercy – you have to adapt to the tempo of the machine. There is a strong dose of wishful thinking in the old socialist adage *Gans het raderwerk staat stil, als Uw machtige arm het wil*, roughly translated 'All the machinery shall halt, if your mighty arm so desires.' The dictatorship of the machine means that you cannot arrive at about seven o'clock to start work. You have to be there dead on seven, because that is when the machine is switched on.

The Dutch are surrounded by clocks

This same modern industry produced the instruments that allowed people to fulfil this requirement, and mass production made them affordable. Alarm clocks started appearing in the shops during the last twenty-five years of the nineteenth century. It was, however, well into the twentieth century before the average worker could afford one. Until then, they were woken up in the mornings by a *porder* – a 'prodder' – a pitiful soul who was paid a pittance to tap on the windows of his clients with a long stick until they heard him and shouted out that they were getting up. Nowadays, alarm clocks are consumer articles with absolutely no prestige value. Even a Rolex, the most prestigious watch in the world, is considered to prove only that the wearer is a show-off.

The Dutch are surrounded by clocks. There is an alarm clock next to the bed. There is a clock in the living room, primarily for decoration. Most kitchens have one, as do most places of work. They are so common that the radio no longer gives the exact time, except for the six beeps of the atomic clock just before the hourly news bulletin.

This situation was not reached without a certain amount of resistance. Some historians describe the recent history of the Netherlands as a disciplinary process, with order and regularity being imposed on the masses, where necessary with a heavy hand. And there were indeed examples of industrial calamities in the last quarter of the nineteenth century caused by the fact that the local population were unable to adapt to a completely different rhythm overnight. They bear more than a passing resemblance to the failed 'development projects' of our own time.

Yet the climate for such a change was most likely far more fertile in the Netherlands than in many other parts of the world. The hard-fought struggle against the water, the eternal threat from the sea, had forced the Dutch to organize and work closely together, and to divide tasks down to the last detail. Secondly there was an elite that 'understood' the demands of this new age. They were used to organizing their lives.

Foreigners will soon notice that the 'holy' diary of Dutch friends and colleagues is full of appointments, meetings and what they call *overleg*. *Overleg* literally means 'consultation' but this is an inadequate translation of what has become an entire concept to the Dutch. It is closer to the English 'in conference', an equally vague and discouraging phrase. Generally, you can get through to the person you are calling without encountering too many problems, even if you only succeed in making an appointment for a later date. But if you are confronted with a colleague or a department secretary who informs you that the person you wish to speak to is 'in a meeting' or 'in *overleg*', you may as well give up.

A meeting is a success only if a consensus is reached

Anyone in a meeting or in *overleg* can be disturbed only in a real emergency, such as a death in the family. Meetings are completely shut off from the outside world. Cell phones offer no solace. Participants in meetings switch them off, usually at the chairman's request. And it is considered very bad manners not to comply with this. If you do persist long enough to get someone out of a meeting, you will almost always hear a hurried, nervous and irritated voice at the other end of the line, hardly prepared to listen to anything you say. This response – non-committal and verging on the allergic – is a product of the compromise culture. A meeting is a success only if a consensus is reached. This requires that everyone follows the entire discussion and participates if possible, even if only with an approving smile now and then. The whole process is disturbed if someone has to leave the meeting and frequently the discussion is held up until they return. For the same reasons, it is simply 'not done' to arrive late or leave early. If it is unavoidable, then good reasons have to be given. Many people who are unable to attend meetings – even if their presence is not compulsory – send a notification of their absence to the chairman, who reads it out at the beginning of the proceedings. Arriving late, cancelling or simply not turning up implies that you do not consider the issues to be discussed or – even worse – the others present at the meeting, sufficiently important to warrant your attention. Their revenge is not to take you seriously in the future. Moreover, if you are not there, you no longer have a voice, a vote to influence the outcome. In a compromise culture, it is crucial to take an active part in the collective creation of thoughts and ideas.

The old regents of the Republic, who could only achieve anything by exercising the greatest caution and finally reaching a consensus, learned this fundamental lesson. If you wanted to have a say, you had to be there. Because it was a matter of voluntary cooperation, decisions made by only a few were ineffective. Towns, regions and provinces imposed no sanctions on those who refused to abide by the

Meetings can sometimes go on until the participants are driven to despair. But, since no one is prepared to blame their own verbosity, there is still no easy way out.

decision of the majority. A good chairman or secretary therefore always ensured that as many people as possible were present when decisions were made.

And then a consensus has to be reached. This is not always easy. Politicians have always devoted great attention to informal *overleg* outside the official conference room to prepare the ground for the compromise they hope to achieve. This is still an important feature of Dutch politics at all levels. The Dutch have an expression for these informal discussions, which frequently take place in private. They say that issues have been talked about in the *wandelgangen*, the name given to the corridors that run through the *Binnenhof*, the traditional home of Dutch parliament.

Bound neither by mandate nor instruction

In spite of all this, reaching a compromise has always been and still is a difficult process. This was particularly true in the days of the Republic, because the representatives of a town, region or province frequently claimed to have no mandate to go along with a certain proposal. They first had to consult with the people they represented and then act on their instructions. During the days of horse-drawn barges, this could sometimes take weeks. Although a threat to national security would normally result in the agreement of all concerned, most decisions became bogged down in endless argument. The central authorities in the Republic succeeded only twice in drawing up a declaration of war before the enemy – no doubt tired of waiting – sent their own declaration to the Binnenhof. The law now specifies very clearly that the representatives of the people – from local councils up to parliament – can make decisions *zonder last of ruggespraak*, 'bound neither by mandate nor instruction'.

This method of working requires that every step of the decisionmaking process be recorded accurately and the decision itself be laid down in writing as unambiguously as possible. Agreements and decisions have to be committed to paper, otherwise there is the risk that they will be interpreted in different ways at a later date. There will then be no higher authority to put an end to the new round of bickering this produces. To this day, the Dutch commit almost everything to paper – the written word is sacred. There is a certain distrust of oral agreements. If an oral agreement is made, and it is to a certain extent official, the parties prefer to follow it up with a written confirmation, which often concludes with the qualification that the agreement is valid unless statement is made to contrary. The written word is law.

You have to exercise self-control

You do, furthermore, have to exercise self-control. There is no room for strong emotions. The meetings of the regents in the days of the Republic were models of polite detachment. If you want to ensure that the final compromise contains as many of your own ideas as possible, you must not allow yourself to lapse into magnificent oratory and theatrical performances. On the contrary, you mistrust such behaviour. You should be cautious in expressing support or opposition. Any suggestion of prima donna tendencies should be ruthlessly nipped in the bud. Not by the forceful presentation your own argument, but by calmly ignoring the guilty party. Rhetoric is not a highly developed art in the Netherlands. Most members of parliament speak in a monotonous tone, often reading from a piece of paper. Only the most capable speakers are not thrown into confusion by interruptions, which are permitted only under certain circumstances. The entire proceedings take place in an air of extreme detachment. It is the argument itself that matters, not the manner in which it is presented. If a speaker puts his case too elegantly, it may even be counterproductive.

Meetings in the Netherlands follow a set pattern. It is not done to challenge the leadership of the chairman. It is their job to give everyone the chance to say their piece and so they are allergic to anything that threatens to interrupt the orderly progress of the meeting. Everyone will try and make it clear that it is the issue under discussion that is at stake and not the persons involved, because – as explained earlier – this has led to bad experiences in the past. It can take a long time to reach agreement. The average chairman will try to reach a general consensus so that, at the end of the meeting, he can safely ask if anyone is in disagreement.

Although this may appear to contradict the above description of the consensus culture of the meeting, there is almost always at least one person in disagreement. If someone strongly opposes what has been agreed by the meeting, he or she will ask that this be recorded in the minutes. It will have no effect on the implementation of the decision and, in many cases, those who opposed the motion will contribute loyally to carrying it out. After all, they lost democratically and everyone knows how they stand.

The regents in the Republic represented a city or region; in the days of pillarization you were a member of a social group, i.e. you had a Calvinist, a Catholic, a liberal or a social-democratic background. This made it more difficult to reach a general consensus. Each pillar rested on a set of general principles that were not up for negotiation. The decision-making process would reach stalemate if people with different sets of beliefs were not prepared to work together. Yet very few chose this extreme, because it meant relinquishing all influence. Well into the 1950s, the Calvinist pillar objected to funfairs as a source of decadent pleasures, spangled palaces of temptation, where Satan kept house. Calvinist political leaders therefore always voted against the issue of permits to fairs and advocated the introduction of an official ban. They had a similarly uncompromising opposition to lotteries, always opposing them in the full knowledge that their proposals would never be passed. Their counterparts in the other pillars respected their position. They, too, had certain issues on which they were not prepared to negotiate. Such issues were always immaterial, with little or no money at stake. After losing the vote, they could always say that they had done their best. In some cases, of course, principles may outweigh one's willingness to compromise. Most Dutch people will not go to this extreme, but there are exceptions. Assuming, however, for the sake of simplicity, that election results reflect the distribution of social beliefs, this is no more than 10% of the electorate. Of the 150 members of the *Tweede Kamer*, perhaps ten to fifteen will always take a position on principle. They represent the very small parties, who are often at loggerheads with each other. In the 2003 parliament, there were five strict Calvinist members divided among two parties, one of whom opposed votes for women. Seventeen extreme-left members were divided among two parties. Eight belonged to GroenLinks, an uneasy alliance of pacifist socialists, communists and Christian radicals, who have difficulty agreeing among themselves. Nine made up the parliamentary Socialist Party, which has left is Maoist roots far behind and is now thriving by advocating populist-left sentiments. The larger political parties have a tendency to tolerate these principled colleagues as a quaint part of national folklore, but their roles are never more than marginal.

But people do listen closely to the consistent arguments of parliamentarians like Jan Marijnissen, leader of the Socialist Party or André Rouvoet of the strict Christian Union. They hear truth in their words. When they see these principled leaders on the television, the viewing public sigh deeply and say that, actually, they are right. It is the 'actually' that is the crux of the matter. If someone is 'actually' right, it means they are but they do not get their own way. If something is 'actually' forbidden, you do it anyway – and without a guilty conscience. The Dutch word for actually, 'eigenlijk', is an important lubricant in the Dutch compromise culture. Just think about all those things that are 'actually' forbidden, but which are tolerated.

In this way, in the margins, radical opinions play an important role. You can scarcely reproach the five Calvinist members for regularly reminding their colleagues of God's punishing hand. Activists in the extreme-left parties often claim that they first proposed ideas that are later adopted across the board. Where the environment is concerned, this is certainly true. Isolated radicals who are not amenable to reasonable argument sometimes prove to be trendsetters. But they are the exception.

In 1934 Jan Gresshof, poet and chief editor of the *Nieuwe Arnhemse Courant*, had a space left over on the front page. Thinking of the nearby *Velperplein*, which was often frequented by the elite of Arnhem, the dignified capital of the province of Gelderland, he wrote the following:

Liefdesverklaring

Ik houd zo van die donkre burgerheren
Die langzaam wandlen over 't Velperplein
In deze koele winterzonneschijn:
De dominee, de dokter, de notaris
En 't klerkje dat vandaag wat vroeger klaar is.
Maar 't kan verkeren.

Zo onmiskenbaar ziet men aan hun kleren
Dat zij rechtvaardig zijn, terwijl de plicht
Die eedle lijnen groefde in hun gezicht:
De dominee, de dokter, de notaris,
Drievuldig beeld van al wat wijs en waar is.
Maar 't kan verkeren.

Op aarde valt voor hen niets meer te leren,
Zij zijn volkomen gaaf en afgerond,
Oud-liberaal, wantrouwend en gezond:
De dominee, de dokter, de notaris,
Voor wie de liefde zelfs zonder gevaar is.
Maar 't kan verkeren.

Zij gaan zich nu voorzichtig laten scheren,
Om daarna, met ervaring en verstand,
Een glas te drinken op het heil van 't land:
De dominee, de dokter, de notaris.
'k Weet geen probleem dat hun na zes te zwaar is.
Maar 't kan verkeren.

Ik hou zo van die zindelijke heren,
Levende monumenten op het plein
In deze veel te heldre winterschijn:
De dominee, de dokter, de notaris,
Die denken uw dichter niet goed gaar is.
Maar 't kan verkeren.

Declaration of love

How I love those gentlemen in black
Who slowly walk across the Velperplein
In the cool winter sunshine:
The minister, the doctor, the lawyer
And the clerk who has finished a little earlier today.
But the tide can change.

Their clothing leaves no doubt
Of their integrity, while duty has etched
The noble lines in their faces:
The minister, the doctor, the lawyer
A threefold image of wisdom and truth.
But the tide can change.

There is nothing left on earth for them to learn,
they are perfect and complete,
Old liberals,[1] distrustful and healthy:
The minister, the doctor, the lawyer,
For whom even love presents no threat.
But the tide can change.

After having their faces carefully shaved,
And with experience and good sense,
They raise a glass to the country:

1 This was frequently used to describe liberals of a stately and conservative persuasion.

The minister, the doctor, the lawyer.
After six, no problem is beyond them.
But the tide can change.

How I love these cleancut gentlemen
Living monuments on the square
In this much too clear winter's sun:
The minister, the doctor, the lawyer,
Who think this poet not quite sane.
But the tide can change.

They did indeed consider the poet 'not quite sane'. Greshoff was fired on the spot.
Too many gentlemanly subscribers had recognized themselves in his words. They
considered the light-hearted satire an attack on their persons and saw to it that its
author was removed from their midst – the same author they had allowed a place
in their company as chief editor. He had overstepped the mark. The discomfort felt
by the gentlemen of Arnhem led to much cheerful indignation in the rest of the
country. But this did not get Greshoff his job back. He moved abroad, and his
'Liefdesverklaring' became one of the best-known poems in the history of Dutch
literature.

Playing the injured innocent

Such sensitivity may at first seem surprising in a country that is proud of its
tolerance. Personal conflicts are, however, more difficult to gloss over than
disputes of a more businesslike or practical nature. For anyone who believes in
the culture of compromise, a direct attack on the personality is difficult to accept.
It is considered a blow below the belt. Indignation is then directed at the attacker,
while the victims can lick their wounds in public and 'play the injured innocent'.
If Greshoff had made old-liberal ideology the subject of his irony instead of
persons clearly recognisable to those in the know, nothing would probably have
happened to him.

The Netherlands suffers from a certain predictability

All in all, this leads to effective cooperation, but never to spectacular change. The
chances of a radical about-turn, no matter the area concerned, are very small. It
does, however, allow all concerned to set out a course which – although it may
never be adventurous – is clear for all to see. The Netherlands suffers from a
certain predictability. Every agreement, each appointment, leads to another and
this produces continuity. You could almost say that society has its own diary, which

is already full quite a way into the future. The real solidity of the whole system becomes clear only in a crisis. In the last century, this happened once only, during the German occupation between 1940 and 1945.

On 10 May 1940, as part of the *Blitzkrieg*, motorized German troops invaded the Netherlands from the western front. Five days later, the Dutch armed forces capitulated. The Queen and the government had fled to London several days earlier, where they set up a government in exile.

Hitler's National Socialism was based on racism. The German people were superior to all others. The Nazis, however, held the Dutch in high esteem. Some of them even considered their neighbours, whose language was closely related to their own, as Germans who had lost their way through a quirk of history. This wrong could now be rectified. Berlin ordered that, if food was scarce, rations for the Dutch people had to be 90% of those for the German occupiers.

Hitler appointed the Austrian Nazi Arthur Seyss-Inquart as *Reichskommissar* in the Netherlands, to run the country now that the government had fled to England. His primary task was to reorganize the Dutch economy as far as possible to serve the

Anton Mussert, the leader of the Dutch Nazis, on an election poster. After the liberation he was executed as a traitor.

Painful scenes in Amsterdam. German soldiers round up members of the Jewish community.

war effort. But he had a secondary, more idealistic mission – to convert the people of the Netherlands to Hitler's sacred doctrine. Until then, National Socialism had not acquired much support in the country. Anton Mussert, leader of the National Socialist Movement (NSB) headed a four-man faction in parliament and, as such, belonged to the marginal figures referred to earlier. Seyss-Inquart was confident, however, that – if he adopted the right approach – he would be quickly cure the Dutch of their misgivings. He found that the Netherlands was a very organized society. With the exception of the government, practically everyone had remained at their posts. This had been ordered in a National War Directive that had been issued prior to the German invasion, to protect the interests of the Dutch people. It was, at the same time, forbidden to help the enemy to wage war. There were no exact guidelines. The document was very vague. Seyss-Inquart left the entire administrative structure intact. He placed his own observers in strategic posts within the apparatus to ensure that everything went as it should and to take action if it did not.

Because they were 'bad'

The time of the German occupation continues to be a cause of heated controversy to this day. The main question is whether, when faced with the test, the Dutch people failed or not. Did we resist, or were we simply cowardly collaborators who changed their loyalties according to the course of the war? The occupation was considered of such importance that, a few months after the German capitulation, the government set up the Netherlands State Institute for War Documentation to keep a record of what had happened. The Institute's director, historian Lou de Jong, acquired a very independent position. The first volume of his monumental history appeared in the 1960s. It was a bestseller, as were each of the subsequent volumes as soon as they were published. De Jong's work provoked fierce debate and destroyed reputations. What he unearthed did not always make for enjoyable reading. He shattered the myth of an intransigent people standing up to the terror of the occupier. Many prominent figures proved to have done things during the occupation – particularly in the early years, when the prospects of an allied victory were still very slight – which, with hindsight, were highly dubious. Were these people 'good' or 'bad'? It was a question, said Jaap Burger, the minister of justice just before the liberation in 1945, of dealing not with people who had done bad things, but with those who were 'bad'. This disturbed memories of the entire period. It was no longer a matter of what happened, but of deciding how 'good' or 'bad' the people involved had been. There was, of course, no doubt about Mussert and his collaborators. Mussert had already been executed as a traitor to his country. Nor was there much of a problem condemning the thousands of Dutch people (rather too many) who joined the 'Westland' ss unit voluntarily. Outside of these obvious cases, however, it was by no means as clear cut.

There is almost complete agreement among historians today that most Dutch people adopted a kind of tactic of accommodation during the occupation. They tried to continue their everyday lives as far as possible and adapted to the changing circumstances where possible. Only a minority chose either active resistance or full collaboration. The majority just let it happen. Historian Chris van der Heijden even gave his study on the Second World War in the Netherlands the title *Grijs verleden* (Grey Past): it was neither black nor white, and certainly not overly heroic.

Another question is, however, more interesting. Was Seyss-Inquart successful in carrying out the orders of his *Führer*? The answer is yes and no. Every time he manoeuvred Dutch individuals and organizations into positions where they had to profess their allegiance, the result was a fiasco. When he announced that students could attend university only after they had signed a declaration of loyalty, 90% of them stayed away. When he placed Nazis in leading positions in the traditional pillar organizations, their members left in droves. Trade unions, for example, simply folded. With a few exceptions, new organizations set up along National Socialist lines remained little more than empty shells. Collectors for a Nazi-based charity known as *Winterhulp*, 'Winter Aid', were simply ignored. The radio in London encouraged this with a famous motto: *Nog niet het knoopje van mijn gulp gaat er naar de Winterhulp–*, 'I'll give not even the button from my trouser fly to the Winterhulp'. The radio and press, controlled by the Nazis, rapidly lost credibility as the war progressed.

That is one side of the coin. But as long as the measures imposed by the occupying Nazis did not demand any show of loyalty, people cooperated with little trouble, sometimes even willingly. This was particularly true in the early years of the occupation. It is clearly illustrated by an excerpt from the illegal newspaper *Het Parool* from 21 August 1942, headed 'The Gestapo and distribution in the Netherlands': 'Every distribution office in the Netherlands has to keep a record of all missing or false ration vouchers or vouchers stuck on the wrong ration cards. The list has to be sent to the Central Distribution Office in The Hague. On 30 June 1942, the heads of all local distribution offices in the country received a confidential letter from the central office that, as of 1 July, a copy of this list has to be sent to the *Deutsche Sicherheits Polizei*, at the Binnenhof in The Hague. In this way, our distribution offices can help to prevent the sending of completely innocent people to the concentration camp for distribution offenders in Ommen. Distribution officials, do not follow these orders. Check less thoroughly or do not send in the lists.'

The illegal press was full of such appeals, together with sad conclusions that these were often ignored out of a misguided sense of duty. The Netherlands had a tradition of trust in the government. Incorruptible and efficient civil servants rarely considered sabotage. They were not only afraid of reprisals – a legitimate fear, considering the lengths to which the Germans were prepared to go – they simply asked themselves each time whether the limit had yet been reached. And, accustomed to making practical compromises, they quickly tended to think that, this time, the demands of the occupier were acceptable. Furthermore, Seyss-Inquart tended to fill vacancies with members of the NSB. The party even had to set up a correspondence course for aspiring mayors. Many public officials defended their decision to stay put with the claim that anything was better than giving up their job to someone from the NSB.

During the occupation, local authorities erupted into feverish activity. Free of parliamentary control, they introduced a flood of new rules and regulations which no longer had to run the gauntlet of public debate. In 1941, they introduced new regulations for road traffic, many of which are still in force today. These were followed by a new, less complex system of income tax. It is estimated that 90% of these new directives were left intact after the country was liberated. In between times, measures imposed by Seyss-Inquart to increase the power of Hitler's totalitarian hand over the people of the Netherlands slipped through the net. Consequently, the Nazis succeeded completely in sucking the economy of the country dry. The authorities generally cooperated in the selection of young men for forced labour in Germany, including – later in the occupation – those who already had jobs. Eventually, all men under 40 had to register. The whole system worked very smoothly.

The history of a murder

It was due to this attitude that the Nazis were largely able to carry out the most criminal part of their programme in the Netherlands – the extermination of the Jews. 'This book portrays the history of a murder' says Professor Jaques Presser at the beginning of his book *Ondergang*, a masterful description of the Final Solution in the Netherlands. The book, which he wrote at the request of the Netherlands State Institute for War Documentation, had a devastating effect. Presser proved conclusively that the Germans were able to isolate, transport and eventually eliminate the Dutch Jews without too many problems because of the cooperation of the organizations involved and the fact that resistance was generally too late and never more than fragmentary. In spite of this, however, the first measures against the Jews were greeted with a mass expression of protest throughout Amsterdam.

There is an atmosphere of resolute defiance amid the grief

In a square near the seventeenth century Ashkenazi and Sephardi synagogues in the centre of Amsterdam, there is a statue of a dock worker. The man is standing, his muscular body tense, his fists clenched, staring defiantly out at the windswept square in front of him. Every year, on 25 February, a crowd gathers around the statue. Wreaths are laid by representatives of the city council and many others who are clearly members of some committee or other organization. They are often old people, but the crowd comprises a wide range of age groups. Often, the more elderly visitors are accompanied by their grandchildren and, now, their great-grandchildren, who they have brought along in the hope that something of the significance of the occasion will remain with them. There is an atmosphere of resolute defiance amid the grief. They are there to commemorate the February Strike. The docker represents all of the city's workers, who downed tools *en masse* on 25 February 1941 in protest at the persecution of their Jewish colleagues. The whole of Amsterdam took part, and even the stock exchange closed for trading as its staff joined in the strike.

The Jews had been persecuted on the streets. A sort of militia of Dutch National Socialists had incited anti-Semitic riots, and the people of the city had come out in support of their Jewish neighbours. The Germans responded by openly intensifying their terror campaign against the Jews. The small underground Communist Party called for a strike. On 25 and 26 February, there was a general strike in Amsterdam and a number of neighbouring towns. On the second day, the occupying forces came out in force to end the protest.

The statue of the dock worker keeps the memory of the strike and the solidarity of the city's workers alive. The annual commemoration not only recalls the heroic deeds of those days but is also a manifestation of defiance against continuing terror and racism. It is of great psychological value to the people of Amsterdam. After the liberation, the Queen granted the city permission to include in its coat of arms the following motto: *Heldhaftig, vastberaden, barmhartig*, 'Valiant, resolute, merciful'.

The square itself is now bare and empty, a place where you would seldom go

The German occupiers made it compulsory for people of Jewish origin to wear this star visibly on their outer clothing at all times. The rule even applied to babies and small children.

This picture of the 'hunger winter' of 1945 is very familiar to most Dutch people. Children scrape out the mess-tins in which sugarbeet soup was delivered to distribution points around the city. The official food rations contained less than a quarter of the daily intake of calories needed to keep one person healthy.

from choice. The magnificent synagogues show, however, that it must once have been the centre of a busy Jewish community. All that is gone. There is a song that describes this loss, written by Kees Manders and sung by Rika Jansen:

> *Als vader weer bladert in zijn fotoboek*
> *dan sta je versteld als hij weer vertelt*
> *Van de Weesperstraat en de Jodenhoek.*
> *Als hij dan verhaalt hoe het leven begon*
> *bij het ontwaken, handel en zaken*
> *Humor en gein, dat was de levensbron*
> *en had je een dag eens geen mazzel gehad*
> *Dan 's-avonds naar de Tip Top*
> *waar je je sores vergat.*
> *Soms riep d'r nog één in 't late uur:*
> *'Ik heb mooie olijven en uitjes in 't zuur'.*
> *Amsterdam huilt, waar het eens heeft gelachen.*
> *Amsterdam huilt, nog voelt het de pijn.*

> When father looks through his photographs
> We are amazed at the stories he tells
> Of the Weesperstraat and the Jodenhoek.
> He tells of how the day started,
> The trade and the business,
> the humour and The wit that was the source of life.
> And if one day you didn't have much luck
> You could go the Tip Top in the evening
> And forget all your troubles.
> Sometimes, late at night, you could still hear
> The call: 'Lovely olives, pickled onions!'
> Amsterdam weeps,
> Where once it laughed.
> Amsterdam weeps, it still feels the pain.

In *Ondergang*, Jaques Presser explains how this happened. The Nazis learned their lesson from the strike and, instead of terrorizing the Jews on the streets, they adopted a more administrative approach. They introduced a whole series of small-scale measures to put increasing pressure on their victims.

The register of births, marriages and deaths introduced by Napoleon now proved its worth. Since it recorded not only name, address and age, but also religion, it was simple to weed out the Jews. Some local officials hit upon the idea of spiriting away the incriminating cards, but this often occurred too late and only on a very small scale. Moreover, in the first few months of the occupation, everyone in the country had received a form to fill in, declaring whether they had

Jewish parents or grandparents. Practically everyone had faithfully returned the form, as one should do with forms issued by the government. This, in spite of the ominous title of the document: *Ariërverklaring*, Declaration of Aryan Descent. A conscientious civil servant in The Hague by the name of Lentz saw an opportunity to introduce one of his pet plans, which the Dutch government had always left on the shelf for reasons of economy. Under this plan, every Dutch citizen would have to carry an identity document. Lentz had designed one, which was almost impossible to forge with the methods available at the time. Seyss-Inquart gave him all the cooperation and support he required. Lentz spent the entire occupation diligently perfecting his system of identification. He never understood why he was so unpopular after the liberation.

When war broke out, the Jewish community in the Netherlands amounted to about 140,000 people. Most were descended from refugees who had fled to the Republic to escape persecution in less tolerant countries. Their special status had officially been abolished in 1795. The Dutch Jews knew that they belonged in the Netherlands. The pillarized society allowed them to retain their own identity where and whenever they wanted without fear of repercussion. Many words with Hebrew or Yiddish origins had become a part of the Dutch language. Amsterdammers proudly refer to their city to this day as 'Mokum', which is derived from the Hebrew word for 'town'. Everyone knows where the word comes from. The unofficial anthem of the capital contains the phrase: *In Mokum ben je rijk en gelukkig tegelijk, geef mij maar Amsterdam,* 'In Mokum I am rich and happy at the same time, just give me Amsterdam'.

Jews never had any reason to mistrust the Dutch government or its representatives. Not even when it issued the *Ariërverklaring*. Not when it fired all Jewish civil servants – at first, on full salary. Nor when it dismissed all Jewish teachers and gave them new jobs at special Jewish schools.

Most Dutch people responded to these measures with some resentment, but considered them at least 'recognizable'. After the February Strike, the Germans set up a Jewish Council for Amsterdam. It was headed by two leading figures from the Jewish community and had a wide range of administrative powers. This, too, seemed acceptable. It was probably a good thing that there was a representative body that could mediate with the occupier. The leaders of the Council soon discovered, however, that they had not been appointed to talk to the Germans. They simply had to carry out their orders. These orders were largely a matter of selecting people for transportation to Germany or even further east. The criteria for selection continually changed. There were of course all kinds of procedures for appeal against selection, or even to be added to the list if one so desired. It was all set up very correctly, right down to the medical examinations. In this way, the Germans were able to increasingly isolate the Jews from their fellow citizens. They devised a way of acquiring the Jews' property without too many problems by forcing them to transfer it to a special Jewish bank. With the cooperation of local authorities throughout the country and under the supervision of the Dutch police, they concentrated the country's entire Jewish community in the area where the statue of the dock worker now stands.

The pace of these measures was determined by the rate at which the death camps in Poland were able to 'process' those who were sent there.

Transportation took place in two phases. The selected groups were picked up and taken to Amsterdam Central Station in extra city trams. They were then taken by train to the Westerbork transit camp near the German border. A freight train packed full of deportees left Westerbork every week bound for the gas chambers in Auschwitz-Birkenau. The trams were driven by employees of the City Public Transport Company. After the liberation, Presser noted with some bitterness that the Dutch rail network had not only survived the war almost intact, it had been extended – with a new stretch of line between Hooghalen and Westerbork. Of the 140,000 Dutch Jews – men, women and children – 110,000 were murdered. That is 79%. In France and Belgium, both of which were occupied during the war, the percentages were 40 and 38 respectively. This is not because the Dutch are more anti-Semitic, it is just that in the other two countries, the people were able to sabotage the Nazi extermination machine more quickly and more effectively. There were protests enough against the persecution of the Jews in the Netherlands – the churches in particular responded very vociferously – but there was too little practical, 'silent resistance'. When the resistance movement, both in and outside the Jewish community, began to set up escape networks, it was already too late.

The longer the occupation lasted, the more the resistance movement, which was made up of a wide variety of groups and individuals, grew and the more it could count on the sympathy of the population. Active cooperation was, however, a different matter. Throughout the war, the entire structure of government and bureaucracy, with the occasional exception, followed the orders of Seyss-Inquart and his officials. The civil servants involved could not comprehend that this was not just another party with whom they had to negotiate, but a totally unscrupulous enemy who was not prepared to talk, who would always demand complete and unconditional compliance. Even when they appeared prepared to adapt, to be – for a brief moment – open to reason, it was never anything more than a strategic marking of time, a pause before clamping down even harder than before.

This does not detract from the heroic deeds of thousands of Dutch men and women who risked their lives or of the undaunted members of the resistance who helped those pursued by the Nazis to escape and sometimes made a significant contribution to the eventual allied victory. In one area, the Dutch resistance was far better organized than its fellow movements in other countries – the publication of illegal leaflets, pamphlets, books and even, eventually, newspapers. Towards the end of the occupation, circulation of illegal papers reached about a million a day, all of which were composed, printed and distributed in secret. The catalogue of illegal publications issued by the Institute for War Documentation comprises hundreds of pages. In spite of the fact that most Dutch people adopted a tactic of accommodation during the occupation, they still wished to express their opinions

May 1945. Emaciated inhabitants of the Randstad wave to English and allied aircraft which are about to make food drops.

– which had not changed – without them being censored. And they were prepared to run a considerable risk do so. The punishment for the possession of illegal publications was imprisonment and internment in a concentration camp; for writing, distribution and printing, it was death.

Yet, at the same time, we realize that it was not a particularly illustrious period in our history. The mistakes made during the occupation will not be made again. The obligation to carry some form of identification is now completely normal in all our neighbouring countries. Any Dutch government that considers introducing a similar obligation immediately finds itself at the centre of a heated debate in which the hated term 'identity card' plays a central role. It was not until 2005 after a long and difficult process, that the government succeeded in introducing obligation to carry ID. Dutch citizens now have to be able to prove their identity. They must produce their passport, driving licence or an ID pass issued by the local council.

Presser's lesson has not been learned. In 1994 the Dutch government decided to make an active contribution to the international effort to end the conflict in Bosnia, where a bloody civil war was raging between the Muslim Bosnians and the Christian Serbs, with the Croats playing a role in the margins. The government agreed to protect the small town of Srebrenica. Srebrenica was one of the 'safe areas' set up in Bosnia to protect the Muslim population against the 'ethnic cleansing' of the Bosnian Serbs, who had the region in an iron grip. A battalion of Dutch UN troops, known as 'Dutchbat', tried to keep the warring parties apart. The battalion – according to UN instructions – was lightly armed and had little authority to respond to direct aggression. The Serb generals and their commander Ratko Mladic rode around in stolen Dutch jeeps, even using them when they came to negotiate with Dutchbat's commanding officers.

It was a perfectly natural step for the Netherlands to contribute troops to the peacekeeping operation in Bosnia. The country is a supporter of international arbitration as a means of solving conflict and is, consequently, a committed and active member of the United Nations. The Dutch army had taken part in peace-keeping operations earlier in Lebanon and Cambodia and, after the fall of the Berlin Wall and the end of the Cold War, the government decided to reorganize the army specifically to participate in such operations. An 'mobile air brigade' was formed and recruitment advertisements were shown on the television, showing Dutch lads in mountainous (and therefore very 'foreign') regions, 'defending' a dam. The copywriter's message was unstated but clear: 'Join the Army – and help to keep the world a peaceful place'. Such recruitment ads are still shown in Dutch television.

Dutchbat, however, was confronted with uncompromising Serbs who were uninterested in working on a peace plan and who displayed completely different behaviour at the negotiating table than the Dutch normally expect. Diplomat and politician Hans van der Broek had already experienced this during his final days as foreign minister. As European Commissioner dealing with Yugoslavia, he had made a long series of agreements with the combatants in the former republic, which were usually broken within 24 hours. The average Dutchbat soldier had increasing difficulty justifying their presence in this cruel civil war. 'Why can't we just let them sort it out for themselves?', they complained to the people at home.

The days that followed were shameful

Then the Bosnian Serbs, under general Ratko Mladic, took over the enclave of Srebrenica without encountering any resistance to speak of. Dutchbat did not fight back. It was not equipped to do so and, in any case, its mandate from the UN did not permit retaliation. Furthermore, the Serbs had taken several hundred Dutch soldiers hostage. The days that followed were shameful. While Dutchbat looked on, the Serbs separated the Muslim men from the women and children. The latter were packed into overfull buses and taken to the front, where they were dumped near the Muslim lines and told to walk the rest of the way. The men disappeared into detention centres for 'interrogation'. Television pictures were shown worldwide of Dutch soldiers in their blue UN helmets witnessing this selection process without raising a finger in protest.

The response to these events in the Netherlands was remarkably calm. Foreign minister Hans van Mierlo stated on television that the Serbs held all the cards, that he was forced to negotiate without 'small change'. And that the first priority was to get all the Dutch soldiers home from Srebrenica safely.

In the meantime, there was increasing evidence of atrocities committed against

Dutch soldiers in very unfamiliar territory: a convoy in Bosnia.

the refugees by the Serb forces. In response to this, the Dutch soldiers were ordered not to speak about what they had seen because loose talk might endanger the lives of their comrades who were still being held. Only Jan Pronk, the development minister, dared to speak out. He spoke of 'genocide' and called on the world community – not just the Netherlands – to respond to the atrocities with a hard hand. His remarks provoked an immediate wave of criticism in the Netherlands and Pronk was accused of putting the lives of the hostages in danger. The hostages, meanwhile, returned to the Netherlands in small groups, because the Serbs had a tendency of releasing their captives in dribs and drabs. A whole contingent of psychologists were at the ready to help the hostages come to terms with their undoubtedly traumatic experiences. The first group to arrive back at the Soesterberg air base were given a heroes' welcome.

There were a few discordant voices. Some commentators suggested that the attention lavished on the 'boys in Bosnia' was disproportionate to that paid to the tens of thousands of Muslims driven out of the enclave – while under the 'protection' of Dutchbat – and now at the mercy of rapists and murderers. Such remarks met with an indignant response from the general public. From the fourth day of the crisis, *De Telegraaf* expressly no longer led with news from Bosnia. The editors, who know the way the public thinks better than anyone, did not want to upset their readership any more than was necessary. The other papers continued to lead with details of the disturbing developments in the Balkans, but support for the

Dutch UN troops meet members of a Bosnian-Muslim militia.

government and for Dutchbat did not falter. There was a general feeling that we had done our best and were not to blame for the failure. The only priority now was to get the boys home in one piece. It all put one in mind of the 'injured innocent'.

One Dutch soldier was actually killed in Srebrenica. This led Alain Franco, who was then the correspondent in the Netherlands for the French newspaper *Le Monde*, to make the following, rather uncomplimentary, comment: 'The death of the Dutch UN soldier Raviv van Renssen was a great shock to everybody. "We are not used to one of our boys being killed in action," said a diplomat who is to take over responsibility for media and cultural affairs in Paris next week. The country was right to be shocked. The Netherlands has fortunately little experience in these matters. The people are not used to their soldiers being sent home in bodybags, burials with military honours, and having the sorrow and grief of the family broadcast into their living rooms. And the government would like to keep it that way. "We are a small country, and we have limited resources," a top official at the foreign ministry told me. "We do not possess great power like France or Great Britain, so there is little we can do." La belle affaire! The Netherlands, the smallest of the large European countries and the largest of the small, which so much wants to play a role on the international stage, has got an attack of cold feet.' Franco advised the Netherlands to adopt a less ambitious foreign policy, if it is not prepared to take risks.

Initially the Dutch government hoped that the problem would eventually go away by itself, but it didn't. Too many people had died. In addition, the Dutch city of The Hague was chosen as the headquarters of the new International Criminal Court, where war criminals from former Yugoslavia and other countries would in the future be tried for their crimes. The government came up with a very Dutch solution to this sticky problem: they commissioned a thorough inquiry into the affair. The task was entrusted to the Netherlands State Institute for War Documentation, which was excellently equipped to conduct research into war crimes and genocide.

The inquiry took many years to complete. A few weeks before the elections in 2002, the Institute published a report several thousand pages long. On the whole, the report confirmed the prevailing view of what had happened at Srebrenica: the Dutch battalion had stood by and watched as General Mladic had organized the genocide. In military terms, Dutchbat was no match for the much stronger enemy force, but the way it responded to the crisis was symbolized by video recordings of Mladic negotiating with the Dutch commander Thom Karremans, which were shown over and over again on television. Mladic called Karremans everything under the sun. The whole conversation was translated into English by an interpreter, and Karremans replied in English, saying: 'I am the piano player. Don't shoot the piano player.' Other recordings showed Mladic giving Karremans a farewell gift when he left the enclave.

Prime minister Wim Kok – who had taken office in 1994 – decided that he and the entire Cabinet should resign in response to the report. As it was just before the elections, it was a symbolic act: by doing so he was officially accepting responsibility for Dutchbat's failure in Srebrenica. And that was the end of the affair. It never came to a serious debate that answered Alain Franco's main accusation. After a short pause for breath, Dutch troops were once again sent to take part in

Commander Thom Karremans will never get the chance to forget the drama of Srebrenica. Here we see him – as a witness to the drama – answering difficult questions.

international military operations, always as an ally of the United States. The Netherlands took part in the occupation of Iraq for a year, and in operations in Kosovo and Afghanistan. In 2005 a Dutch detachment was even sent to the dangerous province of Uruzgan in South Afghanistan.

Since Srebrenica nothing else has gone wrong in military terms. There is a broad political consensus, which is embraced not only by the Christian Democrats and the liberals, but also a majority on the left, that the Netherlands should contribute to peace operations and other military interventions around the world. The rationale behind this is the desire to help achieve a stable and peaceful world, without violence. This calls to mind the First World War, which was also seen as the 'war to end all wars'. Yet only a minority of people in the Netherlands adopt an isolationist position. To do so would, after all, mean that evil would triumph, evil which – since the attack on the Twin Towers – is increasingly sought in the form of fundamentalist Islamic terrorists. This has even led to certain renewed appreciation of the Dutch armed forces. In February 2005, the talent show Idols, one of the most popular programmes on commercial television, devoted one evening to Dutch popular music. To symbolize this patriotic theme, the makers of the programme did not choose clogs, windmills or farmers from Volendam, the home of Dutch pop. Instead they had the mobile air brigade marching across the stage in full uniform, while the Dutch flag flew in the background. There was even a tank, on which the female Idols candidates sat looking lovingly at their soldier boys.

However, whenever parliament discusses the possibility of taking part in operations like that in Iraq, their main concern is the safety of the Dutch troops involved. Every man is born to love his country, as the well-known poem goes, but to die for your country is widely considered a little excessive.

Where does this attitude come from? One explanation is that the Dutch have little experience of foreign domination. They have been accustomed to being governed by their own people for centuries and they do not consider their rulers dangerous outsiders. The people of the area known historically as Flanders, which now constitutes the northern part of Belgium, have succeeded in freeing themselves from foreign domination only in the past fifty years. Here, 'silent resistance' has developed into a fine art. The Flemish have become past masters not only of tax evasion but also at quietly dismantling dictatorial structures. During the Second World War, they were far more successful at deceiving the Nazis than their fellow Dutch-speakers just across the border. The Dutch artist and resistance fighter Eduard Veterman, who was a master forger of false documents, wrote in his war memoirs Keizersgracht 763: 'It was of course comical that the police of a Brussels suburb became "bulk buyers". Belgian government officials were far more active in this respect than their Dutch colleagues'.

After the liberation, both the organization and the staff of the Dutch bureaucratic apparatus remained largely intact. Only those who were overt supporters of the Nazis, such as the members of the NSB, were actually removed from their positions. The situation was not examined with a more critical eye until much later. In 1958, Professor Jan de Quay – who, shortly after the liberation, set up a short-lived 'people's movement' which accepted Hitler's vision of Europe – became the prime minister without provoking an outcry. His deputies all had successful careers. That would no longer be possible today – especially since the publication of De Jong's work.

Belief in the good intentions of the powers-that-be had also survived the war intact and, to a large extent, is still strong today, no matter how much people complain about politicians. The Dutch have a number of objective reasons for this belief. They know that even the largest organizations take account of the individual. They can count on agreements and promises being kept within the agreed period of time. If this does not happen, there are always procedures for appeal. No one has to simply accept a tax demand, an order from the local council or any other expression of power from above. They can object, their appeal will be taken seriously and there is a good chance that they will win. If one or the other party refuses to budge, there are specialized independent courts. This can lead to long-drawn-out procedures which, in many cases, have a deterrent effect. The threat of being taken to court is often used as a weapon. Not because the Dutch are particularly fond of dragging their compatriots up in front of a judge, but because the threat itself generally leads to a new round of negotiations and, eventually, to a compromise that is acceptable to all concerned. It is all a matter of give and take.

They always have some 'small change' in their pockets

Anyone who sits down with a sigh to fill in their tax forms, knows from the outset that the officials at the tax department will most likely not accept all of the deductions they have claimed. They tend to accept this, together with the fact that they will at least get something back. They include a few less probable items, in the hope that the tax people will focus on these and let the others slip through. In the same way, trade unions, employers' organizations and interest groups submit proposals in the knowledge that a large part of what they have presented will have to be surrendered during negotiations. They always have, as it were, 'small change' in their pockets.

You don't get far in the Netherlands without change. This applies as much to the public at large as to sports clubs, school boards and university departments. Everyone is used to having their say and being able to recognize at least a part of it in the final decision.

Anyone who needs the approval of others to realize a plan of some kind, will first conduct an informal survey in the immediate environment to ascertain how feasible it is. In this way, you get some kind of indication of what will be acceptable to everyone. You then draw up a plan which includes a certain amount of loose change. This should consist of items which are not essential to the success of the plan, but which are certain to provoke objections from various quarters. After this, there is a round of consultation with all parties concerned, during which – as expected – objections of all kinds are raised.

Any expression of one's own talent or excellence tends to be counterproductive

Outright rejections are very rare. Comments are usually presented as suggestions for improvement, marginal rather than challenging anything essential. The person submitting the proposals is open to such suggestions and lays his small change on the table, one coin at a time. This requires skill and experience. The quicker he shows his small change, the more the others will demand from him. It is a slow and, for outsiders, sometimes irritating process – particularly as it is so difficult to intervene while the process runs its course. Any expression of one's own talent or excellence tends to be counterproductive. As does any defence of the proposals based on their inherent superiority. Anyone who uses arguments like 'This is the solution we are looking for', 'All our troubles are over' or 'Don't mess around with this, it's already perfect' will only succeed in uniting the opposition against them. Criticisms will then be directed at the essentials of the proposal and the whole thing rejected because the proposer has made it clear that he is not prepared to negotiate, but wishes to impose his will on the others. They feel that their opinions are not being taken into consideration and that they have made no contribution to the issue under discussion. As far as they are concerned, there is nothing more to discuss. Once this happens, the only alternative is the exercise of power. Those in a position of authority, who are higher in the hierarchy, can impose their will, steer the discussion in a certain direction and set limits. But even then it is not advisable to leave no room at all for those in a subordinate position to make their contribution. They will then use the most powerful weapon at their disposal – complete disinterest. They will lose their motivation. They will, as it were, withdraw their creativity. They continue to do everything by the rules, but make it clear to their friends and acquaintances that they no longer really give a damn what happens. Lack of motivation among the staff is a common problem in almost all organizations and companies in the Netherlands, particularly because the law makes it very difficult to dismiss employees simply because they 'don't care'. Managers should be aware of this. Although they might wish to give job applicants an impression of themselves as resolute and vigorous leaders, the socially responsible thing to do is to assure prospective employees that they are always 'prepared to listen' and believe very strongly in the indispensability of genuine *overleg*.

It is more a way exchanging information

As I mentioned before, it is impossible to translate the word *overleg*. The literal translation 'consultation' does not embrace the full meaning of the term in Dutch. It is a form of group communication which aims not so much at reaching a decision as giving the parties involved the opportunity to exchange information. The Dutch spend many of their working hours in *overleg*. This means that they are discussing the state of affairs with their colleagues. They describe in detail the activities they are engaged in and the rest of the group are, in principle, entitled to make comments or ask questions. Superiors will explain their plans to those below them in the hierarchy in detail and inform them of their consultations with colleagues elsewhere in the organization. Everyone, and superiors in particular, gives their reasons for doing or not doing something. They are not afraid of questions, no matter how critical they may be, and take the time to answer them. Tempers very rarely rise during these consultations. If they do, something is wrong.

At the end of the *overleg*, everyone has an idea of what the other wishes to achieve. This is very important if the system is to function correctly. After all the questions, comments and reactions, the limits of a generally acceptable consensus have become more or less clear. Often the chairman will conclude with satisfaction that *de neuzen weer in dezelfde richting wijzen*, all noses are pointing in the same direction, or – in typically Dutch fashion – *de klokken zijn gelijk gezet*, the clocks have all been synchronized. Such *overleg* may lead to practical decisions being made, but more often than not results in little more than an exchange of information. Afterwards the participants can be seen, diaries at the ready, making appointments with each other. Anyone who misses the meeting without giving a clear reason for doing so in advance is treated with disdain. And especially if they had 'something better to do'. Being *in overleg*, on the other hand, is always an acceptable excuse for not being available.

Yet it is considered normal to complain about all this *overleg* and the endless meetings. You soon get the feeling that they make little contribution to efficiency. Most meetings are therefore characterized by a certain degree of dullness and apathy. Boredom is never far away, particularly because the Dutch rarely use their underdeveloped talent for rhetoric. Everyone must be allowed to have their say. This requires a strict and manipulative chairman. Most chairmen restrict themselves to keeping interruptions to a minimum, on the principle that people have the right to finish what they are saying. This may be fair, but does little to make the discussion more lively.

The whole process of *overleg* ensures that the complaints do not lead to this form of communication being employed less frequently. Everyone complains very vociferously, but anyone who does not take it sufficiently seriously does so only to their own detriment. Especially if the other participants are their subordinates.

There is a serious risk inherent in the whole business. The original aim may be lost in endless rounds of consultation and meetings. Compromises pile up until the final result is so watered down that it would have been better not to have done anything at all. This kind of net result is familiar from history lessons on the Republic.

Every organization has a 'beleid', from the government down the smallest local club

There is, of course, an instrument to prevent this happening – *het beleid*. *Beleid* is usually translated as 'policy'. Although this is sometimes adequate, in most cases, like *overleg*, it cannot be translated by any one English term. The word originally indicated a kind of precise and cautious way of working. Anyone who sets about repairing a microscope should not go at it like a bull at a gate, but should be patient and tackle the problem with *beleid*. Typically, a synonym for *beleid* used in this way is *overleg*. Every organization has a policy, from the government down the smallest local club. Philips and Shell have a *beleid*, and so does the printer at the end of the street, with its workforce of four. And, of course, it is all down on paper. The *beleid* describes the aims of the organization and the kinds of activities it undertakes. It also sets limits for these aims and activities. Everything may be very clearly formulated, but more often than not it is pretty vague. The partners involved in discussion of a proposal can determine from the *beleid* whether it falls within the specified limits. Compromises that fall outside these limits can be rejected as not being a part of the *beleid*. On the other hand, elements may often be added to existing activities because they are considered to fall within the bounds of the *beleid*. If, for example, it is the *beleid* of the government to employ more women – as is indeed the case – the personnel departments of the various ministries must direct their recruitment campaigns to take this into account. There can be no debate about this. Anyone who questions it is immediately put in his place. *Beleid* is *beleid*.

Beleid, of course, comes into being through the process of *overleg*, in which everyone concerned takes part. But once it is in place, it rapidly becomes immutable. Everyone knows that they have to act within the limits of the *beleid* – or else. That is why it is accorded such great importance. Those with ambition do their best to be as closely involved in the process of making *beleid* as possible. When talking to friends and colleagues or having a drink in the pub, they will boast of the contribution they have made. In job applications, they will make as much of it as they can, because it demands respect. It is no surprise that the one of the highest jobs in the civil service is that of *beleidsadviseur*, 'policy consultant'.

If people are not satisfied, they blame it on beleid

All this leads to the conclusion, especially in government circles, that problems are caused by a lack – and not an excess – of *beleid*. Interest groups, professional associations and action committees adopt this idea and continually make demands for *beleid* on this and *beleid* on that. Politicians pacify the public with pledges to formulate new *beleid* to deal with their complaints. And if this takes too long, they will soon be pilloried by the media. They can, on the other hand, evade difficult issues by saying that, fortunately, there is a *beleid* that deals with that very problem. There is a good chance that no one will ask what this *beleid* actually entails.

If people are not satisfied, they will tell their friends in the café that there is something wrong with the *beleid*. It is wrong. It is out of date. Or it does not take account of the facts. If it is not changed – and changed quickly and radically – then we shall all (and this is where they stare despairingly into their glass or point accusingly with their index fingers) go to the dogs. There is no other way out.

Beleid is serious business. It is far too easily seen as a solution in itself, and not always out of a desire for an easy life. It is largely due to the fact that most Dutch people – when it comes down to it – believe that most things can be controlled. All it takes is good organization (and if that fails there is always the *gedoogbeleid*, the 'policy of tolerance'). This belief has been reinforced by the process of modernization that began in the last twenty-five years of the nineteenth century and the boundless prosperity that has developed since the end of the Second World War. Modern society is a success story and it leads people to believe that if you take the right measures at the right place and at the right time you will always achieve the desired result.

Beleid is often then a matter of regulating existing processes. The government initially started doing this when circumstances left it with no other choice. Although the Netherlands managed to keep out of the First World War (1914-1918), its economy suffered severely and there were serious food shortages. The complete collapse of the commercial sector was prevented only by a large number of radical government measures. Others were introduced to ensure a reasonably fair distribution of what little food was available. The acute economic depression caused by the Wall Street crash of 1929 also provoked a wave of government regulations and measures aimed at keeping the impact in the Netherlands to a minimum. And it was *beleid* that held all of these measures together in some form of cohesive whole. Consequently, government intervention in economy and society became normal, although there were critics who spoke of 'St. Bureaucratius' and many others who complained that the government certainly seemed to appoint a large number of commissions to investigate a whole range of problems and come up with solutions. Yet this criticism was to no avail. The intention behind all the commissions was to remove the ideological content from the process of formulating *beleid* as much as possible. The whole exercise is, after all, only worthwhile if the result enjoys sufficiently broad support. The parties in the consensus always have to recognize some of their own contribution in the final result, or at least not see too many elements of the opposing parties' viewpoints which – after all – they vigorously opposed during the *overleg*. It is therefore always better if *beleid* appears to be based on facts or scientific research. The commissions are made up of academics or representatives of interest groups, plus a number of 'independent experts'. Everyone hopes that, if the various 'interested' members are unable to find a consensus, the experts – with their knowledge of the facts – will be come up with a solution to suit everyone.

A new group of specialists has developed in the civil service, in interest groups and in some sectors of industry – the *beleidsmedewerkers*, 'policy officials'. These people frequently have departments of their own and their jobs carry a high status. Civil servants always try to include the word *beleid* in their job descriptions, because it gives them good grounds for demanding promotion to a higher salary scale. In the Netherlands, there is nothing political about working on *beleid*. Government specialists are proud of the fact that they can operate efficiently under any kind of political leadership. As good civil servants, they are always 'loyal' to their superiors, whether they be ministers, members of the provincial executive or local councillors. The minister's ideological views will therefore be difficult to recognize in the documents in which his or her *beleid* is laid out. An efficient *beleidsafdeling*, the department responsible for drawing up the documents, is at the centre of a whole web of contacts throughout society. Its work is supported not only by all kinds of special committees, but also by representatives of interest groups and organizations which continually submit detailed recommendations on the content of the *beleid*, frequently in the form of fully worked out draft reports and documents. Countless permanent advisory bodies have grown up around the various ministries which concern themselves with a wide range of issues, from the most general to the extremely specific. The Advisory Council on Government Policy (known in Dutch as the WRR) can concern itself with practically any area it chooses.

The more independent the members of a council or an ad hoc advisory committee, the greater the chance that they submit recommendations that are not considered feasible because they have insufficient *maatschappelijk draagvlak*. This is another Dutch term that defies translation. It roughly means 'support in society', but implies more than simply obtaining the agreement of the general public for a proposed course of action. It is a question of whether the proposals will have a reasonable chance of success when exposed to the network of committees, interest groups and public enquiries that they will have to pass through before the necessary consensus is reached. Recommendations with insufficient *draagvlak* are usually discussed in the media, often after being presented at a press conference, and then disappear into a drawer. *Beleidsafdelingen* are very good at filing away vast quantities of information which only resurfaces decades later when some aspiring historian digs it out while researching for a PhD.

Society, too, has a diary for keeping track of appointments

Beleid is aimed at the future. The Dutch take it for granted that society, too, has a kind of diary for keeping track of appointments. They can leaf back through the planning for the past six months or so, which ensures continuity. Continuity is a 'good thing'. Companies and organizations proudly state the year in which they were founded if it is long enough ago to give them an air of respectability. In their view, there is nothing coincidental about this great age. It is an indication of the foresight of their founding fathers, a characteristic which the current generation of leaders has no difficulty in believing they have inherited.

Many Dutch people strongly believe in the predictability of events. Proposals are frequently dismissed because they affect only the short term. Good *beleid* aims at the long term, or at least, the medium-long term. In practice, this results in a great deal of analysis and brainstorming which is frequently overtaken by developments. There is then a tendency to hang on to the existing *beleid* and to see the new circumstances as incidental rather than structural. Experience has shown that companies and organizations that feel sure of their position are the first to adapt their *beleid* to changing circumstances.

Yet some people still wonder about the value of all this effort. Does *beleid* ever actually help to solve problems? This is a difficult question to answer, because the documents in which *beleid* is laid out are rarely unequivocal and seldom have a single aim. They generally have a number of parallel objectives, or the main aim is divided into components. This multiplicity of aims is related to the character of compromise that such documents always have; their authors try to put as much as possible into them to satisfy as many interest groups as possible. And it does not stop there. In the search for greater effectiveness and workability, secondary policies are devised to suit a whole range of smaller target groups. After all, there are no such things as all-embracing models which you can simply impose on reality, even if you have to break a few corners off here and there. There are always exceptions and specific circumstances which demand special treatment. This ultimately makes *beleid* very complex and its results difficult to measure. It also means that the system of rules and regulations it gives rise to are extremely complicated and difficult to unravel. For example, the level of social security benefits depends on the family situation of the applicant. Two individuals receive more than a married couple, but applicants whose partner is in paid employment are not entitled to a benefit. There are now more than twenty different ways of categorizing people who live together. Social security officials also have difficulties in distinguishing between the categories and complain about their colleagues in the *beleidsafdeling* who are responsible for making the rules which they have to implement as best they can. Reports of ridiculous situations that have arisen as the result of different forms of *beleid* clashing with each other also appear regularly in the media.

Every now and then, politicians attempt to put an end to such undesirable situations. The matter then gets bogged down in parliament, where the representatives of the people speak earnestly of injustice and 'extreme emergencies'. The ministers – or, lower down the ladder, councillors – then fall over themselves to pledge that they will draw up a special *beleid* to address these urgent situations. This led in one notorious case to the failure of an attempt to simplify tax legislation. The original proposal from a committee of experts was amended to such an extent that the new system of rules and regulations was no less complicated than the original one. It was also considered unfair. Too many people fell *tussen de wal en de schip*, between ship and quayside, where – as we all know – you can all too easily get crushed to a pulp.

We passed that station long ago

It is always possible to change *beleid* eventually, but it cannot be achieved overnight. Every single measure has, after all, been discussed at great length. 'That discussion has already been closed' or 'we passed that station long ago' are common and often effective responses to suggestions that existing policy should be reviewed. It is possible to get the discussion reopened only if it can be proved that circumstances have changed to such an extent that the *beleid* is 'hanging in the air', i.e. that it no longer has sufficient *maatschappelijk draagvlak*. This makes the decision-making process in the Netherlands somewhat slow. The Dutch have a word for this: *stroperig*, from *stroop*, the thick syrup they like to pour over their pancakes. Although this implies a certain self-criticism, it has resulted in little more than good intentions. There is a well-known Dutch expression: *Waar gehakt wordt, vallen spaanders*. Roughly translated, it means 'If you're chopping down trees, watch out for flying splinters'. The message is clear – just leave the trees where they are.

Anyone who is likely to be affected by some form of *beleid* or another would therefore be well-advised to follow the process closely and, where possible, become directly involved in it. The usual way to do this is to join in the *overleg*. In their attempts to involve as many people and interested bodies as possible in their activities, *beleidsmakers* promote such participation themselves. It is, after all, a prerequisite for the ultimate legitimacy of their product. The action committees of the 1960s helped them in this endeavour by fighting for the introduction of public enquiries on as many issues as possible. These enquiries are public meetings to which people who are affected by the proposed *beleid* are invited. These may be the representatives of certain sectors, the residents of a particular street or employees in a certain branch of industry. The meetings are in effect a form of *overleg*. The body organizing the meeting outlines its plans, often presenting a number of alternatives. Afterwards, everyone is invited to ask questions and give their comments. This frequently leads to some of those present volunteering to sit on a working group to examine the issues further and present recommendations, which offers them an opportunity to share in the decision-making process.

Again, it is not advisable to swim too enthusiastically against the current, because this is inconsistent with the search for a consensus and the general tendency not to see things in black-and-white terms. Yet there is often an under-current of suspicion at these meetings. Many of those present believe that there is something they are not being told, a 'hidden agenda'. There is only one course of action open if you are suspected of having a hidden agenda – complete openness. No one will actually say anything, but you will notice that your partners in the discussion are increasingly cool and reserved. It is not advisable to bring it up yourself; you should never ask outright: 'So you think I have a hidden agenda?'. The only effective antidote is transparency, putting your cards on the table, providing as much information in as much detail as you can. This is, however, easier said than done. Bureaucracies and similar organizations have a tendency to keep quiet about things that are still being discussed internally. These are sensitive issues. It is very rare that they will come out and say 'We haven't reached agree-ment on that yet' or 'That is a very sensitive issue and any comment might have repercussions for everyone involved'. It is in this fertile soil of silence that sus-picions of a hidden agenda germinate and grow.

During the Republic, the regents held all their *overleg* behind closed doors. The phenomenon of representative bodies meeting in public dates back only to the nineteenth century. Openness was one of the main demands of the action committees that grew up in the 1960s. This initially led to a great proliferation of public galleries. Parties represented on local councils across the country were more or less forced to hold their internal preparatory consultations in public. The openness did not, however, last for long. The more experienced party members simply transferred the real business of reaching a consensus to the *wandelgangen* or to all kinds of informal meetings. Consequently, traditional *overleg* behind closed doors has undergone something of a revival since the 1980s. The negotiations on the formation of the new coalition government in 1994 were more secretive than ever.

In 2002, it was the same story, despite the triumph of the new party led by Pim Fortuyn, who had promised to put a stop to what was known as 'backroom politics'. Mat Herben, who took over as leader of the party after Fortuyn was assassinated, was pleased and only too proud to be allowed to take part in the secret talks with the more established parties.

This form of confidentiality provides ample opportunity to influence the process of making *beleid* by mobilizing external factors. The Netherlands has a free press with relatively little respect for the powers-that-be. Politicians and others who wish to manipulate the process in some way or another regularly take advantage of this. They leak information to the press and journalists are always very pleased with themselves when they find confidential documents in their post. The media devote considerable attention to the information. Journalists will always protect their sources at any price, even though – unlike doctors, for example – they have not sworn an oath of confidentiality. Attempts in the past to discover journalists' sources by taking them to court have always resulted in a scandal, in which the journalist emerges as a martyr for freedom. This is why those in high places who are damaged by such leaks prefer to discover who is responsible by means of an internal investigation. The culprits are very rarely fired. Their careers tend to 'take a dive' and they find themselves excluded by their superiors and colleagues. Leaking confidential information therefore always bears a certain risk. The trail should never lead back to the 'mole', at least not exclusively. The media cannot be punished for publishing 'secrets'. No one will criticize them in public. They will restrict their comments to errors of content on which they will base their counterattack. This, too, will attract a great deal of public interest. The best and most effective way to minimize the impact of a leak – and this is what often happens in practice – is to immediately adopt an attitude of complete openness.

Furthermore, since the 1970s, there has been legislation in the Netherlands, which in principle allows everyone access to all official documents, unless they contain personal information (such as personnel files). The archives of the Internal Security Service – known in Dutch as the *Algemene Inlichtingen en Veiligheidsdienst* (AIVD); the Dutch KGB or, if you prefer, CIA – are exempted from this obligation.

The cloak of charity

Anyone who depends on the machinery of consensus working smoothly is a little afraid of too much mud being stirred up. It leads to conflict and open conflict goes against centuries of tradition. When it flares up, the Dutch are generally at a loss. It is, of course, a signal for conciliators to spring into action. A boss whose sub-ordinates no longer see eye to eye will initially suggest that they all 'sit around the table and talk about it'. If that does not work, experts are called in from outside. Committees of 'wise men' – sometimes with a wise woman or two among them these days – are a popular instrument of conflict management. Judges with two opposing parties in the dock will first make an attempt at reconciliation, so that they will not have to make a judgement, and are very pleased with themselves when – as is often the case – they are successful. Many conflicts are solved in this way. But not all of them. In some cases the hostility runs very deep and can last for many years without losing any of its vehemence. The adversaries should fear isolation – it will be difficult for them to find allies in their immediate environ-ment. Most people want the freedom to talk to who they wish. It is, however, typical of such 'feuds' that the opposing parties attempt to divide those around them into 'friends' and 'enemies'. Most Dutch people, however, do not like such clear positioning and try – usually with success – to avoid both parties. They do not want to 'burn their fingers' on such trivial matters.

If enemies wish to be reconciled, they have to be prepared to forget the past.

This is encouraged by those in their direct environment. You must be prepared to cover certain things with the 'cloak of charity'. This cloak is also frequently used to avert potential conflict. No one likes to see adversaries thrashing out their differences to the very last or, as the saying goes *vechtend over de straat rollend*, 'wrestling with each other in the street'.

It is important that the party concerned does not see this as unconditional surrender. In this way the 'arbitrators' often provide a kind of safety net to ensure that no one falls too far. Top civil servants who find themselves in trouble sometimes 'agree' to an appointment as an 'advisory councillor' to the minister. This is a perfect solution, particularly as there are many advisory councillors with genuine influence. Or it may be widely understood that a certain colleague will be devoting himself to 'special projects' in the future. One solution for politicians who can no longer be tolerated by their fellows is to accept a position as a mayor. It is very rare that, after a conflict or a serious error, the person concerned is *aan de dijk gezet*. This expression, meaning literally 'put on the dyke', dates from medieval times and refers to the practice of banishing offenders from a town, village or region. The legislation on dismissal, which makes it difficult to fire anyone without a clear reason, naturally encourages solutions of this kind, but it also has a lot to do with preserving the atmosphere needed to make decisions on the basis of consensus.

The same approach is used when people make genuine mistakes. In its extreme form this kind of conflict management is known as the putting the affair in the *doofpot*, literally an 'extinguisher'. It has similar connotations to the English expression 'putting a lid on it'. The best example of a scandal being effectively placed in the *doofpot* occurred in the early years of the twentieth century, when the founder of the Calvinist pillar, Abraham Kuyper, found himself in trouble. While he was a minister, two members of his pillar were honoured by the Queen. Their major achievement appeared to have been the donation of large sums of money to Kuyper's *Anti-Revolutionaire Partij* – at least this was the claim of a liberal member of parliament. A council of 'wise men' was set up, who decided that both men would have been honoured even if they had not made the donations. No one believed this. Kuyper continued to deny the allegations, but told the *Tweede Kamer* that *het boetekleed mistaat de man niet* – it was fitting for him to 'wear the hair shirt'. In the debate on the affair, his opponents stated that they had no intention of stirring up the mud any further. The affair was closed. But it was clear that, although Kuyper would continue to lead his pillar and command a great deal of respect, he would never again hold a ministerial position.

Today he would not have escaped so easily, but even now he would not have been put out on the 'social dyke'. The safety net still exists, as was shown in the greatest scandal of the 1970s, the 'Lockheed affair'. Prince Bernhard, the husband of former Queen Juliana, was also the Inspector-General of the Dutch Armed Forces and a leading ambassador of the Dutch business community. As such, he was in a position to exert considerable influence in the selection of new fighter planes. Reports in the media suggested that the Prince had allowed himself to be tempted by extensive sums of money offered to him by the American aircraft manufacturer Lockheed. Again a committee of wise men was set up, headed by one of the country's leading judges. The committee's conclusions confirmed the rumours. For Prince Bernhard, this meant in practice that he was no longer permitted to be involved in the purchase of aircraft or to wear his military uniform in public. This was a very severe punishment for the Prince. The armed forces were very dear to him and he played a leading role in the liberation of the country from the Nazis. The affair, however, did nothing to diminish the Prince's popularity and, after a few years, he started wearing his uniform now and then without raising too many eyebrows. The whole scandal had been defused by the observation of genuine openness. Conflict was prevented by the imposition of a punishment that largely left it up to the Prince to 'do the honourable thing'. And slowly but surely, the cloak of charity spread itself out across the entire affair. When Prince Bernhard died at a very advanced age, a wave of heartfelt sadness swept across the country. Newspaper articles commemorated him as a war hero and as a libertine who, at the end of the day, it was impossible to think bad of.

Lieutenant-colonel Thom Karremans, the Dutch commander in Srebrenica, was given a series of marginal positions when he came back, but he was still promoted. And many a failed director cries all the way to the bank where he picks up the 'golden handshake' agreed when he took the job on in the first place. Anyone who plays the game properly will find that the Netherlands, well organized as it is, is full of safety nets.

The Netherlands is a shipping nation. Is this Rotterdam or Amsterdam? Neither, it is the boulevard in Vlissingen, the second largest town in the province of Zeeland.

4

Trade-oriented

'Holland has stayed Holland because our old folk attended to their business'

From fishermen to merchants and transporters. The Netherlands as a trading nation. Continuity as a basic principle of business. Competition, but not to the death. Cost control. Know your neighbours, for they are all potential customers. International orientation.

Around the end of May and the beginning of June, many Dutch people emerge as lovers of raw fish. Announcements in the media have already set their mouths watering – the new herring catch has arrived. The first batches are usually bought up for thousands of euros by restaurants sporting a row of Michelin stars. After that, the price drops to a few guilders and queues form at the fish stalls on the nation's markets. The Dutch like to eat their herring in the street. In Amsterdam, they use a small fork to pick up small pieces of fillet from a cardboard 'plate', but in the rest of the country, the fish is grasped by the tail and devoured with relish. The stall will often have a large bowl of chopped raw onions through which the herring is first 'passed' to make it even more delicious. In the interests of hygiene, many fish stalls therefore have a notice asking customers to do this only once, preferably before enjoying this traditional delicacy.

The fish has not really been gutted and salted in the traditional way

People born and bred in the Zuid-Holland town of Vlaardingen are also partial to their 'new herring', but many of them eat it with mixed feelings. They point to the red streak near the bones – a telltale sign that the fish has not been gutted and salted in the traditional way. It has been frozen. They insist that these little traces of blood detract from the real taste. Then they lament the decline of the Dutch herring industry. The posters in the fishmongers' windows announce the arrival of the *Hollandse Nieuwe*, but in Vlaardingen, they know better – the fish are all imported from Denmark.

Holland the way a lot of people like to see it. Dutch girls in national costume eating herring in Volendam.

The last survivors of the Vlaardingen herring fleet hung up their nets about thirty years ago, because they could no longer earn a living. This marked the end of a proud tradition that stretched back over six centuries. Every schoolchild still learns that, in 1385, in the village of Biervliet in Zeeland, Willem Beukelszoon invented *haringkaken*. This is a method of removing the intestines of the fish with a single cut of a knife. If the herring are then stored in vats between layers of salt they can be kept almost indefinitely. The only disadvantage of this method is that the longer the fish are stored, the saltier the taste and, after a year or so, they are no longer fit for consumption. This is why the arrival of the new catch was such an event – the taste had not yet been contaminated by the salt.

The herring appear in the North Sea at the beginning of May. In the old days, on the first day of the season, the fishermen would decorate their boats with colourful flags and there would be celebrations in towns like Vlaardingen, Scheveningen and Ijmuiden, and in the many smaller fishing villages. The fleet would set sail that same day, heralding the start of the annual herring race. The first vats to be brought back to shore would fetch enormous sums at the *afslag*, a Dutch auction. Since all crew members received a share of the proceeds, everyone did their utmost to win the race. This explains the nostalgia of the people of Vlaardingen. Today, the harbour is practically empty, although the town itself is thriving. It is home to a large branch of Shell, and Unilever chose it as a site for one of its most important research laboratories. People in the street will point out the creators of

Becel low-fat margarine or Mona desserts, products from Vlaardingen that can be found in every supermarket in Europe and far beyond. In terms of volume, washing powder – from Unilever and other manufacturers – is probably the town's biggest export. The old town centre, where once run-down fishermen's cottages stood together in rows, is now dominated by shopping malls.

The decline of the fishing industry did not, however, bring poverty – on the contrary. People in their thirties and forties remember how, at the end of the 1950s, their fathers – embittered and to no avail – went on strike for a fixed wage instead of the meagre share of the catch granted them by the shipowners. They are aware that it was because their parents had to scrimp and save that the herring industry survived for so long, with its endless toil and obedience to the shipowners in their mansions at the head of the harbour. They themselves have been to college and can afford their own homes because they have a well-paid job at the Unilever Research Laboratory, or at Shell, or at one of the other chemical companies on the other side of the river that stand shoulder to shoulder right down to the coast, thirty kilometres away. Yet they still often feel that they live in a completely new town, one that has banished old Vlaardingen to the local Fishery Museum. They no longer hear the rattle of the steam-powered winches or the thumping of a ship's engine. The only sound of work being done in the town now – if it is warm and the office windows are open – is the occasional beep from a computer. For the past few years, there has been a single lugger moored in the harbour. It is a museum ship and is paid for from donations from the people of Vlaardingen.

Yet there is a connection between the computers and the fish. The enormous schools of herring that used to swim down into the North Sea towards the English Channel made the people living on the Dutch coast into fishermen. And this, in turn, made them into traders. The industrial complexes on the other side of the river belong to the port of Rotterdam, the second largest city in the Netherlands, which projects itself as a 'mainport' and which handles a greater tonnage of goods annually than any other seaport in Europe. This all started in the Middle Ages with small vats of salted herring for the international market. Anyone who studies the history of the towns and cities in the west of the country will discover that, originally, their economies were frequently dependent on fishing. Even as late as the Golden Age, which the Dutch themselves are more likely to associate with international trade, the fishing industry was essential to the preservation of what was the highest level of prosperity in Europe at the time.

An unexpected storm will drive ships up onto the beaches

The port of Rotterdam, the international airport at Schiphol, the Amsterdam Stock Exchange, the trucks that carry freight to the Middle East or Russia and beyond, the international branches of the ABN AMRO bank from New York to Hong Kong – they all have their roots in the fish that tempted the Dutch to man their boats centuries ago. It was through this that they discovered that the sea was not only an enemy, but also a friend which gave them access to faraway lands. But it takes courage to go to sea – even these days, when beams of light from lighthouses penetrate deep into the night, each with its own rhythm, and with computers on the bridge and satellite communications to aid navigation. The North Sea sometimes outwits even the most accurate of weather forecasts and an unexpected storm drives ships up onto the beaches. A number of seamen still perish every year and, in spite of advanced technology and the port traffic control, ships are still required to take a pilot on board who has a long experience of navigating in the treacherous waters.

The medieval sailors depended entirely on their experience to navigate their wooden-hulled ships. Most of them did not even have a compass. They were at the mercy of unpredictable winds that changed direction suddenly and regularly. Once at sea, they had no connection with the shore. Raging storms and pirates were a continual and immediate threat. Modern-day fishermen, who are usually based in Katwijk or Urk and who fish not for herring but cod or delicious sole, use boats with powerful engines. They search for their catch with sounding equipment. Their ship's radio ensures permanent contact with their home port. If anyone is seriously injured or sick, a helicopter appears to take them to hospital. Their forefathers were left to fend for themselves and to the fickle hand of fate – fishing was a risky business.

This made the fishermen into tough survivors

This made the fishermen tough survivors. The crew of a fishing boat knew that they depended on each other and that, in principle, everything outside the boat was a threat. 'And the spirit of God moved upon the face of the waters', says the book of Genesis. This was all they had to believe in. Dutch fishermen still tend to be very religious, generally preferring a strict form of Calvinism, with its belief in a vengeful God who will save only a few and who sends raging storms to punish man for his wickedness. They are also extremely independent characters who will allow nothing to stand in their way when there are fish to be caught. When the Ministry of Agriculture, Nature Management and Fisheries imposes quotas as a result of agreements made in the European Union to prevent the sea being overfished, even the strict Calvinists among the fishermen showed unprecedented creativity in evading the watchful eyes of the inspectors. The orthodox fishing village of Urk, where on Sunday only the leaves on the trees move in the wind, is also famous for its many illegal bars in sheds and garages.

Fishing taught the seamen how to survive the dangers of being at sea and they ventured further and further from their home ports. Gradually they accumulated the knowledge necessary for merchant shipping to develop, initially in the seas of northern Europe, later as far as the coasts of Turkey and, by the end of the sixteenth century, throughout the world. Dutch cities became emporia where products from the far corners of the earth were bought and sold. It was not simply a matter of import and export. Transit was perhaps even more important, and a tour through the port of Rotterdam will show that this is still the case today. Gigantic containers are hoisted from ships' holds and mounted straight onto the back of trucks. Dutch truck drivers are known throughout Europe and they have that same resilience, independence and stubbornness that kept their ancestors alive on the open sea.

Zie ik Hollands vlag op verre kust, dan juicht mijn hart 'victorie', When I see the flag of Holland on a far coast, my heart cries 'victory'. This line comes from an old song that children used to learn at school. It has now been filed away as a dubious example of obsolete imperialism, but the emotions it describes are genuine. The average Dutch man or woman will feel a swell of pride when they see the imposing building of the ING Bank, complete with its Dutch lion, on the Avenida Paulista in Sao Paulo; or when they discover that the Alaska milk powder for sale all over Manila was produced in Noord-Brabant; or when they go for a drink in a bar in Hong Kong and run into a group of rough-talking compatriots, who turn out to be tree-growers from the village of Boskoop, in Zuid-Holland. 'Not bad going for such a small country', they think to themselves. When you belong to a population of only sixteen million, there is a certain prestige in seeing companies from your homeland playing a leading role in faraway countries.

If you encounter them at sea, they will rob you

'A pirate state lies on the sea, Between the Scheldt and Eastern Friesland!' Even the Dutch sometimes find themselves believing this, not without a certain secret pride. It is a quotation from 'Max Havelaar or the Coffee Auctions of the Dutch Trading Company', a nineteenth century novel in which the author, Eduard Douwes Dekker (known to his readers by his pseudonym, Multatuli), revitalized Dutch literature all on his own. The book is a devastating indictment of criminal colonial and trading practices with the kind of power usually associated with Joseph Conrad. It exposed a collective guilty conscience that now causes many a shiver at the sight of a Dutch flag flying in a foreign land. There is an ancient Chinese text that, after praising the Dutch for their seamanship, says: 'But if you encounter them at sea, they will most certainly rob you.' Most Dutch people know this quotation, but are unsure what to make of it. And the image of the Dutch merchant with a Bible under one arm and his cash book under the other has long been a cliché in the business world. 'Go and sell what thou hast, and give it to the poor ... and come and follow me,' said Jesus to the rich young man. The man chose to keep his riches and 'went away sorrowful'. This story from the Bible is well-known to both Calvinists and Catholics and most Dutch people have to admit to themselves that, like the young man, they 'go away sorrowful'.

Christendom, as such, has little in common with the business world. Business practice has traditionally been more closely related to sin. Catholics considered it against the will of God to charge interest for lending money right up to the end of the Middle Ages – a belief that is being revived by modern-day Islam. The first Calvinists were a little less strict about this, but they too had their doubts about the pursuit of riches. It was wrong to accumulate money for its own sake. *Geld maakt niet gelukkig.* 'Money can't buy happiness.'

This has, however, never been a reason for the Dutch to neglect their bank accounts. A seventeenth century sea captain was supposed to have said that he would 'sail to hell and back if it would earn him a couple of farthings'. Yet the ambivalence of this position remains. The effect it has on the lives of the rich needs no repeating here, but it also has an impact on the way the Dutch do business and on the way in which they calculate their opportunities and risks. There is another saying: *Zo gewonnen, zo geronnen,* roughly equivalent to the English expression 'Ready money will away.' You will not find many people in the Netherlands who believe in 'getting rich quick'. Wealth is the result of a long and continual process. This is not to say that a swindler with a get-rich-quick scheme will not find a sympathetic ear in the Netherlands, but he will have to have a very convincing line of argument. Once the whole affair is exposed, the media are more likely to express delight at the misfortune of the victims than indignation at the criminal practices to which they fell prey. There is no pleasure as great as that caused by the sufferings of others and no one will show an ounce of sympathy for those who have lost their savings, like those who victims of the ICT crisis shortly after the start of the twenty-first century.

What happens on the stock exchange during boom periods lacks what previous generations called 'solidity'. Before you do business with someone you should make sure that they are solid. That is to say, not too impetuous, careful with their money and, if possible, with many years of experience in the same area of activity. There is little respect for anyone who moves from one thing to another. An obituary to Benk Moret, one of the founders of the renowned firm of accountants Moret, Ernst & Young stated his credentials very clearly in the second paragraph: 'Moret came from a family of accountants.' It added: 'He was an administrator and an entrepreneur with great vision, daring, energy and decisiveness, determined when it came to important matters, flexible and prepared to compromise about things that he did not consider essential.' And of course, all kinds of evidence is proffered to support these claims. Under Moret's leadership, the firm expanded steadily, frequently through mergers with competitors. He had a vision that resulted in a process of continual growth. The obituary made no mention of spectacular coups or commercial *tours de force,* even though they doubtlessly occurred.

Similarly, on the 40th anniversary of the tugboat king Murk Lels of Smit Internationale, an employee wrote the following ode to his widely respected boss:

Mastermind in towing business
Undisputed salvage king
Ruler of the world's best tugboats,
Knowing prizeman in the ring
Let your house flag in the future
Eager wanted colours be
Let there always be employ for
Smit's towing company.

Lel's major talents are clear: he never gave up and he assured continuity and – at least this is what the amateur poet hopes – this would remain the case in the future. Lel's obituary closed with this poem, in spite of the fact that he was the director of a very adventurous company. Smit Internationale goes to the help of ships in distress and salvages wrecks. This is often on a 'no cure, no pay' basis. Or it may be a race against other companies, with the first to fix a line winning the contract or – if the vessel has been abandoned – claiming ownership. Yet the poet does not recall any of the undisputed salvage king's more exciting ventures. For him it is important that the company flag keeps flying. For him, that was Murk Lel's great achievement.

A good businessman does not put all his eggs in one basket

A good businessman does not put all his eggs in one basket. He is prepared to take risks, even big ones at times, but all-or-nothing situations have to be avoided at all costs. This mentality was already in place in the late Middle Ages. Merchants preferred to take out shares in a ship or several ships rather than have a vessel or fleet of their own. If a ship then fell prey to the whimsical North Sea or to the ever-present pirates, they did not lose everything because the risk was sufficiently spread. This arrangement also meant that other merchants were seen not only as competitors but also as colleagues with whom you might cooperate in certain circumstances. Anyone who aimed at continuity was not afraid of the fight, but would think twice before allowing it to become a matter of life and death. This attitude survives today. The Dutch business community has a large number of sector organizations which have all kinds of agreements with each other. The Royal Federation of Printers, for example, has developed a set of standard contracts which contain no agreements on prices but do cover a lot of other matters, like the minimum period of notice that has to be given to cancel the graphic preparation of a magazine. When times are hard, it may be possible to negotiate these conditions with hard-pressed printing companies, but in normal circumstances no one would think of undercutting their competitors by offering more lenient terms.

Price agreements used to be not unusual in the Dutch business community, until they were banned by the EU at the end of the twentieth century. Newspapers, for instance, have coordinated their subscription rates for many years, and a price war at the kiosks is inconceivable. In such a climate, it is a small step for company directors to consider merging with their competitors. This can lead to monopolies. The formation of monopolies was forbidden more than a century ago in the United States. A similar debate took place at the same time in the Netherlands. Politicians, with the liberals at their forefront, hit upon a different solution. They decided that monopoly companies – and they were thinking primarily of companies that provided public services, such as the gas supply or the telephone and, later, public transport – should be owned by the government. This would enable the representatives of the people to ensure that the monopoly was not abused. As a result, municipal councils, provincial authorities and the central government became entrepreneurs. This ideology held sway until the 1980s, when it was replaced by a new wave of privatization, the reasons for which will be examined later. That development did, however, force the government to introduce anti-monopoly legislation, like that in the United States. The Netherlands also has a growing number of bodies whose task it is to ensure that the market operates freely. This entails a form of regulation which some people see as merely adding new tentacles to the octopus of government bureaucracy.

Government regulation of the private sector represents the continuation of a tradition that stretches back centuries in Dutch and European history. In the Middle Ages, practically every trade or craft was organized into guilds aimed at

This replica of one of the VOC ships that used to sail to the East Indies is moored in the old Navy dock in Amsterdam.

protecting the interests of their members. Rules with the power of law ensured that competition did not get out of hand and that individual members could not expand to an extent that could threaten the survival of others. In some cases, technological developments were forbidden, because they would provide their perpetrators with an unfair advantage. The training of new members was tightly controlled and the guilds tended to impose increasingly difficult requirements to deny access to newcomers as much as possible. The rule of the guilds lasted until the French invaded in 1795 and brought with them freedom of entrepreneurship.

In 1596, the first Dutch ships reached what is now Indonesia and broke the monopoly that Portuguese seafarers had enjoyed for over a century. The large number of expeditions that followed the safe return of these first explorers led the government to intervene. It encouraged all the new investors to work together in the *Verenigde Oost-Indische Compagnie*, the United East India Company. The bait was an undisputed monopoly on trade in goods from Asia. The officially sanctioned piracy in the Caribbean – aimed at ships from hostile Spain – was later organized in the same way under the auspices of the West India Company, which also acquired a monopoly on the transport of slaves from Africa to North and South America.

Both companies were among the first to issue shares that were traded on the Amsterdam Stock Exchange. They were run by a form of Governing Board but operated on a fairly decentralized basis. The two companies also wished to secure a monopoly on purchasing. They tried to get their suppliers to agree to a kind of contract for an unlimited period which would not permit them to do business with other companies – from France or England, for example. This was frequently a question of who had the greatest firepower at their disposal. The companies had to 'conquer' strategic points, where they also held the political power and could, if necessary, finance entire armies to keep the place under their control. This eventually proved too expensive for the West India Company, but its counterpart in the Orient was in a far better financial position. It became the largest company in the world, a position which it maintained for at least 150 years, making it the first genuine multinational. Throughout most of its existence, it paid out reasonably high dividends to its shareholders. The company finally failed as a result of the high cost of preserving its purchasing monopoly and because it became bogged down in its own vast bureaucracy. But 200 years is still a respectable age for any company to reach.

The patroness of the city received goods from all over the world

The façade of the seventeenth century City Hall in Amsterdam is decorated with a relief showing, in the eyes of its civic leaders, the basis of the city's prosperity – it shows the patroness of the city receiving goods from all over the world. The message is clear – Amsterdam was one of the world's leading ports and its success

– as I have already said – lay not in import or export but in the transhipment of goods on Dutch ships. Certain goods, such as tobacco or sugar, were also processed. The descendants of the North Sea fishermen had become carriers of cargo and they completely dominated the European merchant shipping industry. Practically all the grain exported from northwest Europe was shipped from Dutch ports and it was a long time before other countries – particularly England and, to a lesser extent, France – were able to catch up. They succeeded only by pursuing protectionist policies that eventually broke the dominant position of the Dutch traders.

The leading merchants in the Netherlands came from the ruling regent families and their ideas had a considerable impact on the country's foreign policy. This was consequently based on a single immutable principle – the Netherlands was in favour of an international system in which there were as few obstacles to trade as possible. Most wars during the illustrious Golden Age were fought with that aim in mind. But wars are expensive and merchants tend to assess their costs with a critical eye, especially if they do not produce the desired effect quickly enough – and, as time went by, this was more and more often the case. As a result, they adopted a policy of neutrality which was increasingly presented as a matter of principle. The Netherlands tried to stay on good terms with as many foreign powers as possible to ensure that business could go on without being disrupted. This continued to be the basic *raison d'etre* for the neutral position maintained by the country right up until the German invasion of 1940. It closely resembled the traditional Swiss policy of neutrality. At times, there was even a tendency to don the pure white cloak of pacifism and civilization to disguise the real reason for its neutrality.

The German occupation put a stop to this policy for good. The Netherlands joined the Western alliance and became a loyal member of NATO. At the same time it emerged as a champion of supranational cooperation. It was one of the founding members of the European Community. The means may have changed, but the end is the same – to create a system where the international movement of goods is restricted as little as possible. In 2003, the people of the Netherlands voted *en masse* against the new European Constitution. But this had nothing to do with free trade and everything to do with the fact that the EU was intervening in more and more areas of daily life, so that people were afraid that they would end up trapped in the endless rules of the bureaucracy in Brussels. The Constitution – which was in fact nothing more than all existing EU legislation brought together in one enormous document – contained few guarantees for democratic control. That was already clear from the opening words: there was no 'We, the people of Europe....', but a list of heads of state in alphabetical order. The first words of the European Constitution were therefore: 'His Majesty the King of the Belgians'.

Today, as in the past, the Netherlands assigns great importance to international law. In front of the City Hall in Rotterdam, Europe's largest port, there is a statue of the seventeenth century regent and scholar Hugo de Groot, the founding father of this belief in the need for supranational regulation. His major work, the *mare libero*, argued that the seas should be open to all and that the sovereignty of coastal states should not extend further than three miles from the shore. The three-mile distance was not arbitrary – it was the maximum range of the largest cannons of the time. De Groot's ideas became generally accepted and survived almost up to the present day. The principle of the open seas has, however, been considerably eroded by the exploitation of natural resources under the seabed. The belief that these resources should not be the sole property of the coastal states but should be shared by all mankind and, therefore, controlled by the United Nations is popular in the Netherlands. This is no surprise – for a small country with such a short coastline, this would be the best deal.

Anyone from outside the European Union who tries to find a market for their products in the Netherlands is in for a surprise. The doors of the EU are wide open for most raw materials, unless they are freely available in the continent itself. Those who offer manufactured or semi-manufactured products, however, will find that, the more complex processing their products have undergone, the higher the import duties they will have to pay. The EU has even imposed quotas on the import of certain products, such as textiles and tapioca. This is, to say the least, not entirely compatible with the lofty principle of free access to international markets. It is therefore not uncommon to hear the word 'hypocrisy' used in this respect around directors' tables and at ministries of economic affairs in developing countries. The Netherlands defends its approach officially by claiming that a small country cannot follow its own course without suffering the consequences and that it always makes a plea for free trade in discussions with the other members of the European Union and in international fora. And, indeed, diplomats and ambassadors always have evidence to hand to support this claim. Yet critics at home frequently suggest that Dutch companies could perhaps be a little less compliant in toeing the official line. They are accused of giving priority to the cash book above the Bible. Whatever the reason, the Netherlands has come little further than good intentions. And if outsiders complain of fine talk, weakness and hypocrisy, the response is that, after all, everyone is entitled to their opinion.

You should not steal from your own purse

The Dutch have an expression: *Je moet geen dief zijn van je eigen portemonnee.* Literally, it means 'You should not steal from your own purse'. This attitude – 'If we don't do it, someone else will' – is deeply embedded in the Dutch way of thinking and most people are prepared to accept it for what it is – cynicism. They would rather be seen as cynical than naïve.

And besides, what is all this talk of free trade? The Netherlands has a centuries-old tradition of government intervention in the economy. Real free trade existed only during the period of liberal domination in the nineteenth century and that lasted only a few decades. The State's tendency to take over companies with a monopoly has already been mentioned. But it went further than that. In 1902, the government set up state-run coal mines because the privately operated mining sector was – in the eyes of public opinion – too chaotic. The crisis caused by the First World War led to much more direct economic intervention, to which everyone soon became accustomed. A new wave of intervention followed the 1929 Wall Street Crash. The driving force behind this was the former managing director of Shell, the anti-revolutionary Hendrikus Colijn. The government naturally had the tendency to surround this increased involvement in the economy with all kinds of *overleg*, accustomed as it was to making decisions on a consensus basis. The business world not only got used to this intervention, but actually began to request it. Company directors request help from the government if their organization or the entire sector is in some kind of difficulty. The State, for example, stepped in several times to save Fokker, the Netherlands' only aircraft manufacturer. It also intervened to prevent Daf, the truck builders, from going bankrupt. Such measures sometimes involve hundreds of millions and, in the case of the dying shipbuilding industry, billions of euros. The State always provides support only on the condition that the company involved carries out a reorganization. This form of intervention has not always been successful. The Dutch shipbuilding industry, once a world leader, still failed to compete with new and cheaper shipyards in South-East Asia even after the government pumped billions of euros into it. Fokker's directors were unable to get the company out of the red and it is now nothing more than a fond memory. Daf's private car sector was taken over by the Swedish company Volvo in the 1970s, an operation which required a large injection of funds from the government. The cars that roll off the production line today are the result of a joint venture between the company itself, the Japanese manufacturers Mitsubishi and the State. The company continues to be far from sound.

The State repeatedly fends off the invisible hand

This policy of intervention is generally defended with the argument that it fights unemployment.

Another effective argument in favour of bailing out large companies on the verge of collapse is that, if they go down, they will take a large number of suppliers and other companies with them. In this way, the State repeatedly fends off the invisible hand that Adam Smith projected as the best regulator of the economy. Smith's hand, however, is resilient and always bounces back. The fiasco in the shipbuilding industry led to a scandal and a parliamentary enquiry. Ever since, the government is cautious about where it spends its cash and the critics of such policies have grown in number. They consider government intervention too defensive, aimed only at preserving economic sectors which an advanced industrialized country can better leave to others. Intervention, if at all, should be directed towards new, more promising areas of activity.

Many people may agree with this in their hearts, but it does not rise to the surface too easily. In a society based on consensus, vested interests can exert considerable influence. This makes it very difficult to leave a particular economic sector to its fate. The entire Dutch agricultural sector would collapse immediately if the government and the EU abolished the extensive system of subsidies and protectionist measures. The agricultural lobby is, however, far too powerful and influential to allow anything like that to happen. Furthermore, a country may have military-strategic reasons for wishing to produce a large proportion of its food supply itself. Left to its own devices, the invisible hand would cause a great deal of disruption, particularly in the short and medium term. There is a gigantic food-processing industry closely related to the agricultural sector which is essential to the Dutch export market.

This all seems incompatible with the fact that, since the 1980s, more and more Dutch politicians sing the praises of the free market. And not only that, they drew conclusions from it. The argument that had once been used to justify public ownership of companies – that where economic monopolies emerge and competition is lacking, democratic control is necessary – that argument from the early twentieth century was long forgotten. Private initiative and free competition – it was preached from all sides – would lead to better quality and lower prices. The fall of the Berlin Wall and the demise of the Soviet Union proved the superiority of democratic capitalism. In addition, a wide range of EU agreements to prevent the distortion of competition forced the state to play a less active role. As a consequence a wave of privatization swept across the country. Municipalities and other authorities transferred ownership of public housing to housing associations, which had originally been set up to build good quality, cheap houses for members of the working class, but which now had to act as property developers. Public transport was privatized and the rules regulating taxi services were scrapped. Around the turn of the century the same happened to the energy companies.

If you take a taxi, you are generally in a hurry. You don't have time to ask twenty taxi drivers to make you an offer, so that you can choose the one with the best price-quality ratio. So you are dependent on the first taxi that stops for you. The deregulation of the taxi sector led to an enormous growth in the number of taxis, a fall in the quality of the service and much higher prices. The housing associations were unable to solve the worsening housing shortage in the Netherlands, while the real estate sector experienced a price explosion around the millennium. In the recession that followed it took much longer for a house to be sold, but the prices did not go down. The quality of public transport – now in the hands of a number of monopoly companies – plummeted and embittered users observed that the only things that never arrived too late were price increases.

The privatization of the state postal and telecommunications company resulted in other problems. The postal services and electronic communications were split into two separate companies. KPN, which was responsible for telephony, had to compete with providers from throughout the world, who had established themselves on the Dutch market at the end of the twentieth century when the whole country started using mobile telephones. KPN meanwhile was on the verge of failure, as a result of bad investments, and it looked as though the Netherlands would lose its only national telecommunications provider. A strict austerity policy saved the company, at least for the time being. It is now facing new problems, as internet telephony and increasingly cheap mobile calls render the fixed line network obsolete. KPN is now hoping to survive by offering a range of combinations of internet and cable television.

Why did privatization so rarely lead to the paradise that it had promised? Defenders of the free market said it was because it was conducted in typical Dutch compromise fashion. Some elements of the market had been introduced, but there was no evidence of the invisible hand. The government continued to set the level for house rents. The rail company had been privatized but the railways and other infrastructure were not. And privatization had resulted in a massive expansion of the control bureaucracy already referred to earlier. If the market was really left to work freely, they said, ordinary people would reap the benefits. Now they were getting the worst of both worlds.

There was a lot of support for this argument, but others claimed that privatization had been a serious mistake and that the government should retrace its steps before it was too late. A new term of abuse was invented: market fundamentalism. As if economic liberalism was another radical faith, like those that had been the cause of such insecurity in the early years of the twenty-first century. Such reasoning took strong hold in a country which had always been proud of its organizational strength and its moderate approach to ideology and religion.

A third objection to further privatization was nationalist in nature. Sectors vital to the Netherlands, like energy and telecommunications, were now prey to foreign hands. That limited the influence that the government could bring to bear, and threatened the country's independence.

A maze of rules and regulations

Every new government declared when it took office that it would take strong measures to reduce the surplus of rules and regulations. Most of them left more behind than were there when they started. In 2003, the second Balkenende government promised to scrap a third of all rules, but three years later, they had nothing to show for it. That is only very marginally the fault of the government itself. Practically every week, parliament called on the Cabinet to 'tackle' one problem group or another. All that tackling necessarily meant a lot of extra rules, which then had to be refined and adjusted if they proved to be unjust in practice. It is a never-ending story, and in the country's bars and cafés, the excess of rules is an endless source of complaint. Why not try this interesting experiment? Tell all your friends at the table in the café that they are right and argue in favour of deregulation in an area that is close to their hearts: opening times for cafés, for example, or professional quality requirements for people in different occupations. They would then protest even louder. Then you would see why the Netherlands will always be a country of rules and regulations.

Anyone who wishes to set up a company in the Netherlands will therefore find themselves confronted with a maze of rules and regulations reminiscent of the old guild privileges. Many branches of trade and industry demand that people intending to start a business have some kind of diploma. In the case of the retail trade, the local authorities decide how many shops of a certain kind they want in a particular area. This is frequently based on the requirements of the sector organization itself, which wishes to subject competition to strict rules and make life difficult for *beunhazen*. A *beunhaas* is someone who operates a business without having the required know-how or, in the terms defined by the sector organizations, does not have the right qualifications. Because the organizations usually provide the required training themselves, the requirements are strict and candidates require a thorough knowledge of the area if they are to succeed. Anyone who does not get over this hurdle is not officially permitted to operate in the sector. In this way, the received traditions of the sector are preserved.

Quality is the main priority – and with good reason

A stroll through any town centre or a glance in the newspapers, with their countless advertisements in which companies try to outdo their competitors in praising their products and services, shows that the Netherlands is, above all, a free-market economy where a company's success depends in the first instance on it finding the right combination of quality and price.

Quality is the main priority – and with good reason. The strength of the economy has never been its competitive prices. The Netherlands is not a cheap country. Its companies have to survive by providing service, reliability and good quality. The country is simply not cut out for the bottom end of the market. And, if that ever was the case, that position has now been amply filled by low-salary countries. In the 1970s, with the exception of a few specialized companies, all the country's textile manufacturers folded. The same fate befell the shipbuilding industry.

This alone, however, is not enough for a company to survive against international competition – particularly from Asia. Generally speaking, Dutch producers of technologically simple articles and semi-manufactured products do not have an easy time, except in sectors where the Netherlands has a traditional lead, such as cheese, flowers and fresh vegetables. And even in these sectors, competition is increasing steadily. Dutch companies now have a tendency to transfer production to low-wage countries. Philips, for example, has transferred many of its production activities to countries like China. Dutch policy-makers comfort themselves with the thought that the Netherlands has a successful future

Relaxing on the beach at the Hook of Holland. The ship is just leaving the port of Rotterdam. The number of pensioners in the Netherlands is growing rapidly and there is a widespread fear that there will not be enough young people to maintain the country's prosperity.

as a knowledge economy and an international supplier of high-quality products and services, but in the early years of the twenty-first century it was clear that they may have not got off quite that easily. India, for example, can supply those high-quality products and services just as well and at a much lower price. For the first time in almost a century, parents no longer took it for granted that their children would have a higher standard of living than they had.

In the international services sector, the Netherlands also found itself facing fierce competition. That was bad news and the signs had been on the wall for many decades. The Dutch merchant fleet, for example – one of the top ten in the world in the 1950s – is of little importance today. Shipowners now sail largely under the Panamanian or Liberian flags. But in areas where the Netherlands has undisputed know-how – such as dredging or a wide variety of other civil engineering activities relating to water or water management – business is thriving. Since the enlargement of the European Union with the accession of new member states from Eastern Europe, the road transport sector in the Netherlands has come under pressure from Polish, Czech and Slovakian haulage companies. Some Dutch companies have responded by moving their operations into the lion's den, from Rotterdam to Gdansk, or from Amsterdam to Warsaw.

There is an observable shift from industrial production to the provision of services. This is a common trend in all highly developed economies, but in the Netherlands, it has an added dimension in that it is entirely in keeping with the

Some work simply cannot be done by a machine and no one from the Netherlands is prepared to do it. Here seasonal workers from Poland are sorting onions.

country's historical traditions. The Netherlands was, after all, the home of the great trading houses and the banks they needed in order to operate. It possessed no natural raw materials on which to build up an industrial base. At least, that was the general belief until the 1960s, when it was discovered that the country was sitting on a gold mine in the form of a natural gas bubble of OPEC proportions.

In Germany, the Netherlands' neighbour and by far the largest trading partner, it was a different story. Since the last quarter of the nineteenth century the German government had promoted the build up of an enormous industrial apparatus, which is still the basis of the country's phenomenal prosperity. Such a policy has never existed in the Netherlands. Industrial development did occur, but was largely the work of visionary entrepreneurs rather than the result of a concerted effort by the government. And, of course, there was undoubtedly a knock-on effect from Germany. The lack of a genuine industrial policy has been the subject of regular public debate right up to the present day.

This may be the reason why industrialists and entrepreneurs rarely achieve national prominence. The reputation of Ruud Lubbers, who – as prime minister – dominated Dutch politics from 1983 to 1994, was based on many things but not on the fact that he came from an extremely successful family of industrialists. Lubbers also did his best to keep this in the background, as did his predecessor in the thirties, Hendrikus Colijn. Colijn enjoyed great trust as a principled Calvinist. His career at Shell had nothing to do with his electoral successes.

Free entrepreneurship carries a high social status

How would average Dutch parents react if their daughter came home with a businessman? Or – in the new age of emancipation – their son, with a business woman? It is very unlikely that they would be shocked, because free entrepreneurship carries a high social status. People will proudly tell you if they have their own business. A traditional mother might still prefer to see her daughter turn up with a doctor (preferably a surgeon) or a professor on her arm, because these professions are held in even higher esteem. Nevertheless, the business sector enjoys a great deal of respect. Another illustration of this is the confidence that Dutch employees tend to show in their employers. In most cases, they believe in the company and its products and will become very defensive in the face of outside criticism. This pride, however, applies to the product first and the boss second.

Dutch employers therefore have little difficulty in exercising their authority, as long as they follow the traditional Dutch pattern of *overleg* and justifying their decisions. Shipbuilder Bartel Wilton, one of the most respected directors in Rotterdam in the 1950s and 1960s, once declared: 'You have to make the most of the circumstances, cooperate with the people you work with and ensure that errors do not occur as a result of misunderstandings.' On the issue of the statutory requirement for a Works Council, he said: 'In a cold climate, you put on warm clothes. You don't change the climate that way, but you do make it easier to live with. It is the same in business. You still have employers and employees, but they have to find a way to get along.' Wilton was known to some as 'Red Bart'. This suggestion of socialist leanings has been attributed to a surprising number of Dutch entrepreneurs – most of which have been upstanding liberals or Christian Democrats. It simply means that they are the kind of person you can talk to, someone with whom you can make a good, practical deal to suit the demands of the situation.

Entrepreneurship based on a sound knowledge of the market

This, too, may have its roots in the Dutch merchant tradition. The commercial spirit in the Netherlands is concerned not so much with building up industrial emporia as with delivering a specific quantity of goods to a certain place at an agreed price. This is entrepreneurship based on a sound knowledge of the market. It means making the right offer at the right time so that the customer takes the bait. You can only succeed in this if you have a thorough basic knowledge of the sector you are working in and of the circumstances of your potential customer, and can make a good estimate of how much they would be prepared to pay and what they are worth. There is an old Dutch saying: *Je moet weten wat er in de wereld te koop is*, 'You must know what's on sale out in the world.' For the Dutch, success in business demands a keen interest in what is going on in the outside world. This attitude is reflected in society at large. Until well into this century, the newspapers printed the foreign news on the front page, before the national and local news. And in that order of priority – from international down to local. During the Golden Age, Amsterdam, the merchant city, was arguably the most important information centre in the world. Large companies like the United East India Company had enormous networks, which enabled them to gather information on their competitors and which were therefore significant instruments of industrial sabotage. If you wanted to know the latest news about everything and everyone, you had to go to Amsterdam. Resourceful businessmen turned this into an export product. In 1620, for example, printer Broer Jansz started publishing an English version of his weekly newspaper and shipping it to London. The first English daily paper, the Daily News, which appeared in 1702, printed proudly under its name that it contained all reports from the *Opregte Haarlemse Courant*. The *Gazette de Leyde*, a French-language paper published twice weekly in Leiden, had a wide European readership and was the most reliable source of news across the continent for more than a century. The Netherlands long ago lost its leading position as a collector and distributor of news to other centres like London, Paris and New York, but the interest is still there.

Foreign books can be bought even in the smallest places

The Dutch have believed since the Golden Age that knowledge of more than one – and preferably more – foreign languages is an indispensable component of a good education. Every child that progresses further than the primary school – and, since the mid-twentieth century, this means all children – obtain a basic knowledge of English and, in most cases, French and German. Until the 1960s, it was compulsory for further education students to take all three foreign languages in their final examinations, except those following lower and intermediate technical courses. Since then, they may drop two of the three, but by then they have had two hours of lessons a week in the language for a period of two years.

The Netherlands is the leading importer of books from Anglo-Saxon countries in the non-English-speaking world. Foreign books can be bought even in the smallest provincial towns, as can newspapers and magazines. In the last quarter of the twentieth century, Dutch institutes of higher education started offering courses in English on a large scale as a special service for foreign students. In 2006 there were more than 1,200 courses available, often in very specific and specialized subjects.

Until the Second World War, France and Germany competed fiercely for first place in the market for foreign publications in the Netherlands. Britain was consistently in third place but, after the liberation, English started to dominate. You only have to look in any bookshop or station kiosk, with their wide assortment of paperbacks from the larger British and American publishers, for proof of this. They are not there for the tourists. You can buy the Times Literary Supplement, *Die Zeit*, the New York Review of Books or the *Nouvelles Literaires* at most railway stations. Or, if you prefer, Barron's, the Financial Times, the European edition of the Wall Street Journal, the *Handelsblaat*, Fortune or *24 Ore*.

Foreigners who wish to practice their Dutch complain that they get little chance to do so. The Dutch tend to switch immediately to English, or even to the native language of the person they are talking to, if they can speak it. This is also a throwback to the old merchant tradition. It is always better to speak the language of your business partner than for him to speak yours. That is also why little effort has been made to increase the influence of the Dutch language in the world, particularly in comparison with the concerted campaigns of the British or French, or even of a relatively small country like Sweden. The Dutch always express their admiration when a foreigner proves to have mastered their language, after which they will often switch directly to English, so that the listener's only option is to claim not to speak it. The same applies to educational institutions. During the colonial era, the Dutch rulers in Indonesia preferred to speak Malay – or what passed for Malay in their view – than their own language, and they were not at all pleased if a 'native' proved to speak Dutch.

Since the 1960s, the Netherlands has become a country with a large immigrant population. Given the attitude described in the previous paragraph it was to be expected that neither the government nor the private sector took the initiative

Integration. Newcomers to the Netherlands now have to prove that they have a good command of the Dutch language and know something of Dutch society and history.

Integration is a favourite theme for TV satire. This is a scene from the popular programme on the public channel 'Man bijt hond' (Man bites dog).

to ensure that the newcomers learned to speak Dutch. More highly educated immigrants – for example, university professors – sometimes lived here for decades without learning a word of Dutch. They simply communicated in English. At the other end of the social spectrum, a few basic words learned at the workplace were enough to get by. And when the government did start to take an interest in the welfare of the newcomers, it was to enable them to learn about their own language and culture at primary school. Since 9/11 that has all radically changed. The governments wants all immigrants to take compulsory integration and language courses. Anyone wanting a residence permit to live in the Netherlands – for example, to come and live with their spouse – must first pass their integration and language examination at the Dutch embassy in their own country. This is a clear break with the past.

Many Dutch people are convinced that they can speak foreign languages, particularly English, rather well. This can be very irritating, particularly for immigrants of Anglo-Saxon origin. They find themselves faced with countless mistakes and minor errors and receive answers to their questions, posed in carefully perfected Dutch, in a highly personalized interpretation of Shakespeare's idiom. Dutch people can often be heard to claim that they 'speak English far better than they write it'. In the words of an American with 20 years' experience of the Netherlands: 'This is a typical example of their over-confidence. But, in comparison with many other nationalities, the Dutch do speak surprisingly good English'. In spite of this, she concluded that many Dutch people over-estimate their mastery of the language.

This is a matter of argument. For the Dutch, a foreign language is an instrument. They learn it to enable them to communicate. They start communicating when they have learned only a few words and are not ashamed of making grammatical errors. Educational television offers courses in a variety of languages, with Indonesian and Mandarin Chinese being surprisingly popular choices. The courses are designed to enable people to conduct a simple conversation, and also provide considerable background information on the customs and practices of the country where the language is spoken.

's Lands wijs, 's lands eer. This Dutch expression, meaning literally 'a country's wisdom is a country's honour', is roughly equivalent to the English expression 'When in Rome, do as the Romans do'. Another Dutch saying *De klant is koning*, the customer is king, reflects the same sentiments. When the King of Thailand announced that he wished to be addressed in the future as an Emperor, the representative of the United East India Company wrote the following words to his superiors: 'It is, after all, certain that his majesty wishes to be addressed by his subjects in the Siamese language as nothing more nor less than *pro ponte suekka*, which means nought but Supreme Lord. But we, to keep ourselves out of out of the line of fire, shall refer to him as "His Majesty," leaving it to his discretion how he should interpret this.'[2]

As this example shows, there is a solution to everything. About the same time, the company's representative in the Indian town of Negapatnam, a certain Van Dielen, used to receive his Indian clients in true local style, complete with temple dancers. This roused the indignation of the strict preacher in the town who wrote to Van Dielen's superiors: 'That director Van Dielen, in the presence of the other members of his board and their wives, did arrange such a feast of Balthazar with the playing of cards and throwing of dice and did summon and admit such heathen whores and diabolic artists with the beating of drums and the playing of other pagan instruments, singing songs of damnation and felicitation, which they had dedicated to the devil but days before, combined with the foulest dances of prostitutes, ballets, masquerades and devilish spectacle.'[3]

After an investigation into the affair, the preacher was dismissed. Van Dielen's superior commented: 'Not all sources of offence are of the same nature but do vary greatly according to different occasions, customs, places, times and peoples and, if the greatest of caution is not observed, offence will often be given rather than taken.'[4]

's Lands wijs, 's lands eer, indeed. The merchant had to be something of a chameleon. Dutch people who spend any time abroad do not retain their language and customs for long. The children and grandchildren of the tens of thousands of emigrants who left the country in the early 1950s to start up elsewhere – particularly in Canada, Australia, New Zealand and Brazil – have little to betray their origins

2 'Immer dit is seker dat sijn maijt, in de Siamse taale van zijn eijgene onderdanen niet anders aangesproken en genaamd werd dan pro ponte soekka, hetgene niet ander beduijt dan Opperste Heer. Maar wij, om ons eenerzijds buijten schoots te houden, noemen hem sijn maijesteijt, differerende de verdere uijtlegginge daarover aan haar eijgen discretie'

3 'dat 't opperhoofd van Dielen tot presentie van de andere raadtpersonen met hare vrouwen, daartoe aanstellende een expresse belsjazzarszars maeltyt tot kaartspelen, dobbelen suypen ende heeft ontboden ende toegelaten de heidense schandhoeren ende duyverskonstenaars met trommelen schellen ende andere pagodische instrumenten klinkende, singende vervloekte liederen ende gelukwenschende gesangen, die sij den duyvel daags te voren opgeoffert hebben, vermengt met de vuylste hoeredanse, baletten, mascaraden en duyvelsche vertooningen'

4 'alle ergernissen sijn niet van een en dezelfde natuyr maar besondere gelegentheden, zeden, plaatsen, tijden en volkeren koomen darin groote veranderinge te veroorsaken, welke wanneer men deselve niet met alle voorsigtigheid aenmerkt, soo gebeurt 's dickmaels dat 't word in plaats van een gegeven een genomen ergernisse'

(unlike their counterparts from Germany or Greece) other than their surnames.

Dutch society, on the other hand, is very open to external influences. The intelligentsia grumble now and again about Americanization, and the detrimental effects of the 'McDonalds culture', but generally speaking there is little to stand in the way of such influences. Since the beginning of the 1950s, the younger generations have followed American – and, to a lesser extent, British – trends very rapidly. They are increasingly exposed to them on television. Since the 1980s, the television cable network has reached even the most remote areas of the country so that most households can receive not only Dutch but also French, German and English programmes, plus a number of satellite channels, including MTV. This, in itself, is perhaps not so remarkable, but the Netherlands is also often a world leader when it comes to adopting international products and trends. This can also be seen in the rapid expansion of broadband internet. Nearly the whole country was online with a broadband connection within a year of it becoming available.

For this reason, companies frequently use the Netherlands to try out new products. These are, on the other hand, not always adopted totally wholesale, but are frequently adapted. Very few restaurants offer traditional Dutch cuisine. The hungry passer-by will see a wide range of pizzerias, Greek and 'Chinese-Indonesian' restaurants, which are increasingly being joined by Indian, Turkish, Surinamese, South American and Ethiopian establishments. *Shoarma*, the meat

Patates frites, *French fried potatoes, were imported from Belgium. You can buy them in a snack bar or a 'chip van' on the side of the road. Try a 'patatje oorlog', French fries with mayonaisse and satay sauce. In the past five years or so, more and more snack bars have been taken over by members of the Chinese community, but they still offer traditional Dutch fare.*

snack from Israel, have also become very popular in recent years. This development is not restricted to the centres of large cities but is perhaps even more apparent in provincial towns. With a very few exceptions, these restaurants and snack bars aim at a wide public and not only at their own particular ethnic group.

The Dutch themselves, accustomed to an international cuisine, increasingly cook foreign dishes at home, using ingredients they can buy at any supermarket. Traditional Dutch cooking – stews, pap and all kinds of dishes based on meat, potatoes and vegetables – is clearly on the decline. Pizzas and Asian rice dishes – have practically become an indispensable part of the weekly menu. Even more so now that a growing number of people have their meals delivered to their homes, which is completely alien to Dutch tradition. It was a custom introduced by immigrants, particularly from Turkey and Morocco, and the pizza courier has now become a Dutch phenomenon. Dutch restaurant owners have not yet followed their example. You can order delivery of a *döner kebab* with French fries and garlic sauce, but you won't find anyone who will bring you sauerkraut, brown beans with bacon pieces or steak with mushrooms and fried potatoes.

Yet visitors from abroad who are served up dishes from their home country frequently notice a difference. It may be minimal, but it is there, nonetheless. The food may taste less spicy or perhaps a touch sweeter. It is difficult to explain how or why this happens, but restaurants do make concessions to the Dutch palate. This means that dishes must not contain a lot of spices, because their guests will soon find the food too hot. The traditional potato-based diet makes little use of herbs and spices. True cosmopolitan food-lovers are aware of this and give each other the addresses of places where such concessions are not made. These purists are, however, very much in the minority and most foreign dishes therefore acquire an unmistakable Dutch taste. As the food snob complains loudly of their blandness, you find yourself thinking: *Doe maar gewoon, dan doe je al gek genoeg.*

The best places to 'go native' are the bookshops with their shelves full of English and American publications. But nowadays they also have a wide assortment of foreign books recently translated into Dutch. In this way, the Dutch public has been introduced to Russian, African and South American writers. These translations are always given considerable attention in the serious media and, if the number of new translations appearing on the shelves is any indication, they clearly sell well. Many of them are available in cheap paperback series, costing around ten euros a copy. The translations are always from the original language and not from the English version, because the Netherlands – with its traditional knowledge of foreign languages – has many competent translators. A typical example is August Willemsen, whose translations of the main works of Brazilian literature have made him one of the most well-known intellectuals in the country. It comes as no surprise that Willemsen is also a witty essayist on a wide variety of subjects ranging from his own profession to such diverse topics as alcoholism and Brazilian football.

Once again, translated foreign literature is not only available in the large city

Traditional Dutch grocers' shops have all made way for supermarkets. Immigrants are now reviving the corner shop.

centres. Small bookshops out in the provinces also offer a wide selection. Around the corner from my house is a small shop, where French, German, English, Turkish, Polish, Russian, Arabic, Italian and Spanish newspapers are available every day. And I live in the suburbs of a provincial town, not on a canal in Amsterdam. Foreign visitors who tune in to a Dutch television channel are often pleasantly surprised to discover that foreign programmes are not dubbed, as they are in Germany and France. All foreign series and films are broadcast in their original language with Dutch sub-titles. The same applies to the big screen, except in the case of Disney cartoons and other films intended for small children who are unable to read. The Dutch love to poke fun at their German neighbours, who dub everything; they make endless jokes about the cowboys or – even worse – Frank Sinatra, who babble away at them in German if they happen to zap past a German channel. It has regularly been predicted that this will all eventually lead to the decline of the Dutch language. But until now, the language has shown no genuine signs of decay. Foreign-language media – such as a daily newspaper in English – have never really caught on.

Scientific researchers do have a tendency to publish in English, but that has more to do with increasing specialization. Since genuine colleagues are few and far between, it is necessary to be able to communicate with a broad international public. But in the immediate surroundings of the university or the laboratory, Dutch remains the working language and foreigners who stay here for any length of time without learning Dutch will find that this ultimately leads to isolation and considerably hinders their ability to function on a day-to-day basis, even though universities and institutes of professional education offer so many courses in English.

An aversion to nonsense and a love of hard facts

This merchant spirit has another major characteristic – an aversion to nonsense and a love of hard facts. One of the most famous lines in Dutch literature, which comes from Multatuli's Max Havelaar, goes as follows: *De lucht is guur en het is vier uur*, 'The air is raw, the clock strikes four'. It is uttered by Batavus Droogstoppel, a partner in the company of Last & Co, Coffee Brokers. Droogstoppel is making a case for 'truth and common sense'. He says: 'Holland has remained Holland because our old folk attended to their business, and because they had the true faith. That's all there is to it!' And later: 'I've no objection to verses in themselves. If you want words to form fours, it's all right with me! But don't say anything that isn't true. "The air is raw, the clock strikes four". I'll let that pass, if it really *is* raw, and if it really *is* four o'clock. But if it's a quarter to three, then I, who don't range my words in a line, will say: "The air is raw, and it is a quarter to three". But the versifier is bound to four o'clock by the *rawness* of the first line. For him, it has to be exactly four o'clock, or else the air mustn't be raw. And so he starts tampering with the truth. Either the weather has to be changed, or the time. And in that case, one of the two is false.'

Batavus Droogstoppel, coffee broker, is a caricature. He is clearly the 'bad guy' in the book, causing even his creator to exclaim with indignation at the end of the book: 'Halt, wretched spawn of sordid moneygrubbing and blasphemous cant! I created you. You grew into a monster under my pen. I loathe my own handiwork: choke in coffee and disappear!' Caricature or not, there are still plenty of Droogstoppel-types around today. Many Dutch people have difficulties in recognizing aspects of their own character in others. Multatuli's stereotype is built up from character traits that you frequently come across in Dutch society.

Elsewhere in Max Havelaar, Droogstoppel claims that he never has to ask the way anywhere twice, 'for I always know how to get to a place when I've been there once, because I always take such careful note of everything. I've made a habit of doing that in business.' The Dutch merchant spirit does indeed demand a sharp eye for the facts of a situation. All forms of pretence have to be exposed. You have to take care of business and not spend a cent too much. Everything else is pure fantasy. Dutch parents whose children do not take life seriously enough will be told: *De zaken gaan voor het meisje*, 'business comes before girls' or, to use a common English expression, 'business before pleasure'.

This means that many conversations – no matter what the subject – soon take on a financial tone. *Wat koop ik daarvoor?* is a common response if someone is asked to help in some way or take part in some sort of activity. The question, 'What can I buy for that?', has taken on a general meaning, but its origins are clear – what will the person concerned get out of it? This attitude may lead to stinginess, but rarely to a fear of making investments that do not provide immediate profit. Van Dielen, the man who arranged such lavish parties in Negapatnam, was also prepared to donate funds for the building of Hindu temples. Even in the seventeenth century, they knew that goodwill could be very profitable.

Anyone who goes bankrupt has ruined his reputation for good

A debtor can count on little sympathy. Anyone who goes bankrupt ruins his reputation for good and will have great difficulty in winning back the confidence of his creditors. Until well into this century, the Reformed Church community in Friesland excluded bankrupts from Holy Communion, their most sacred religious ceremony.

Because he did not commit suicide after going bankrupt, as gentlemen were required to do in his circles, the family of Rotterdam old-clothes dealer Herman Heyermans Junior broke all contact with him. He subsequently moved to Amsterdam, where he became one of the country's greatest playwrights, frequently compared with Ibsen.

The reverse can also happen. Timber merchant Dirk Witte was also a songwriter with a talent that few have surpassed. His funeral was attended by the *crème de la crème* of the Dutch art and entertainment world. His family, however, were proud to observe that there were also many friends and colleagues from the timber trade. In spite of his hobby, Dirk has always kept a solid head on his shoulders.

Since the 1970s, the Dutch have become more used to living on credit. A large part of the money they lend is used to buy consumer durables, like cars. Few can afford their own house without winning the national lottery, so most people with their own homes also have a heavy mortgage to go with it. A house is, of course, a long-term consumer durable, so many see it as an investment in the future.

Significantly, most Dutch people are very selective in using their credit cards. They prefer to use their bankcards to pay electronically so that the money is automatically deducted from their current accounts. This means that they are not in debt for a single moment. In spite of this, a growing number of people are finding themselves in financial trouble. Particularly those at the bottom of the social scale are confronted with debts that they have no hope of paying off, even though the amount they owe may seem reasonably small to those who are better off. Anyone who buys household goods 'on tick', usually from mail-order firms, eventually finds themselves inundated with small monthly repayments. When this happens, there is a safety net. There are a large number of municipal credit banks who are prepared to take on the problem of clearing the debts. This generally means that the creditors have to settle for less than they are due. They usually agree to this because otherwise they would never see any of their money again. Government bodies, such as the tax department and the energy companies, prove to be the least willing to reach a settlement. The debtors themselves have to tighten their belts for a couple of years. The credit banks offer their help under strict conditions. They take responsibility for paying fixed costs, such as rent and energy bills. The debtors then have to live on what little is left. They also receive guidance with keeping the household budget. Anyone who refuses these conditions is left to their fate.

Around 2005, an estimated 200,000 Dutch families were in serious debt: according to the debt collection agency Intrum Justitia, 'serious debt' entailed amounts of around 15,000 or more, and at least 11 different creditors. In that same year, the population as a whole was in the red to a total of 7.6 billion euros. Every day, television commercials offer a 'solution' to these problems. They show a happy couple buying an expensive kitchen, which they could afford thanks to a low-interest personal loan. Credit companies have been engaged in aggressive advertizing since the end of the 1990s. They offer low interest rates. That often means a very long repayment period, and the creditors will do everything they can to keep their customers. Just fill in a form on the internet and the money will be on the way – at least, that's what the ads promise.

Princess Laurentien gives a helping hand at the Voedselbank, *where people on very low incomes can come and collect food packages. The rapid growth of these food distribution centres in recent years indicates a widening gap between rich and poor in the Netherlands.*

Minister of finance Gerrit Zalm responded in a very Dutch way. First he called on the aggressive credit companies to regulate themselves. When they didn't, he announced government measures. He proposed changes to the law which would restrict the options for consumptive borrowing, unless there was substantial security to back it up. In this way, in patriarchal fashion, he resolved to protect people wishing to take out a loan against themselves.

Compared to the people of the neighbouring countries, the Dutch proved to be very thrifty. The ICT boom had tempted many of them to speculate on the stock market, but once they realized that shares could not only rise spectacularly, but also fall, most of them went back to saving their money. At the end of August 2005, the people of the Netherlands had a total of 211 billion euros in savings accounts. And that in a country with a population of 16 million. Nor does it include money in pension schemes or property. At the same time, the national debt was 215 billion euros. No wonder that Dutch financial analysts are so keen to express their concern at the low rate of saving in the United States. On the other hand, this also justifies the conclusion that all those savings reflect a mentality of risk-avoidance. It is therefore not surprising to hear that, in this land of caution, a young Bill Gates came up against a wall of *doe maar gewoon, dan doe je al gek genoeg* advice and Droogstoppels who found his plans far too poetic to risk financing them.

They have a lot to do

Asked how things are going, most Dutch people will answer that they are busy. They have a lot to do. They are always full of new plans. The attitude they wish to project is not one of calmness and leisure, but of great vigour and activity. Bosses across the country can often be heard to respond to enthusiastic employees coming to them with a new proposal: 'Put down the main points in a short memo and mail it.' The implication is that they do not have the time to read long and complicated arguments and that an idea of any importance can always be formulated in a few hundred words. The boss will then be the one to decide whether the idea has any merit. Lubbers and his successors tried to give added impetus to this vigorous approach. The 'starting entrepreneur' was the model citizen. They would find a 'gap in the market' and find a way to fill it, benefiting not only themselves but also – by creating jobs – society at large. Even non-profitmaking organizations and government departments adopted this new 'market-oriented' approach. The jargon of the private sector penetrated the formerly closed world of the civil service. Courses in economics and business studies experienced a period of enormous growth. Yet the word around which the social debate centred was not 'entrepreneurship', it was 'management' – the ability to give dynamic leadership to an organization. Student associations seeking sponsors did not present themselves as tomorrow's entrepreneurs, but as tomorrow's managers. Captains of industry prefer to be seen as the enthusiastic managers of their companies than as directors who sign enormous contracts.

Every year, fifteen to twenty thousand of these 'starting entrepreneurs' set up new companies. This is not a very high percentage for a country with over 16 million inhabitants. When it comes down to it, most Dutch people prefer to express their dynamism within an existing organization with a proven history of continuity. They seek positions in management, resulting in a strong increase in the number of managers.

Around 2004 that resulted in a wave of complaints from the government and private sector. Professionals at grassroots level, like doctors and teachers, said that all the rules imposed on them from above left them no room for manoeuvre and destroyed their pleasure in their work. They spent more time, they said, filling in all kinds of forms for their superiors than doing their actual work. The managers with their shiny briefcases seemed to be going the same way as the hippy do-gooders of half a century previously: they were dead wood to be cut away, full of talk and far too expensive. Even the prominent vvd politician Marc Rutte joined the ranks of the manager-haters.

In the meantime, interest in the pure science subjects was declining and university departments could only keep themselves afloat by attracting young PhD candidates from China, India or Russia. The private sector then complained that the Netherlands was ruining its leading technological position for good.

Another primary concern is cost control. This is, of course, an ever-present problem for company directors, since unnecessary costs reduce profit. But Dutch managers devote particular attention to the problem. A saving today is almost always preferred to potential revenue in the near future. If income falls the response tends to be to cut back on expenditure. Planned investments are scrapped and less profitable activities are stopped, even if their prospects for the future are promising. This is called in Dutch *de tering naar de nering zetten*, not spending more than one makes or 'cutting the coat to suit the cloth'. It closely resembles the regime imposed by the municipal credit banks on their debtors.

The national budget deficit is therefore a common subject of public debate. It is always seen as a matter of grave concern and ministers of finance devise policies aimed at providing a lasting solution to the problem. The response to serious economic setbacks is unfailingly to reduce expenditure and never to cover the shortfall by printing more money. Ex-businessman Hendrikus Colijn, prime minister during the economic crisis of the 1930s, believed that the country would only survive the depression by making financial adjustments. He pointedly rejected a Keynesian solution of government investments to get the private sector back up and running. The same applied to devaluation of the Dutch guilder. He held on to the gold standard until 1936, years longer than neighbouring countries like France and Great Britain. The strong guilder was a source of great pride to Colijn and when the Netherlands also abandoned the gold standard, he saw it as a capitulation.

The recession of the 1980s produced a new wave of cutbacks, but this time based on different arguments. The government claimed, to put it in simple terms, that a guilder spent by the government was a guilder that could not be invested by the private sector. Once again, the value of the guilder was protected jealously. Since then, inflation has been almost negligible, compared to the 1970s, when – much to everyone's concern – it sometimes rose to between six and eight percent a year.

When the economy recovered strongly in the second half of the 1980s, the government saw no reason to put a stop to its policy of cutbacks. The parties that formed the new government in 1994 worked on the basic assumption that they would have to save a further 9 billion euros. Reports on renewed economic growth and falling unemployment had no impact on their resolve. They could also feel the warm breath of the media in their necks, who were keen on exposing most proposed cutbacks as juggling with figures. The same media always devote considerable attention to *meevallers* and *tegenvallers*, unexpected extra revenue or costs, which the Ministry of Finance regularly brings to public attention. These are usually tax revenues or social security expenditures that were unforeseen in earlier prognoses. *Tegenvallers* are a powerful weapon for a minister of finance who wishes to push through more cutbacks; *meevallers* are a godsend for hard-pushed ministries, such as education and social affairs, who are under continual pressure to bring down costs.

Among the general public, a fairly broad consensus developed that the Netherlands was 'too expensive'. It was pricing itself out of the market because salaries were too high. Not that everyone actually ended up with such a large amount on their bank accounts every month – it was the high taxes and social security contributions that pushed costs up to such irresponsible heights. All kinds of complex models were devised to establish a link between increases and decreases in government spending and the rise and fall of unemployment in the private sector. Minister of finance and PVDA leader Wim Kok therefore announced in the summer of 1994, while engaged in the negotiations to form a new government, that the cutbacks would lead to 350,000 new jobs in four years. Commentators observed that, since the early 1980s, no self-respecting politician goes anywhere without their handheld. They need it to draw up 'income scenarios' and 'cost-revenue analyses' and to calculate their impact on unemployment.

In practice, 1.6 million new jobs were created in the 1990s, because the entire global economy was experiencing an unprecedented boom. At one point the Dutch national budget actually showed a surplus instead of the customary deficit. When, straight after the millennium, the ICT bubble burst, The Netherlands went into recession. The centre-right Balkenende governments immediately resorted to the tried and trusted policy of imposing cutbacks, enabling minister Zalm to keep the budget deficit at a low level. That led to an increase in the tax burden for the man in the street, which the prime minister described as 'the sour part'. This was a reference to the well-known Dutch saying that, to get to the sweet part of an apple, you sometimes need to bite through the sour part. At the same time, Balkenende and his ministers sung the praises of people taking their own responsibility. This theme, too, had come into vogue since the Lubbers era in the 1980s, as the people of the Netherlands tried en masse to adjust to a society that no longer offers – to them as individuals, to companies, to government departments or to non-profitmaking organizations – the continuity that was formerly accorded such importance.

For many, this has been a painful experience. In a certain way, it has put them back in the same position as the herring fishermen six and seven hundred years ago. They sail, with their frail craft, on a stormy and unpredictable sea. But – in spite of its dangers – the fishermen, the merchants and the explorers never allowed the sea to daunt them.

Many Dutch people find something attractive about this new uncertainty. They like to show their dynamism and flexibility. They relish the challenge. But still, they heed the old seamen's motto: *Kalmpjes aan, dan breekt het lijntje niet*. Be careful and the line will not break. A good sailor is prepared to take risks but is never reckless. In uncharted waters, he will drop a line to plumb the depth. He will always resist the pull of the land, until he is certain that there are no dangerous currents. Because, after all, the most important thing is to get home safely.

The traffic on the main motorways is monitored on video screens, so that prompt action can be taken if congestion starts to build up. Despite these high-tech systems, there are tailbacks during the rush hour which are only too frequently more than a hundred kilometres long in total. Widening existing roads or building new ones might move the jams elsewhere, but it doesn't solve them completely.

5

Privacy-minded

'Be a prince in your own square metre!'

Reserve as a basic character trait. Caution in contact with strangers. Keeping emotions under control. Respect for the privacy of another. Freedom of choice and conformity combined. Money does not buy happiness. A relationship for spiritual contentment, work for self-respect. Loneliness. The restrictions imposed by 'gezelligheid'.

A café in the Netherlands can be a very sad place. There may be two or three men at the bar who would most probably like to talk, but there will be empty bar stools standing resolutely between them. Only the most talented of barmen can break through such loneliness. Most of them are content to serve up the drinks in silence.

In the Netherlands there is a distance between people. Literally. The Dutch will sit next to someone else only if there is no alternative. Even in the bus or train. If they are all packed together during the rush hour, they will pull in their stomachs, as if to say: 'I am touching you, but I don't really want to. I am trying to make myself as thin as possible. It's not my fault, I'm really doing my best.' Anyone who fails to observe this rather forced ritual is asking for trouble. They will be seen as another one of those dirty foreigners who rub themselves up against you in public places.

Physical contact is avoided as much as possible. People from cultures where there is less distance between people, such as the Arab countries, notice this immediately. They find that the people they talk to will back off continually until the minimum acceptable distance has been restored. A test conducted among my colleagues proved that this is about 70 centimetres. There was no significant difference between men and women. Yet lovers will stand in each others' arms at the bus stop, kissing without embarrassment. They walk down the street with their arms around each other's waists. Or they will lie, bodies entwined, on the beach. If there are no empty seats left on the tram, a polite young man will stand up or he might allow his girlfriend to sit on his knee. No one minds this, but you will notice that they look away. It is not done to stare at such scenes of intimacy. Many people will even make it clear that they have not seen it at all.

Television pictures of foreign dignitaries embracing at the foot of the aircraft steps are greeted with amazement. For many Dutch people this only confirms their suspicions that these people are not to be trusted. Decent people keep their distance. If they do not, then there is something going on. Couples in love – as long as they are heterosexual – are permitted to make an external show of their affection. In the most modern parts of the country, such as the more progressive parts of Amsterdam city centre, you may see two men walking hand in hand, but it is still very rare and not considered acceptable by most people. In any case, a couple will present themselves as such. The 70 centimetre barrier may no longer be between them, but it is a clear signal to others that, for them, it applies more than ever.

You don't talk to complete strangers

The Dutch have a reputation as being a little dour and unapproachable. They will frequently agree with this view of themselves, but then add that, once the ice is broken – a very appropriate choice of expression – they are hospitable hosts and faithful friends. It is difficult to say the extent to which this is true. Everyone has their own character and some seek more contact than others. But there can be no denying that the way the Dutch communicate creates a barrier between them and people they do not know.

You simply don't talk to complete strangers. People in public places will not easily strike up a conversation with those around them, unless there is good reason. If you ask the way, or some other question that is not of a personal nature, you will receive a detailed answer. But it is very unlikely that you would be invited to join a group of strangers at a table in a café. In the trains, the passengers maintain a stony silence, with their faces buried in a newspaper or with their iPod cutting them off from those around them. There may be a buzz of conversation here and there, but it generally comes from groups of friends or people who work together.

This is all in sharp contrast to the picture I painted earlier of a society in permanent communication, in perpetual search of compromise. So why do people talk to each other so little? The Dutch will answer that they are minding their own affairs, not impinging on the privacy of others. They are afraid of being a nuisance. They will speak only if there is a common theme to bind the group together. If a train stops out in the middle of nowhere, and there is a delay of half an hour so that everyone's carefully arranged plans are thrown into disarray, conversations will soon start. But once the delayed train arrives at the station, the common theme disappears and the animated conversations and open-air gatherings come to an end.

Many Dutch people believe that this lack of contact with others is on the increase. Interviews with older people almost always contain complaints about it. The main theme – which comes in many variations – is that people used to be more united as a group. They helped each other. No one does that nowadays, everyone is too concerned with themselves.

The question is, what do they mean by this? The Dutch make a clear distinction between strangers – who are nothing to do with them – and friends. It is possible that, as time has passed, the circle of friends and relations has grown smaller. There is evidence to suggest that this may be true. With the exception of the mass migrations to the cities in the west of the country around the turn of the century, the Dutch traditionally tended to stay put. Families would live in the same villages and towns generation after generation. The enormous economic development since the end of the Second World War largely put a stop to that. I can still remember how, in the 1950s and 1960s, my father and his five brothers would gather at their parents' house on a Sunday, together with their families. They were connected to other families in our provincial town by a complex web of relation-ships which meant that the circle of friends and relations was always large. Today, not a single Van der Horst of my generation still lives in the town. The family is now spread across the country and I have not seen the majority of my cousins for perhaps twenty years. I hear of them through the family grapevine. My own brother lives in a completely different part of the country (actually only fifty kilometres away, but to the people of this small country, that is a long way). This effectively prevents the development of close networks of relations, such as the family had in the 1950s. This network was largely made up of separate families who all lived within a few streets of each other and whose parents had also known each other.

These extended family networks have been destroyed in the modern age and this makes the consequences of keeping one's distance even more marked. It is easier to become caught in a vicious circle of loneliness. Old women in particular fall prey to this. Their average life expectancy is 81 and, as in most countries, they tend to outlive their husbands. Behind their impeccable white net curtains, they endure their unhappiness in silence, because they find it difficult to express their emotions. They put on a brave face and hide their misery from outsiders. This is due partly to pride, partly to embarrassment and partly because they don't want to be a nuisance. The obvious thing to do is to bring these lonely people together, and many attempts are made. They are, however, rarely successful because the loneliness is often partly founded on the desire to be left to one's own devices and not be dependent on anyone. The result is a contradiction that is not easy to solve and produces a feeling of powerlessness. There are countless organizations in the Netherlands prepared to provide assistance to people in trouble – but the average citizen has the tendency to leave them to their fate.

Foreign visitors, particularly from Africa and Asia, are shocked when they see the old people's homes where younger generations can dispatch their parents and keep them out of sight. They consider this shameful evidence of a lack of love for one's parents and of a sense of responsibility. But this is not the philosophy behind the system. The homes give their residents the opportunity to live their lives according to their own norms. They do not need to adapt to the wishes of their children or vice versa. As elsewhere, the compromise culture plays a leading role in families. Older people wish to be taken seriously and not to spend the rest of their lives in a situation of permanent give and take. In spite of their age, they want to retain their independence and their privacy. This is impossible if they have a room in their children's house. Yet, in some ways, there is good reason for Asian and African visitors to respond to this system with such aversion. Many old people complain that a visit from their children every couple of months is not often enough, and that they do not see as much of their grandchildren as they would like. But they still consider their option of living in an old people's home a significant acquired right.

In spite of this, most Dutch people will try to postpone the day on which they move into one of these places. And the government provides them with every support. Most people agree that the elderly should stay independent as long as possible, preferably in their own homes. The prospect of moving to an old people's home is only seriously considered when, in spite of help with the cleaning and meals delivered to their doors, they are no longer able to fend for themselves. *Oude bomen moet je niet verplanten.* You should not uproot old trees. People have the right to stay in their own homes and surroundings as long as possible. A perfect symbol for this mentality is the rollator, the wheeled walking frame that has become a familiar sight on the streets since the end of the last century.

Elderly people in the Netherlands want to remain independent and mobile as long as possible. The rollator helps them to do that. Here we see a practical lesson in which the secrets of this simple yet wonderful invention are revealed.

It is a Dutch invention, which allows elderly people to continue to move about independently: a rollator is essentially a very simple trolley, with handles to steer and a handbrake. You can lean on it for support as you walk. Ideally, it will also have a basket for shopping. Thanks to this simple invention, countless elderly people are spared a life of isolation in an old people's flat. The rollator helps them to keep the independence they so cherish for as long as possible.

Taking all this into account, you ask yourself how that boy and girl who kiss each other completely without embarrassment at the bus stop ever managed to meet in the first place when everyone so jealously guards their own privacy. The answer is obvious – they started off as acquaintances, or rather, their two networks of family and friends came into contact. They found a themselves in a situation where they could talk about a common theme. And one thing led to another.

The explosive development of clubs and associations

Anyone who is not a part of some network of relations or other, giving them an opportunity to talk about matters of common interest, soon becomes lonely. This may be one of the reasons for the explosive development of clubs and associations in the Netherlands, particularly involving sports and hobbies at local level. Although the sport or hobby is the main reason for taking part, social contact is of more than secondary importance.

This system is becoming less and less effective. As the population becomes more mobile, it is increasingly difficult for individuals to build up networks of this kind. Spiritual leaders and social workers see loneliness as a serious social problem. Opponents of reductions in social security benefits often use the argument that the unemployed will then have less money to spend on subscriptions to clubs and will become isolated. In spite of their highly developed sense of privacy, most Dutch people are afraid of isolation. They prefer to function as part of a group and most believe, in the last instance, that life can only be lived to the full if shared with a partner.

Finding a partner is, however, not always an easy task. At least, it has become increasingly difficult in the past thirty years. Traditionally, as in the rest of Europe, the family was the basic unit in the Netherlands. You got married in your early twenties, had children, promised to be faithful 'till death did you part' and you kept your marriage vows. You did not have a lot of choice. Until the 1950s the social pressure on couples to stay together was enormous. The Roman Catholic Church did not officially recognize the annulment of marriages and, although the Protestant Church permitted divorce, few took advantage of the right. This was unquestionably connected to the fact that, in the Netherlands, the man was traditionally seen as the breadwinner, while his wife tended to the housekeeping and the children. This was so deeply embedded that, even as late as the 1950s, female civil servants automatically received an 'honorary discharge' when they got married. The cultural watershed of the 1960s – and, without doubt, the mass availability of the contraceptive pill after 1963, which allowed women to decide for themselves whether they wished to bear children – put an end to this traditional system of relationships. Living together without being married – previously considered little better than prostitution – became normal. Sex before marriage – until then a taboo subject – was generally accepted. Under new legislation, 'irreconcilable differences' were acceptable grounds for divorce, hitherto only granted if one of the partners admitted to adultery (a precondition that came to be known as *de grote leugen*, the great lie). The social security system guaranteed that partners without their own income would receive at least a minimum benefit, making it easier in practice for relationships to break up.

This change in the economic importance of the marriage contract was perhaps the most significant factor in the break up of the traditional system. In less prosperous times, economic security is an important part of what people experience as 'happiness'. In modern society, economic security is guaranteed for practically everyone. Consequently, other – less material – factors become more important, and relationships are assessed entirely on their emotional quality. The character of the partners and how they interrelate are far more important that how much either of them earns. The quality of the relationship is paramount. If it is not considered optimal, the partnership may break up.

Because of the national respect for privacy and, compared with Asian or African cultures, the loose contact with other family members, couples in the Netherlands become very dependent on each other. Staying together till death do you part is no small task when average life expectancy is between 75 and 80. Relationships have to last a very long time and the love has to be very strong if the partners are not to become bored with each other at some point. This is particularly true if you are not prepared to live a life of disappointment and if you are not satisfied with less than a partner who is a source of pleasure around the home, leads a regular life and brings in a reasonable salary every month.

Beauty fades away, and the ugliness remains

Romantic love in its purest form has, more than ever, become the standard for happiness. Weddings themselves often have the character of a fairy-tale. Western fairy tales traditionally end with the sentence 'And they lived happily ever after' and most modern Dutch couples will settle for nothing less. Ultimately, they apply the same norms as Goocheme Sallie, a popular film and stage character in the 1930s. The aged working class lad from the backstreets of Amsterdam sang a well-known song, with lyrics by Philip Pinkhof:

> *Je bent niet mooi, je bent geen knappe vrouw.*
> *Je nagels zijn voortdurend in de rouw.*

Toch wil ik van geen ander weten.
Omdat ik zoveel van je hou.
Al ben je ook een beetje vreemd van ras
Toch ben ik danig met jou in m'n sas.
k'Wil van een ander nooit iets weten
Omdat ik zoveel van je hou
Wat verdriet, mooi ben je niet
Vooral wanneer je kijft
Al ben' je geen plaat
Schoonheid vergaat.
Maar weet de lelijkheid die blijft,
daar moet je maar aan wenne.
Al zijn je kleren ook van satijn
en doe je niet mee aan de slanke lijn
Toch wil van veen ander weten.
Omdat ik zoveel van je hou
Al zijn je haren niet gepermanent
en is 't gebruik van zeep je onbekend.
Toch zou ik jou niet willen ruilen
voor zo een maag're modeprent.

You're not too pretty, you're not a beautiful woman,
And your nails are always dirty.
But I would never look at another
Because I love you so much.
Even though you're a bit of a strange lass
When I'm with you I feel like a king.
I would never look at another
Because I love you so much.
It's a pity, you're not so pretty
Especially when you nag.
You may not be a picture,
But beauty fades away.
And you just get used to
The ugliness that remains.
Even though your clothes are not of satin
And you're not much of one for dieting
I would never look at another
Because I love you so much.
Your hair may be in need of a perm
And a bath might not be out of turn
But I would never trade you
For some skinny dolly bird.

Doctor seeks Eve, no older than 40

The fact that fewer and fewer people succeed in finding a relationship that meets these high emotional requirements is illustrated by a phenomenon that has become commonplace in the last twenty years – the 'personal ad'. Until the advent of the Internet at the end of the 1990s, personal ads were a growing source of income for newspapers and magazines. They then moved online and hundreds of dating sites emerged catering for a wide range of tastes and preferences, up to and including sado-masochism. These ads paint a reasonably good picture of what people understand as 'happiness'.

In 2006, the dating site Relatie-Planet reported that 1,337,197 singles had advertized on its pages. They said things like: 'I am a bitch, I am a lover, I am a child', 'Sweetie', or 'I'm looking for a man or woman to be my mate, my best friend and my lover.' Gissy was looking for a man 'with a great sense of humour, a free spirit who also understands the spiritual side of life'. A woman who 'loves life and laughter' and whose motto is 'bar, beer, a glass of wine' was looking for 'attractive, fun, spontaneous and optimistic men'. Men describe themselves on the site as spontaneous, sociable, sporty, cheerful and honest. One wrote: 'Do you think that intimacy is important but also attach a lot of value to freedom? Be careful, I love to be hugged, I love spirituality and a good conversation, and especially I love to laugh and, if necessary, cry.' He was looking for a 'happy lady who loves life'.

There are a lot of nice people out there

One noticeable thing about these advertisements, they tend to emphasize the positive side of the advertizer's character. There are a lot of nice people out there. Very few of them make any reference to money or material possessions, or give any details of the advertizer's income. They do, however, contain a great deal of indirect information.

Anyone registering with a dating site has to give a lot information about themselves: the colour of their eyes, their hair, their weight, how tall they are, their hobbies and interests. But they are never asked about their social status or income. That is not done, though they are asked about their education. Terms that occur frequently in personal profiles on the Internet are 'equality' and 'good conversation'. There is a general consensus that these requirements can be fulfilled only by someone with a comparable education. This apparently reasonable demand is, however, a cover for an age old source of social differentiation – status. Since the Second World War, educational qualifications have in many respects replaced what former generations referred to as 'social standing'. There used to be an enormous gap between the gentleman farmer and his farm labourers, between entrepreneurs, shopkeepers and simple workers. These differences would often be manifested in their manner of dress. The sons of shopkeepers did not marry factory girls, and a farmer's daughter would not dare to come home with a young farm labourer. It happened, of course, but it was asking for trouble. With the democratization of modern society, such attitudes have become unacceptable, but educational qualifications have emerged as a good substitute. The implicit assumption is that a university graduate will hardly be able to conduct a decent conversation with someone who has only had an intermediate technical education or has a diploma in home economics, let alone set up house on any equal basis. Intelligence and creativity are directly linked to educational achievement.

This, of course, says nothing at all about the countless relationships that develop without the help of ICT. At the most, the internet reveals a little about the ideals of the people who present themselves on it. But, because they describe the ideal partner, they are an important source of information on what many Dutch people would like to see in the perfect relationship. The fact that, just as anywhere else in the world, *l'amour* plays the game according to its own rules, makes little difference. I myself have never been in love with anyone who conformed perfectly to my image of the ideal partner and I believe that this applies to most people.

It is therefore remarkable that the requirements continue to be so high. The fact that most Dutch people now live outside of the traditional family unit illustrates that, in spite of the unabated desire to form a partnership, they are less prepared than ever to make concessions. You might wonder whether this change is for better or for worse. The dramas of divorce have become an ever-present feature of modern society; but perhaps they are still preferable to the sorrow born silently by many partners in former generations as they preserved the pretence of a successful marriage.

Work is good for one's personal development

In addition to a relationship, the modern individual needs one other thing to be fulfilled as a person – a paid job. At least, there is a widely held consensus that work is good for one's personal development. It is a source of self-respect and of contact with others. People without work for any period of time find themselves 'on the margins of society' and feel that they 'no longer belong'. Full employment is therefore one of the main aims of all political parties. They may not agree on how it is to be achieved, but they are unanimous on the end itself.

Work has become a scarce commodity in the Netherlands. 57% of people be-tween the ages of 16 and 64 have a paid job – a total of about 7.3 million, including all those with part-time jobs (sometimes amounting to only a few hours a week). This means that, in a country with a population of over 16 million, 45% of people are in employment. The rest are at school, retired or living off some form of benefit. These figures are the source of grave concern in the Netherlands and it is widely believed that the number of people out of work is growing rapidly. This is, however, not the case. In 1970, 58% of people between 15 and 64 had jobs. In 2004 that percentage had risen to 73.1%. By way of comparison, the figure for the EU as a whole was 63.3%. The difference lies in the percentage of people who wish to work. The Netherlands was traditionally a country where the husband was the breadwinner and the wife stayed at home. Partly as a result of the second wave of feminism, this situation has changed radically. An increasing number of women wish to make careers for themselves and are receiving the active support of the government.

Not that women were afraid to go out to work in previous generations. Most girls looked for jobs after they left school, making a contribution to the upkeep of the family and saving the rest for their *uitzet*. This was their 'bottom drawer', originally consisting of bed linen, but later covering the whole range of household goods that would give them a good start when they got married and gave up their jobs to look after their own home.

Until well into the 1970s, there was a particular type of school, the *Middelbare Meisjesschool*, which was originally intended for the daughters of well-off families, who would later marry the sons of the gentry, many of whom would have had a university education. The future model wives were taught modern languages, cultural history and literature so that they would later be able to converse on a whole range of subjects – in French if necessary – but not too deeply, over a dinner that they had also prepared themselves. The girls who attended the MMS were not able to go on to university.

Very few women actually went to these schools. Most parents considered it unnecessary as their daughters would be getting married later anyway. This has now all changed dramatically.

Personal relations are political

This change was symbolized by what came to be known as the 'second feminist wave'. Female activists in the 1960s noticed that they were often left to make the sandwiches while the men did the talking. At the beginning of the 1970s, they emerged as a group with a wide variety of demands, which they presented under the motto: *Het persoonlijke is politiek*, 'personal relations are political'. They claimed that existing relations between the sexes – also between couples – were repressive for women. They said that keeping a household was also work, and demanded that men do their share. Their aim was to achieve a situation in which the percentage of men and women in paid employment reflected the demographic balance between the sexes. They pursued this aim through a policy of positive action. Best-selling author Maarten 't Hart noted that they were always concerned with higher positions and were not interested in the 'feminization of the dust-cart', but his reservations gathered little support. The image of the housewife changed. From a respected mother-figure who ran the home, she was degraded to a stupid drudge who sacrificed herself so that her husband – a 'fallocrat' and oppressor – could pursue his wonderful career. The feminist novelist Renate Dorrestein christened this sorry figure a *theemuts*, a tea cosy. The second feminist wave never became a mass movement, but it acquired considerable support in leading circles and among the intelligentsia. A moderate form of positive action – exemplified by the policy of giving preference to women candidates if job applicants had identical qualifications – was introduced throughout the entire government apparatus. The media, across the political spectrum, expressed their support for the feminists' demands. Universities set up courses in 'Women's Studies'. Increasingly well-educated women started participating in the labour market. At present, about half of further education students are female, although they still tend to avoid the technical subjects. It has become very unusual for women to give up their jobs because they are getting married or going to move in with their partner. It still happens frequently when they decide to have children, but many couples wait until they are well into their thirties to start a family when it becomes a matter of 'now or never' for the woman.

There is little left of the second feminist wave and all its radicalism. But the protagonists of the 1960s and 1970s do enjoy the respect of younger generation, who now wear fashionable clothes and high heels. Ambitious young women in the Netherlands are, after all, no longer political activists but power girls, who use everything at their disposal – beauty and brains – to move forward in their personal careers. The majority of young women do not of course do this at any cost: more than men, they prefer part-time jobs, even though that might affect their chances of promotion and for making steps up the social ladder.

Women who don't do this often have difficulty finding a suitable partner. Power girls too prefer men with the same or a slightly better education. Some observers say that modern women should follow the example of the macho men and just choose a hunk, even if he does earn a living working on a building site. Power girls might agree with that in their dreams, but not in reality. Whether they follow their heads or their hearts is not for us to decide.

In the summer of 2006, during an upsurge of the national economy, 350,000 people were registered as unemployed. That did not include those retiring early or drawing disability benefits. The pressure this places on the benefit system is compounded by the belief – which is becoming increasingly popular across the political spectrum – that many of the unemployed do not make sufficient effort to look for work, but prefer to live off their benefits, sitting 'on their lazy butts' all day in front of the television. The government takes a wide range of measures to restrict access to benefits. Every now and then, there are scandals as employers are unable to find labour for seasonal work. A recurrent example of this is harvesting asparagus, heavy work which is so badly paid that, even when compared with the lowest of benefits, it is not worth the effort. So the asparagus is picked by migrants, since the fall of the Iron Curtain often from former Eastern Bloc countries. In addition, there proved to be a considerable demand for well educated and skilled workers of all kinds. Despite the unemployment, because many Dutch people without jobs did not have the right qualifications, many Dutch companies found themselves forced to take on skilled Polish labour.

Experience has shown that people who are unemployed for more than two years have little chance of ever finding another job – if for no other reason than that their own desperation eventually gets the better of them. These people form the hard core that accounts for slightly less than a third of the total number of unemployed. What is it that keeps this hard core intact? Since the 1980s, the belief has been growing that the social security system itself is the cause. The unemployed are insufficiently encouraged to find work. Anyone who finds paid will only earn slightly more than they receive in benefits, and perhaps, because of taxes, even less. In modern political jargon, this is known as the 'poverty trap'. Politicians to the right of the political spectrum have a simple solution: lower the level of benefits and people will always be better off in paid work. It is this way of thinking that has brought the purchasing power of benefits down over the past quarter of a century. The decrease was accompanied by a shift in public opinion. In the 1960s and 1970s, unemployment was seen as a social problem. If you couldn't find a job it was society's fault. These days, this reasoning is rejected as too simplistic, even

The Dutch are getting older, but the older generations are healthier than ever – and very active. Why sit and stare out of the window if you can still kick a ball around? These grey-haired veterans are being honoured for past triumphs.

in left-wing circles. There is now a widespread belief that people are perfectly capable of improving their lot and that they should not be subsidized if they prove too lazy to do it for themselves. That was the underlying idea behind the social policy of the social democratic-liberal governments of the 1990s, but it only really became dominant during the centre-right governments of Jan Peter Balkenende. Under Balkenende the Invalidity Insurance Act (WAO) was replaced by the Work and Income Act (WIA). Instead of determining the degree to which people were unable to work, under the new Act, the emphasis was on what people *could* do. The unemployed were informed that they had to 'make every effort' to find work. Employers had to do their bit, by reserving appropriate jobs for invalids

Since about 2002-2003, many municipalities expect something back from people on social security: they have to do simple production work for a couple of days a week. The argument is that this will prevent them from no longer being accustomed to working. In Schiedam this resulted in an immediate reduction in the number of people claiming benefit by half. A large number of them clearly preferred to lose their benefit than to go to work.

The idea that everyone must earn their own living as far as possible, is based on a very old tradition. Calvin's work ethic survived the hedonistic and anti-religious storms of the 1960s. And liberal self-reliance is only possible if individuals are able to stand on their own two feet. Around 2000 a new dimension was added to the problem: the average age of the population rose because, since the widespread introduction of the pill in the sixties, Dutch people were having fewer children. Economists made calculations to work out how a decreasing number of working people could provide sufficient funds to ensure that a steadily growing proportion of the population could enjoy a happy and healthy old age. Pension contributions threatened to become prohibitive, unless everyone who was able actually worked for a living. And not only that. People would have to keep on working for longer. All early retirement schemes from the 1980s were scrapped and even the retirement age of 65 was no longer safe. Experts predicted that, in the future, the retirement age would be raised to 67 or even 70. A change, they added, which was justified, since people were living much longer than they used to. Anyone retiring at 65 now would probably live for another 20 years or more, while in the last 25 years of the nineteenth century, when the retirement age was originally set at 65, they could expect to last another two or three at the most.

On the other hand if you are over 45 your chances of finding a job are very slim indeed. Very few companies will employ you, despite the fact that in the Netherlands leaders in business and the civil service are often in their fifties themselves. And despite the constant lamentations in the media and in parliament, that the experience and strength of the older generations is indispensable in the world of work.

You can be yourself behind your own front door

Men and women in the Netherlands today therefore have to acquire for themselves two scarce commodities – an emotionally satisfying relationship and a paid job. In this respect, the most successful are the *tweeverdieners*, couples where both partners have jobs. If their relationship is also sound, they are in luck. Furthermore, since it is still assumed that salary levels have to be sufficiently high to maintain a family, working couples have more financial room to manoeuvre. They can afford a holiday in Thailand or the Dominican Republic (exotic, faraway places are becoming increasingly popular) or a mortgage on a house. The interest on mortgage repayments is tax deductible and the traditional aversion to lending money for the acquisition of material possessions does not extend to buying a house. The belief that a house will increase in value over time is deeply entrenched and is not affected by temporary dips in the property market.

A decent home of their own is one of the main priorities for most Dutch people. You can be yourself behind your own front door. As soon as young people have their own source of income – their first job or a student grant – they start thinking seriously about leaving home. From humble beginnings – a room or a single-floor flat – they will gradually move on to better things as their income increases. A new word has even appeared in the Dutch language to describe this process: *wooncarrière*, literally a 'residential career'.

Through a wide variety of consumer surveys, a picture has developed of what Dutch people see as their ideal home. It is not a flat, but a house of their own –

Most people in the Netherlands would prefer to live in a house with a pointed roof and a garden front and back. But the country is too small for that, so most have to live in an upstairs maisonette or an apartment. So some architects like to experiment – here we see, after the hanging gardens of Babylon, the hanging apartments of the Netherlands.

In global terms, the birth rate in the Netherlands is low. Immigrants soon adapt to the Dutch custom of 'few, late and planned'. Once the baby has been born, the happy parents make no secret of it. This is probably a joke by neighbours or colleagues.

preferably detached, but a semi-detached or terraced house will do – with a front and back garden. In most cases, the wish remains unfulfilled because, just as with a job or a satisfying relationship, such houses are difficult to come by. The Netherlands is small and, with the exception of Bangladesh, is the most densely populated country in the world. Due to lack of space, house builders are forced to construct high-rise apartment blocks, particularly in the urbanized areas in the west. Since the 1970s, however, low-rise housing has once again become fashionable. The designers of new estates have discovered that – with a little creativity – they can fit as many people into the same surface area in 'regular' houses as they previously did in four or five-storey apartment blocks. After all, there had to be sufficient space between these blocks if the estate was to offer reasonable living conditions for its residents. 'Hong Kong'-type solutions, with high-rise blocks built shoulder-to-shoulder, were never a realistic alternative.

Many of the people living in flats or upper-floor maisonettes dream of a house with a garden. It is difficult to say why this is. If you ask them, they will say that a garden is 'nice for the children' or that it is 'pleasant to have a bit of greenery outside the door', but there is often a municipal park nearby that would fulfil this function. It is possible that they are nostalgic for their agricultural roots, but this is unlikely – gardens are generally used for decoration, rather than for growing vegetables. Perhaps a patch of land in front of and behind the house fulfils some deep-lying desire to extend one's own private terrain, the place where you can 'be yourself'.

The boom of the 1990s brought this desire to the surface even more. The supply of houses could not keep track of demand and prices went through the roof, partly because interest rates on mortgages were also very low. House buyers were happy, because their mortgage repayments were affordable. By the year 2000, however, it had become almost impossible to buy a house on a normal salary and since then a decent house is only within reach of couples who are both earning.

On the market for rented accommodation too, demand exceeded supply. Because the government imposed strict limitations on rent increases, waiting lists got longer until potential tenants had to wait years before finding a house. In 2006 the government estimated that hundreds of thousands of extra homes needed to be built. The problem was that the government had long ago stopped building houses. It could therefore only provide incentives for investors, such as housing associations and property developers to do so. And so, for house-seekers, it became more and more difficult to find that special place where you could feel completely be yourself.

Being yourself is a problem that was described perfectly 70 years ago by songwriter Dirk Witte. His lyrics have now become a part of the classic Dutch repertoire:

> Je leeft maar heel kort, maar een enkele keer.
> En als je straks ánders wilt, kun je niet meer.
> Mens, durf te leven.
> Vraag niet elke dag van je korte bestaan:
> Hoe hebben m'n pa en m'n grootpa gedaan?
> Hoe doet er m'n neef en hoe doet er m'n vrind?
> En wie weet, hoe of dat nou m'n buurman weer vindt?
> En – wat heeft 'Het Fatsoen' voorgeschreven?
> Mens, durf te leven!
> De mensen bepalen de kleur van je das
> De vorm van je hoed, en de snit van je jas
> En – van je leven.
> Ze wijzen de paadjes, waarlangs je mag gaan
> En roepen 'of foei' als je even blijft staan.
> Ze kiezen je toekomst en kiezen je werk.
> Ze zoeken een kroeg voor je uit en een kerk
> En wat j' aan de armen moet geven.
> Mens, is dat leven?
> De mensen – ze schrijven je leefregels voor
> Ze geven je raad en ze roepen in koor:
> Zó moet je leven!
>
> Met die mag je omgaan, maar die is te min.
> Met die moet je trouwen – al heb je geen zin.
> En dáár moet je wonen, dat eist je fatsoen.

En je wordt genegeerd als je 't anders zou doen.
Alsof je iets ergs had misdreven.
Mens, is dat leven?
Het leven is heerlijk, het leven is mooi.
Maar – vlieg uit in de lucht en kruip niet in een kooi.
Mens, durf te leven.
Je kop in de hoogte, je neus in de wind.
En lap aan je laars, hoe een ander het vindt.
Hou een hart vol wan warmte en van liefde in je borst.
Maar wees op je vierkante meter een Vorst!
Wat je zoekt, kan geen ander je geven.
Mens, durf te leven!

You only live once and life is so short,
If you change your mind later, it's already too late.
So dare to live life to the full.
Don't ask every day of this short existence
What would my dad or my granddad have done?
Or what would my cousin or my friend do?
And who knows what the neighbours would think?
And what is the 'Right Thing To Do'?
So dare to live life to the full!
Others tell you the colour of your tie,
The shape of your hat, the cut of your coat,
And – of your life.
They tell you which paths you're allowed to take
And call you to heel if you stop for a while.
They choose your work and your future,
The pub where you drink, the church where you pray,
And what you should give to the poor.
Do you call that living?
The others – they write the rules
They give you advice and they call as one:
This is how you should live!

They say: here is a friend, but this one's no good
And you should marry this one – whether you want to or not.
Go and live there, it's the right thing to do.
And then they ignore you if you do it your own way,
As if it were a terrible crime.
Do you call that living?
Life is a fine and a wonderful thing.
But spread your wings and don't get trapped in a cage.

Dare to live life to the full.
Keep your head high, your nose to the wind,
And don't give a damn what others may think.
Fill your heart with love and with warmth.
And be a prince in your own square metre!
No one can give you what you are looking for.
So dare to live life to the full!

Don't give a damn what others may think. It clearly takes courage to 'dare to live
your life to the full'. It brings nothing but trouble. The 'others' will soon be on your
back. You do not behave according to their rules and the fact that this rubs them
up the wrong way is clear from the uniformity of their small gardens and that the
furnishings of their houses are often so predictable. Who are they, these 'others'?
A few years after the success of *Mens, durf te leven*, singer Louis Davids enthralled
packed theatres with a portrayal of his audience. Davids was honoured with the
nickname *Die Grote Kleine Man*, the Great Little Man. The entire song can be
encapsulated with the words: 'The little man carries the can.'

Dempsey gaat weer aan het boksen en krijgt weer 'n dik miljoen
Om zich 'n kwartiertje te laten stompen
En zijn tegenstander, als ie wint, een half miljoentje meer
Want die kereltjes die laten zich niet lompen!
Wie snakt er naar zo'n baan, zou, kreeg ie het gedaan,
Voor twee tientjes al zijn kiezen uit zijn kaken laten slaan?

Dat is die kleine man, die kleine burgerman
Zo'n doodgewone man met 'n confectiepakkie an
De man met zo een uitgesneden linnen frontje an
Zo'n zenuwelijer, hongerlijer van een kleine man.

We verzorgen onze medeburgers tegenwoordig best:
Als je niet werkt krijg je achttien gulden premie.
En dan zijn er veel slampampers die zijn liever lui dan moe
Want die denken: nou achttien piek, die neem ie!

Ze schelden allemaal op patroon en kapitaal
En wie is weer de dupe van dat vrijheidsideaal?
Dat is die kleine man, die kleine burgerman
Zo'n hele kleine man met een confectiepakkie an
Eén met zo'n imitatie-jaeger onderbroekie an
Zo'n minimumlijer, zenuwelijer van een kleine man.

Dempsey earns more than a million when he steps back in the ring,

For fifteen minutes of punching and pain.
And his opponent, if he wins, gets half a million more,
You can't pull the wool over a fighter's eyes!
Who would want a job like that, getting paid
A few guilders to have their teeth smashed in?

That is the little man, the small and decent man,
The very little man wearing his off-the-peg suit,
The little man with a dicky on his chest,
The poverty-stricken, nerve-wracked, little, little man.

These days we take good care of our fellow man
If you can't get a job, they give you a handout of eighteen guilders.
And there are lot of layabouts who prefer to be lazy than tired
Who think: eighteen guilders for nothing, I won't say No to that!

They all complain about the bosses and their capital
But who is the real victim of that ideal of freedom?
That is the little man, the small and decent man,
The very little man wearing his off-the-peg suit,
The little, little man in the Jaeger-copy underpants,
The poverty-stricken, nerve-wracked, little, little man.

There are several other verses to the song but, without an explanation of Dutch society in the thirties, they would be incomprehensible to the reader. They show the Little Man to be a monument to jealousy. He believes himself to be the victim of everyone who does not wear an off-the-peg suit, from vice-admirals to unemployed good-for-nothings, from the idle rich in their villas to overpaid sporting heroes. He is the stereotype of the resentful, lower middle-class citizen, the *petit-bourgeois* who rejects everything that is not a part of his narrow world. In retrospect, it is not so surprising that lyricist Jacques van Tol hosted a pro-Nazi radio programme which included an anti-Semitic version of his most successful work. After the war, the 'little men' treated him in typical fashion – he remained one of the country's most productive songwriters, but his name was never mentioned.

Anyone who wishes to be decent imposes considerable restrictions on their behaviour

It is also typical that the *Kleine Man* is still widely seen as a brilliant apologia for the hard-working loner. Singers who include it in their repertoire can count on loud applause before they have sung the first note. Yet the basic characteristic of the little man is that he does not dare to live his life to the full. He feels that his square metre is under threat, but he never uses that scarce space to create something unique. Everything he does complies with what Dirk Witte refers to as *Het Fatsoen*, what commonly passes for Decency, the 'Right Thing To Do'. Since the advent of Pim Fortuyn and Jan Peter Balkenende, this is now known as 'norms and values'. That sounds a little more philosophical, but like the Decency of earlier generations, norms and values mean standing up for old ladies in the tram, not getting angry if something irritates you and being polite to the people around you.

Anyone who wishes to be decent imposes considerable restrictions on their behaviour. Witte himself was a 'decent' man – he ran the family timber business. His songs may have been something of an escape valve for the enforced decency within which he had to live his life. That is why they were accepted. A decent man may make unconventional statements now and then, as long as they do not affect his daily behaviour. And if that does happen, punishment is swift and merciless, as Witte himself was aware: 'And then they ignore you if you do it your own way'. The price of non-conformism is isolation. Like Big Brother, 'they' are watching you.

They may be watching you, but they are not very likely to take any steps against unconventional behaviour, either collectively or as individuals. They have too much respect for another's privacy. The media regularly report stories of children living in large towns and cities who have been abused by their parents for years while the neighbours simply pretended not to know anything was going on. Or perhaps they genuinely did not notice anything strange. People in the Netherlands have a blind spot for what others do in the privacy of their own homes. The neighbours will often be heard to say: 'We never had much contact with that family anyway'.

Fatsoen shares a common root with many similar words in other languages. It is clearly linked to the English 'fashion', and in eighteenth and nineteenth century texts you sometimes find it used in this way, to describe clothing. But it now has a far wider application. The definition in the Van Dale, the standard dictionary of the Dutch language, is one of the longer entries: 'Everything that is considered to belong in the realm of common decency and acceptable behaviour, whether in the moral or the formal sense (that is good manners in the widest meaning of the term), and particularly what is understood as conventional.' A very careful choice of words! The use of the passive form cleverly evades the question of who decides where the limits of decency lie. It is also very clear that *fatsoen* has a great deal to do with appearances, otherwise the concept would not be described by a word that originally referred only to clothing. It is concerned with the way people behave in public. You can walk around naked in your own home, if you so wish, as long as the curtains are drawn. In other words, it is a system of norms and rules of behaviour which have developed as part of the collective process. If you want to belong, you have to abide by these norms, or at least appear to do so to the outside world.

Older people often complain that traditional *fatsoen*, just like norms and values, is on the way out. This may, however, not be entirely true; *fatsoen* is not so much being eroded as fragmented. Society is being divided up into a plurality of collective 'spaces', each with its own form of *fatsoen*. This is entirely compatible with the basic social principle that each group should be given its own space in which to develop as it pleases. Staying with the example of walking around naked, a good illustration of this is nude bathing. When it became popular in the 1970s, most bathing resorts set up nudist beaches. Wearing a swimsuit is not optional on these beaches, it is forbidden by general consensus. It is also inadvisable to sit up on the dunes fully clothed and ogle the naked bodies running around in front of you. You will soon receive a visit from a delegation of 'heavies', whose muscles are all the more impressive for being totally exposed. They will inform you in no uncertain terms that you are offending the *fatsoen* of the beach. You either play by the rules, or you stay away – there is no middle way.

These naked defenders of decency have something in common with the residents of the small town of Staphorst, in the Province of Overijssel. The latter are strict Calvinists and are very serious about observing the Sabbath as a sacred day of rest. Even driving a car is considered to be in conflict with the Will of God. The faithful do not wish to be confronted with such sinful behaviour as they walk to the church for morning and evening service. They therefore walk along the middle of the street and do not get out of the way of any vehicles that may chance to come along. If drivers sound their horns or try to accelerate past, there is a good chance that the locals will defend their beliefs with their fists. The people of Staphorst, like the nude swimmers, do not wish others to offend their *fatsoen*.

Anyone who lives in a community with many practising Christians who still like to see the Sabbath observed would be ill-advised to cut their grass or repair their car in the street on a Sunday. Clean the car in the garage, but don't make too much noise. Of course, it is everyone's right to do as they please and the radicalism that still rules in Staphorst is rare. Nevertheless, most Dutch people have a mental signal that is triggered if they fear that their actions are likely to give offence. This places considerable limitations on individual behaviour in its more extreme forms. An Asian anthropologist suggested that so many Dutch people leave their curtains open in the evening to show passers-by that, inside too, nothing is going on that may cause offence. This is clear evidence that the Dutch have a strong tendency to conformity and, if true, it is bad news for those from the *'Mens, durf te leven'* school. Then you would be better off humming to yourself in secret or joining a sub-culture that does not demand such extreme individualism. That should not be too difficult. Even sado-masochists have magazines and through which they can contact fellow s&m enthusiasts. The magazine is, however, sent to them in a plain envelope. That is perhaps understandable, but the same applies to the *GayKrant* – with a circulation of over 26,000, the world's most widely read magazine for homosexuals. In spite of the fact that homosexuality is broadly accepted in the Netherlands and that the law forbids discrimination against gays, most readers consider it safer if the postman or the neighbours do not know that they are subscribers.

No one wants to risk giving offence. You never know who might turn out to be the little man in the off-the-peg suit. With such a wide variety of clothing available these days it has become very difficult to spot him at first glance.

Is this true all the time and everywhere? The people of the Netherlands have never been particularly bothered about the fundamentalist Christians in their midst, as long as they stayed in their village enclaves in places like Staphorst and Stavenisse. But it is a different matter if, as has happened in recent decades, people with a similar lifestyle appear in the middle of their large cities. One of the consequences of mass migration from Turkey and Morocco, Islam has become the second largest religion in the Netherlands and, in many towns and cities, you now see minarets among the church towers. Since the early 1990s, Islam in the Netherlands has experienced a sort of reformation. The traditional popular Islam of Turkish and Berber origin started to be replaced by a modern interpretation, which nevertheless presented itself as the true Word of God. The old traditions had to make way for literal compliance with what was written in the Koran and the

Rita Verdonk, Minister for Integration and Immigration, offers her hand to an imam. He refuses to shake it, however, because his interpretation of Islam forbids him from touching any other woman than his own wife. A clash of cultures: the minister feels insulted and the imam feels that he has been placed in an impossible position. During a later visit to a mosque, Queen Beatrix decided not to shake hands and chose another form of greeting that showed the required respect and cordiality.

Hadith, a series of stories about the Prophet Mohammed which had been passed down through the generations. The symbols of this fundamentalist interpretation of the Islamic faith were the headscarf, the veil and the long robes which its female followers donned en masse. The men restricted themselves to wearing a beard.

These reborn believers read in the Koran all kinds of instruction about a strict division between men and women. Men were not allowed, for example, to touch any women other than their mothers, sisters and wives. The more radical among them rejected practically all worldly pleasures, including music. And they advocated application of the Sharia, traditional Islamic law.

And so it happened that when the liberal minister for integration and immigration in the second Balkenende government, Rita Verdonk, approached a strict imam with an outstretched hand, he apologized that his faith forbade him to shake hands with a woman. 'Then we have a lot to talk about,' replied the minister. This instantly made her the mouthpiece of much discontent among the public, who found this urban fundamentalism much less acceptable than that of the villagers of Staphorst. This strict form of Islam was widely seen as a threat and, especially since the attack on the Twin Towers on 11 September 2001, its followers were seen as a fifth column secretly planning to take over. In many people's eyes, a strict Islamic lifestyle had nothing to do with traditional Dutch *fatsoen* or modern norms and values. These critics were always very quick to claim that the Koran condoned the beating of women and that the repression of women and a hatred of homosexuality were essentials of the Islamic faith.

Few people actively caused any problems for Islamic women who chose to wear headscarves or veils, but it was made clear to strict Muslims that their way of life would be met with widespread disapproval. Anyone who is themselves too visibly in public, can feel the disapproval of those around them. In the new century that approval was all too often associated with antisocial behaviour. In the media the focus was on a new phenomenon: groups of young people hanging around in street. Teenagers of both sexes would hang out at the local shopping centre or – even worse – actually take over a corner of it. They are showing that they have an 'urban' lifestyle; the young men are machos and the girls are bitches. They come across as a little threatening. That – the shoppers think to themselves – is what has become of our norms and values. People have always been critical of youth, but it has a new edge to it, if a segment of public opinion fears the end of all values and talk about the young scooter-driving hooligans on the market square in the same breath as terrorists who fly airplanes into the World Trade Centre. That creates a feeling that there is no end to it and that the 'others' no longer recognize any limitations on their behaviour. Part of the Dutch tolerance for different faiths and lifestyles is the principle that people must always know when to stop, especially in public. In a country full of minorities, you should be proud of your beliefs, but not wear them on your sleeve. Dutch citizens are only princes and princesses in their own square metre. Anyone indulging in imperialism – by imposing their lifestyle on others – is asking for trouble, because they are also attacking the foundations of Dutch society. Women can therefore defend their right to wear a niqaab on the same grounds of non-discrimination that make gay marriages possible. However, if you vociferously demand the right to put your women into niqaabs while in the same breath condemning gay and other lifestyles, you will get a hard time, for you are pulling away the cornerstone of the social contract in the Netherlands.

You don't want to burden others too much with your own emotions

When my father died, it was up to me – as the eldest son – to say a few words at the cremation. I drew up a short speech summarizing the basic principles by which my father had lived and explaining why the cremation service was not religious in character, in spite of my father's Catholic upbringing. He had foresworn his faith in the 1960s. Since many of the people who attended the service would probably not have seen my father for many years, I thought it a good idea to ask a number of friends and colleagues for their comments on what I intended to say. This proved to be a bad idea. Few of them were willing to comply with such an extraordinary request. They did not even know how they should respond. I frequently ignore certain accepted norms of behaviour, but this time I had gone too far. I was inviting people to enter a private world in which they clearly felt that they did not belong. I was giving them access to my emotions, but that also meant I was forcing the door behind which they kept their own concealed. I was making an unexpected attack on very sensitive terrain.

This made my mother study my speech even more closely. Not because she wished to influence what I said, but because she wanted to know what was coming. She, too, did not want to burst into tears during the cremation service.

It was a solemn occasion. It was permitted to show one's grief, but not with outbursts of sobbing. In such situations, you have to keep a 'stiff upper lip' and show that you are completely in control of yourself. In doing so, you not only show respect for yourself, but also for others who would perhaps not know how to respond to outward displays of grief. We in our family had always been suspicious of the true depth of sorrow or of joy, disliking people who cried or laughed too loudly, believing them guilty of melodramatic or theatrical behaviour. The service went entirely according to plan. There was an atmosphere of silent dignity and we all kept our tears to ourselves.

Even by Dutch standards, this perhaps went a little too far. We Van der Horsts have perhaps hidden our emotions away behind a particularly thick wall. Many Dutch readers will then be a little perplexed when they read the story of my father's funeral, but the mechanism behind it will be familiar to them. You should be economical in expressing your emotions and shield them from others because they are private. And, at the same time, you do not want to burden others with them. They belong in your own square metre and not 'out there'.

This is perhaps not entirely true. You may be able to express your feelings – in a controlled way – in a safe environment. For example, to someone in a professional capacity. In the past, this was the monopoly of preachers and priests. Listening, offering consolation and good advice was – and still is – the main component of the service they provide. This is why they are rarely praised for the quality of their liturgical talents. Their strength lies in their ability to alleviate suffering, their wisdom and the moderation they practice in their contact with others.

But secularization is well advanced in Dutch society. The Netherlands now has the greatest concentration of psychiatrists in the world. You can permit a psychiatrist to enter your own square metre in the same way that you can admit a plasterer, painter or electrician to allow them to do their work. These people do not bring in their personalities, but knowledge of their chosen trade. So the psychiatrist always has a box of tissues at the ready – here you can and may cry as much as you please.

Nevertheless, Dutch society is full of unexpressed sorrow. This causes psychological damage that does not heal overnight. A famous photographer, who lost two children in a road accident, found respite from his grief when he visited the Sahel. He was able to talk about the tragedy there without people being shocked. They knew what it was like to lose their children and they treated grief as a perfectly natural phenomenon. The Dutch tend to leave people alone with their sorrow and loss, as though they do not dare to touch it. And those who are suffering keep their feelings to themselves. This makes grieving a long and lonely process.

In recent years, a number of extremely successful television programmes seem to have undermined this aversion to outward displays of emotion. It started with dating shows in which, by playing a sort of game, the contestants choose a partner to go on holiday with. On their return, they reappear on the show and tell the studio audience and the viewers how it all went. By far the most popular show of this type tried to bring together couples who had broken up and to turn long-standing animosity into friendship. The host acted as a conciliator. He did not actually enter the homes of the people he was hoping to reconcile, but would take them to a caravan nearby where they would be shown a videofilm of the other partner, who would declare their love for the injured party or promise to mend their ways. Tears would flow freely and the final reconciliation would take place in the studio in front of the live audience.

A show that went a step further was Big Brother, a Dutch idea which was imitated around the world. Different kinds of people were brought together in a large house, and their every move was captured on camera. Viewers were enthralled: What would happen? Who would fall in love with whom? Would they end up in bed together? Big Brother was a massive success. In no time it was followed by reality soaps, in which the rich and famous were filmed going about their daily business. The high – or perhaps, low – point was a series in which TV personality Patty Brard took an enema together with a large number of friends. They all seemed to empty out on the screen, in all senses of the word.

All appearances to the contrary, the success of these shows actually reinforces the Dutch tradition of not burdening others with your problems. The 'victims' do not expose their suffering or joy to a small number of individuals who are physically present, but to an anonymous unknown mass of people. There is no interaction. This is television as therapy. Sorrow can be expressed openly, public reconciliation can take place, joy and happiness need no longer be suppressed, while the others, the onlookers – even though there may be millions of them – remain at a distance. The television proves to be a perfect escape valve for emotions that would otherwise stay bottled up. And the members of the audience, in their turn, need not be embarrassed about this public show of emotion. For them, too, there is no opportunity to interact. They can satisfy their curiosity without having to suffer the consequences. They do not have to look the other way, as they do when the see the couple kissing at the bus stop or when the neighbours start fighting on the stairs. Suffering and happiness may be expressed, as long as it is at a distance. And, of course, they can consider themselves fortunate that they have never had to expose themselves in such a way, and certainly not literally.

Friendship rarely provides a safety net for survival

The programme that has been reconciling all those enemies since 1992 has a snappy title: All You Need Is Love. As I said before, happiness is a matter of satisfying immaterial needs and this is the basis of a genuine relationship. Friendship rarely provides a safety net for survival. People who find themselves in financial problems will not easily turn to their friends for a loan. You might go on holiday with friends, you will visit each other's homes, but the friendship should not become entangled with material debts. Furthermore, the door of the Dutch home is not always open, even for the closest of friends. Many people dislike visitors who arrive uninvited. It messes up their plans and, since they were not expecting guests, they generally have nothing to offer them and feel that they are failing in their duty as hosts. In practice, it will generally not be as bad as I suggest, but the principle remains the same.

In contrast to many other peoples, the Dutch never allow for a possible unexpected extra mouth to feed at the table. It is simply 'not done' to turn up uninvited at a friend's house around dinner time and afternoon visitors will be expected to leave again around five, because the evening meal is traditionally eaten between six and seven. If they stay any later, the hosts will start to feel uncomfortable. They cannot start cooking until the guests have left. If they do, it is tantamount to inviting them to dinner and they do not have enough food to do that.

The first way to solve this problem is to try and make it clear to your guests that it is time for them to go. You can do this primarily by allowing each topic of conversation to run dry, by remaining silent instead of responding. Some very direct people might then stand in front of the window and say: 'Well, it's dried up now, you can be on your way' – especially if the sun has been shining all day. If this does not shift the more tenacious of guests, the invitation to dinner will then follow, but it will not come from the heart. People only visit each other at dinner time in the Netherlands if they have been expressly invited to do so. The invitation will then generally be for a clearly stated time. You must not be late, and certainly not cancel half an hour before, because a dinner invitation is a serious matter. It means breaking one's normal routine, extra shopping and a lot of work. For these reasons, there is always something a little festive about having people to dinner. You cannot serve them just any old dish. It must at least be a little more elaborate than your average daily meal. Other types of invitation – 'Drop round for a drink this evening' means from eight o'clock on, after dinner – should also be taken seriously, if a specific day or time is mentioned. Only when a Dutch acquaintance leaves you with *Wij zien elkaar* – 'I'll see you around' – or *Wij moeten snel eens een afspraak maken* – 'We'll have to make a date to meet some time soon' – can you be sure that you can safely take your leave with no strings attached.

And so the Dutch live their lives in the quiet privacy of their own square metre. 'Home' is one of their most cherished concepts. It is a familiar theme in television commercials. Home is where the soup is. And the coffee. If you want to see the ideal Dutch family in action, watch the coffee commercials. Once the coffee is on, the situation becomes *gezellig*.

'Gezelligheid' is a form of behaviour, of communication

Gezelligheid is another Dutch word that defies translation. It describes an atmosphere that the Dutch proudly believe is unique to them. The word itself is closely related to *gezelschap*, company. It is a form of behaviour, of communication, which keeps the people involved together because they appreciate it and it makes them feel good. *Ongezellig* behaviour on the part of one of the participants can ruin the atmosphere entirely. And the chance is always there because in a café or at a party, it is no longer necessary to search for a consensus. People are there for fun. They can and do stand up for their opinions. Controversial statements can be heard from all corners. The danger then is that the *gezelligheid* will be disrupted if someone does not permit another to voice their opinions and attacks them personally.

My mother and father used to visit my grandparents every Sunday. My uncles and their families were also expected to appear, and each of them took two cigars for my grandfather. Everyone was given a cup of coffee and then they would settle down to argue about social problems. They never talked about family matters, that would be too close. I was a small child at the time, but I remember my father rising to his feet and – as if he were addressing a mass gathering – declaring: 'The tram is a prehistoric means of transport.' He said it very emphatically, making it clear that he would tolerate no objection to this clearly true statement, but my

Old-fashioned Dutch gezelligheid. *This is a traditional birthday celebration. No one takes anything for themselves – the hosts pass round the drinks and snacks, making sure of course that no one goes without.*

uncles nevertheless entered into a heated argument with him on the subject. I saw my aunts looking at their spouses, warning them not to go too far, but they did not intervene.

I remember another occasion when this happened. It was in the 1950s, when the Cold War was at its height. My father had just made another of his controversial statements.

'Then', said my uncle Anton, 'you are a Communist'.

'Of course I'm not a Communist'.

'You are a Communist'.

Then my grandmother intervened. 'Easy now, boys,' she said 'There's someone lyng sick in bed next door.' She used to tell us children that too, when we were making too much noise.

Then my aunt Eugenie, uncle Anton's wife, said: 'Give it a rest, Anton, let's keep it *gezellig*.' All of my aunts forbade my uncles from talking about politics at family gatherings, because we were all there for the *gezelligheid*. My mother said once, after we had returned from a funeral: 'It's terrible really, but it's always so *gezellig* afterwards.'

Gezelligheid is a common good and everyone has a moral duty to preserve it. The main component is communication, contact between two or more persons, often – depending on the nature of the occasion and of the people taking part –

facilitated by the consumption of coffee, tea, alcohol or even weed (passing a joint around is a very successful means of breaking the ice). Anyone who disrupts this *gezelligheid*, this togetherness, is in for trouble, as the seventeenth century biography of admiral Michiel de Ruyter clearly illustrates:

'Once, on a horse-drawn barge, someone uttered scandalous things in his presence against the Government and he responded with great severity, saying that he was a servant of the Land and that he could not tolerate such language. He ordered the speaker to be silent and, after several warnings, told him that if he did not cease his slanderous accusations, he would order the captain to put him ashore. When all this was to no avail, he seized the troublemaker, picked him up and, strong as he was, set him overboard not far from the land, where he concealed himself.'

The admiral, who had a hero's reputation throughout Europe, could be a little short-tempered. Those who disrupt the *gezelligheid* these days need not fear that they will be manhandled, except in a café where the drink has been flowing a little too freely. They will, however, be studiously ignored and will notice that it is increasingly difficult for them to draw up a chair and join in the conversation around the table. They have not respected the principle of 'each to his own' and such behaviour is not easily forgiven.

Be warned – De Ruyter did not set the man overboard because of his opinions, but because of the way he presented them. Someone like that did not belong in the saloon of a barge, where the whole group had to spend many hours cooped up together and *gezelligheid* was the best remedy for boredom. The admiral wanted only to prevent the atmosphere from being ruined. In spite of his personal piety – he read theological books for pleasure – his biographer claims that he was not a quibbler. 'He was always loath to hear other forms of Christianity, or even those who live outside of Christendom, being condemned wholesale. He preferred to reserve judgement. Although he saw no reason for hope, since there is no salvation without Christ, he himself not only observed that this was true, but also recognized an unfathomable deepness. Wishing to be charitable in judgement of both, he left the matter to the Will of God. He was also greatly displeased when those who were misguided in their religious beliefs were the subject of mockery and scorn.'

The *gezelligheid* that is found among groups of friends on café terraces is a continuation of the harmony that ought to reign in the household. The Dutch word for living room, *huiskamer*, itself suggests a cosy, homely atmosphere. Once the stove has been lit, the room is *gezellig*. *Zet die tv nou eens af en laten we gezellig naar bed gaan*, people will say to their partners. 'Switch off the television for a change and let's go bed.' The use of the word *gezellig* is intended to make the suggestion sound more enjoyable than what the other person is doing at the time. Similarly: *Wees eens gezellig en leg dat boek weg*, 'Put your book down and be a bit sociable.'

Gezellig can also be used to describe a room or a home. Some houses may be furnished in modern styles, with their cool colours and sharp contrasts, while others – perhaps with more traditional interiors – are really *gezellig*. *De Rotterdammer*, the now defunct daily newspaper, advertized itself as *Een gezellige krant!*, believing that it, in doing so, it would create the right homely image to attract the Protestant families at which it was aimed.

Kees van Kooten and Wim de Bie, two of the Netherlands' best known cabaret artists in the latter part of the twentieth century, produced the perfect description of *gezelligheid* in their song '1948'. Ironically enough, it is set to the music of Gilbert O'Sullivan's 'Alone Again'. The loneliness is there, but in a very different form.

> *Buiten huilt de wind om 't huis*
> *Maar de kachel staat te snorren op vier*
> *Er hangt een lapje voor de brievenbus*
> *En in de tochtigste kieren zit papier*
> *Wij waren heel erg arm*
> *En niemand hield van ons.*
> *Maar we hadden thee en nog geen tv*
> *Maar wel radio en lange vingers*
> *We gingen nog in bad*
> *Haartjes nat, nog even op*
> *Totdat vader zei: 'Vooruit naar bed'*
> *Dan kregen we een kruik mee*
> *Gezichten op 't behang*
> *Maar niet echt van binnen bang*
> *Toen was geluk heel gewoon.*
>
> *Buiten huilt de wind om 't huis*
> *Maar moeder breit een warme sjaal*
> *En het ganzenbord op tafel stond er*
> *De volgende morgen nog helemaal*
> *Ook gingen wij naar 't bos*
> *Daar zijn we toen verdwaald*
> *Van de weg geraakt, carrière gemaakt*
> *Heel die pannekoekensmaak vergeten.*

Outside the wind is howling round the house
But the stove is turned up to four.
There's a flap in front of the letter box
And the draughts are stuffed with paper.
We were very poor
And no one loved us,

But we had tea and no TV,
Just the radio and sponge fingers.
We all had a bath, got our hair wet
And were allowed to stay up for a while
Until father said: 'Off to bed',
Then we were given a hot water bottle.
There were faces on the wallpaper
But we weren't really scared, back then
When we were always happy.

Outside the wind is howling round the house
But mother is knitting a warm scarf
And the board game was still on the table
Untouched the following morning.
And we went to the woods
Where we got ourselves lost,
Couldn't get back and made our careers
And forgot the taste of pancakes.

The italics in the last four lines are mine. To the Dutch, the woods often represent wild and untamed nature, even though most woods in the Netherlands today have been planted. In the woods, the trees are high. You can see little sky and nothing of the horizon that are so familiar out in the open polders. The woods are a strange world, where you soon lose your sense of direction. *Iemand het bos insturen*, to send someone 'into the woods', means to let them down or abandon them.

The woods signify insecurity and danger. Van Kooten and De Bie described the lost haven of *gezelligheid*, from which they have been exiled as they have pursued their careers. They are a living testimony to *Mens, durf te leven*. They went their own way. But, with hindsight, they realize that they have lost their ways and that the *gezelligheid* has gone forever. That feeling of complete safety and continuity has dissipated for good into the mists of time. They now have to survive in the cold light of reality. The warmth – so often associated with *gezelligheid* and, as is shown by the references to the stove, the water bottle and the scarf, one of the main attributes of this paradise lost – is the price they have paid for success and freedom.

It is this that stops people from turning their back on the *gezelligheid*, and going out into the wide world, or at least giving the princedom on their square metre the appearance of an absolute monarchy.

The air is permeated by the stifling smell of sprouts

Yet much modern literature deals with attempts to escape hearth and home, traditions and all forms of *gezelligheid*, which are now seen as suffocating. This passage is taken from the first and still best known work of this genre, *De Avonden* – The Evenings – written by Gerard Reve and published in 1947. When this great writer of the people, as he came to be known, died his funeral, on 15 April 2006, was almost a national event:

'While she cleared the table, his father went to lie down on the divan, decided to take off his shoes, sat for moment staring in front of him and then stood up and walked to the bookcase. Just before he reached it, he slipped, his left leg shot up in the air, but he regained his balance. 'Whoops!' shouted his mother. 'He's alright', Frits said. 'You don't need to yell so.'

His father took a book out of the bookcase, went back and lay on the divan, and pushed his free hand through his hair. 'Uh oh, the stove', said his mother. She looked at the fire and added: 'It's burning away fine in there. Don't touch it. Just leave it as it is, with the kettle keeping it open.' She showed them how the aluminium kettle had to rest against the top of the flap of the stove, so that it stayed open a little. 'Otherwise it will all be burned up within an hour', she explained. She went into the kitchen.

Frits looked at the clock. 'Everything is lost', he thought. 'Everything is ruined. It is ten past three. But the evening will make up for a lot.'

Reve paints a similar picture to Van Kooten and De Bie, but to him it is an oppressive prison, in which the bars are formed by narrow-mindedness, hypocrisy and fear of the unknown. And the air is permeated with the stifling smell of sprouts. Sprouts are a kind of miniature cabbage with a slightly bitter taste, and most children hate them. If they are boiled for a long time, a penetrating odour fills the whole house. The smell is a reminder that the vegetable is as good as tasteless (boiled for only a few minutes, sprouts are delicious, but this is the modern method of cooking them. Traditionally, they were left on until all the taste had been boiled out of them), that what little taste they do have is bitter. It recalls their sallow green colour, so representative of the colourless nature of existence itself. The smell of sprouts can be invoked by the uninspired words of a colourless politician, the cliché-ridden reports of a burned-out media commentator or the exaggerated caution of a company director.

Where *gezelligheid* reigns, there are always those who believe they can detect the smell of sprouts. For them, it is not liberating, but confining. The unwritten rules no longer help you to be yourself in company, but enforce uniformity in thought and deed. All colour fades. You feel that you would like to give everyone a 'good kick in the butt'. Silently, you revolt against what you now see as *lulligheid*. *Lullig* is yet another of those Dutch words that covers a multitude of meanings in English.

The Dutch-English Van Dale charmingly translates it as 'shitty, cruddy, crappy', but *lullig* extends to a whole range of unpleasant aspects of human nature. If you accuse someone of being *lullig*, you may consider them feeble, stupid, mad, lacking in character, nasty or irritating. The word crops up in a wide variety of common Dutch expressions, such as *Doe niet zo lullig* – Don't be such a shit – or: *Zo'n grote vent op een vouwfiets is een lullig gezicht* – A large man like that looks like a wanker on a fold-up bike. *Lulligheid kent geen tijd*: this is how the well-known columnist Nico Scheepmaker paraphrased the expression *Gezelligheid kent geen tijd*, roughly equivalent to the English 'pleasant hours fly past'.

On the Internet, they throw all caution to the wind

The requirement to be *gezellig* and to hold oneself in in public keeps the people of the Netherlands on a tight rein, so that they are forced to live a life of *lulligheid*. For the past ten years or so, however, they have found a place where disapproving looks cannot make them abide by the rules: the Internet, the virtual Netherlands. There, often under the cover of a nickname, they throw all caution to the wind and, from what they say, you can tell that is especially the Little Men (and Women) in their off-the-peg clothes who can finally say what they really feel and create the impression, as they type away frantically on their keyboards, that they are avidly embracing the sentiments of 'Mens durf te leven' and daring to live life to the full. The most popular site to do this is the weblog *Geen Stijl*. *Geen stijl*, literally 'no style,' can mean in Dutch that something is out of fashion, but also, interestingly enough, that something is anti-social or not done. *Geen Stijl*, which was bought out early in 2006 by the visionary management of the popular daily newspaper De Telegraaf, presents scornful criticism of the events of the day, in a way that exactly reproduces the tone and style of the Little Man in the jargon of the twenty-first century, of the baseball cap and hip-hop. On 8 May 2006 the site carried the following comments on what was considered to be excessive police behaviour after a party in the village of Pijnacker:

> *kudthippies. moet je maar in een fatsoenlijk dorp wonen.*
> fucking hippies. You should go and live in a decent village.
> daskapitalist 08-05-06 @ 10:31

> *dat krijg je met die media-geile crimefighters met prestatie contracten. com-municeer met de burger via de accept giro of de lange lat. laten we eens wat aan die politiestaat doen voordat het echt te laat is..*
> that's what you get with publicity-obsessed crime fighters with per-formance contracts. communicate with the people with a direct debit fine or a long stick. let's do something about the police state before it's too late...
> SloopKogel (Demolition Ball) (wie zijn 08-05-06 @ 10:32

Ze zien er inderdaad wel gevaarlijk uit die gasten! Waarom niet gewoon meteen met scherp schieten? Wat een gezelligheid, hadden de heren van het kontneukende ambtenarenapparaat -herstel- smeris een cursus frustratie leauzen??

They look pretty dangerous, those guys! Why didn't they just use live ammo and be done with it? What fun, had the brown-nose bureaucrats – sorry, the cops – been on a frustration-release course or something??

de melkboer (dairy farmer) 08-05-06 @ 10:33

Fijn he, de ME. Ik kan me een namiddag in Den Haag herinneren. Toen gingen ze lekker 'studentje slaan'. 250 mensen moesten zich bij de EHBO laten behandelen. Daarna mensen laten voorkomen. Omdat wel iedereen schuldig moet worden bevonden vragen ze dan een random andere agent even te getuigen dat de 'verdachte' in kwestie met stenen gooide of zoiets dergelijks. Ja, de politie, je beste vriend.
Laten we hopen dat er dit maal wel een paar van die klootzakken ontslagen. Vooral de leidinggevenden. Want die zijn verantwoordelijk.
Nice guys, eh, the riot cops? I remember one afternoon in The Hague, when they came to have a bit fun beating up students. 250 people had to go to emergency. And then a bunch of guys had to go to court. And because everyone had to be found guilty, they got a random cop to testify that the 'suspect' had been seen throwing stones or whatever. That's the police for you – your best friend.
Let's hope they sack a few of the bastards this time. Especially the top brass. They're the ones who are responsible for it all.

ShimoKura 08-05-06 @ 10:33

A contribution on plans to introduce immigrants to the natural environment in the Netherlands generated a lot of comments, including the following:

Als de allochtone medemensch belangstelling had voor de natuur was ie er gaan wonen. In alloland zit tussen de stortplaatsen nog heel wat meer natuur dan hier. Bossen vol vrijheidsstrijders, stropers en bijtende beesten - dat dan weer wel.
If our fellow man of foreign origin was interested in the natural environment, he would have gone and lived in it. There's a lot more nature in between the garbage tips over there than there is here. And forests full of freedom fighters, poachers and wild animals....

boomklever2 (nuthatchz) 08-05-06 @ 13:17

Geef ze een graties rondleiding op de sexparking
Give them a free tour of the casual sex parking spots
Traag (Slow) 08-05-06 @ 13:22

In 2006 *Geen Stijl* received a little under a thousand reactions like this every day – and that was after the site moderator had removed the more extreme contributions. It was one of the first weblogs in the Netherlands. Less than four years after the phenomenon first arrived, there were some 600,000 blogs in the country, most of which were hardly active. A number of them however were outlets for very outspoken opinions, on which the contributors made no attempt at all to keep it *gezellig* of within socially accepted limits. Anyone getting to know the Netherlands only through the Internet is confronted by a cacophony of seriously conflicting opinions, slanging matches and virtual fist fights. That is by no means unique: it is becoming clear throughout the world that Internet communication does not always bring people together, to put it mildly. But in the Netherlands, the contrast between actual and virtual reality is very marked. Are all these weblogs perhaps a safety valve to ensure that the social cooking pot does not boil over? Or do they reveal a reality which has long been kept in the dark by the blanket of pillarization and the compromise culture? And if the latter is the case, are we not sitting on a volcano that is waiting to erupt? It is much too early to answer this question. Or to speculate on whether we are living in a Jekyll and Hyde society. Perhaps it is good to remember that, in the heyday of the pillars, there was just as much polemic discussion in the media that was read by the grassroots members – although of course, in that Victorian past, not an indecent word was spoken. In this light it is more appealing to choose the safety-valve model. Nevertheless there are many indications of a hardening of social attitudes and relations in the country.

It was this reality that partly led to the rapid rise of political newcomer Pim Fortuyn in 2002. He also tapped into another Dutch tradition of paternalism and consideration for others. Freedom was a great thing, but ended where that of another began. And the government must be prepared to protect people from themselves. Fortuyn tended to present his social criticism in terms of law and order. He attacked the policy of tolerance and promised to take a hard line on 'antisocial behaviour'. What it boiled down to was that Pim Fortuyn wanted to use the mighty hand of government against anything that threatened to disrupt traditional *gezelligheid*: junkies, Muslims, large companies and administrative conglomerates with their heartless mania for regulation, technocratic leaders and their a-political committees of experts in The Hague. After Fortuyn was assassinated, political parties – including those on the left – took over many of his ideas. In government circles, a new term came into vogue: *bemoeizorg*, which was used to describe involuntary or unsolicited care. As in the 1950s, anyone who overstepped the mark, got a visit from the social services. In Rotterdam, where Pim Fortuyn's party dominated local politics between 2002 and 2006, *stadsmariniers*, urban marines, patrolled the streets in problem neighbourhoods to force people to behave decently. Some local councils made people on social security benefits work for a couple of days a week, usually in municipal gardens or sheltered workshops, so that they could get used to the discipline. Newcomers to the Netherlands had to integrate as soon as possible. Rotterdam – Europe's largest port and an international transit centre – adopted a directive to this effect. Foreigners had to speak Dutch on the streets, if their conversation could be heard by passers-by. In 2006, left-wing parties won the municipal elections, but this did not lead to the end of *bemoeizorg*. On the contrary, the left just carried on in the same vein and announced an active policy aimed at antisocial behaviour and people who refused to conduct themselves according to the generally accepted norms of decency and order. At first sight, there seemed to be something of a cultural sea change under way. But that is not necessarily true. Since the murder of Pim Fortuyn, it has become fashionable for politicians to echo the rumblings of discontent in the country's bars and cafés in their speeches and statements. But that does not mean that they then follow up with effective measures. The country is regularly shocked by tragic stories of children being neglected, abused and sometimes even murdered, while the authorities have ignored countless warning signals and not removed them from their homes in time. Few official bodies clearly actually implemented the policy of *bemoeizorg*.

Despite all the rhetoric, the average Dutch person will not offer a helping hand unless asked to do so. This applies as much to individuals as to organizations. The initiative never comes from the helper. The most surly of passers-by will show you the way when you are lost, if you ask. But you can stand shivering in the rain for half an hour, while the wind keeps threatening to blow away the map in your hand, and no one will ask you if they can help. People in need of assistance or information have to go in search of it for themselves. There is a whole complex network of government bodies, associations and organizations set up purely to help people in a wide variety of ways. But you have to find them yourself. Rotterdam even has a Help and Information Centre to guide people through this labyrinth. You only find the right place by being referred to it. But once you are there, you will receive their every cooperation. Some organizations are so keen to be of assistance that they try to help people they can actually do very little for. This is particularly true of bodies that provide grants of various kinds. Grants are particularly suited to this way of working, because they usually give people a helping hand in some way or another but are provided only on request. Not wishing to send people away empty-handed, these organizations frequently refer unsuccessful applicants to other bodies where they might have more luck. These will then most likely give the client the same treatment. This polite form of rejection is known as *van het kastje naar de muur sturen*, sending people from pillar to post. It eventually drives people to distraction, especially those who do not understand the reasons for it. They think that they are being tricked and *aan het lijntje gehouden*. This expression, literally 'dangling on the end of line', means that a decision that is important to someone is continually postponed in the hope that they will give up and not come back. This is a very effective way of not having to provide a service without actually refusing outright. For foreigners who are not familiar with Dutch society, this frequently leads to a lot of unnecessarily wasted time. They apply to some organization or other for a grant of for assistance. They are told that their proposal or application is very interesting but unfortunately falls outside the criteria for acceptance. They are then given a list of other organizations that might be able to accommodate them. If this happens more than once, it is likely no one is genuinely interested in the proposal. There is only one way to find out – ask what is wrong with it, what the weak points are, why it is unacceptable. You will need a thick skin if you go this far, because this service will be provided with equal enthusiasm, most probably in no uncertain terms and with no respect for your feelings. After all, you did ask for it. It is, however, worth exposing your-self to such possible humiliation. You may finally realize that, until now, you have been chasing an illusion. Or, perhaps, a number of feasible alternatives will emerge.

A similar attitude is observable in many teachers, particularly at university level. With a few exceptions, who are frequently considered eccentric, they are generally unwilling to tell their students that their achievements are below par. They prefer to precede criticism with praise and therefore emphasize those areas in which the student in question has done well before moving on to make a number of critical remarks. It is very likely that the kind words are a sugar coating intended make the bitter pill a little easier to swallow.

In the business world, managers and other bosses have bitter pills aplenty to dish out. The problem for the recipient is to see through the sugar coating to the true meaning as soon as possible because, in the end, the pill will have to be swallowed anyway. 'Perhaps', your superior will say, 'it is time for us to go our separate ways'. Or: 'Perhaps your undeniable talents can be put to better use elsewhere'. But ask 'Where?' and you will receive a vague reply.

I speak from experience. While I was still a student, I was thrown out of a freelance job. This happened very unexpectedly and was, I thought at the time, totally unjustified. Now – sadder, wiser and older – I can recognize the signs that I failed to see at the time. My colleagues had accompanied their praise for my work with small criticisms – and the criticisms were always the same. My boss tried to cheer me up. Perhaps I could realize my potential elsewhere.

'But your company is the only one in the country in this field', I replied. 'And you take on the staff. That doesn't give me much of a chance.'

'Where there's a will, there's a way', he said. 'Look at Beckenbauer (he was a famous German footballer at the time). He doesn't keep to any pre-planned pattern of play. He goes his own way. He is as stubborn as a mule. But he is the one who gets that vital goal.'

'So, if you were the manager of the German national team, you would never have selected Beckenbauer?'

Touché, I thought. But the boss lost no time in escorting me personally to the door. I have never seen him again. Once a particular course of action has been decided upon, there is no going back. The discussion may continue, but only to explain the decision in greater detail. Anyone who responds emotionally or with the slightest signs of aggression only gives the other an opportunity to bring the whole painful experience to an end. The rules of the game have been broken. My boss wished only that he could fire me in an atmosphere that was as *gezellig* as possible. I ruined that for him.

Perhaps Beckenbauer would never have been selected for the Dutch national team. The antics of the Brazilian footballer Romario during his time as a player in the Netherlands bear witness to that. Romario comes from a culture where the people at the top live by a different set of rules. They can ignore the laws that apply to the mass of the people and generally get away with it. They celebrate this almost unlimited freedom by adopting a particularly brash kind of individualism. This made Romario – who played sublimely during the 1994 World Cup – totally unsuitable for the Dutch premier division club PSV Eindhoven. The Brazilian followed his own rules when it came to training and other agreements with the club. He more than made up for this with his dazzling performances in games, but never became the undisputed hero of the fans. His criticisms of the manager, his fellow players and the club directors – superficial in his eyes – eventually proved to be very fundamental. PSV and Romario parted company, and the star went to Barcelona. At the Spanish club he encountered similar problems with the Dutch manager, Johan Cruyff. Nevertheless, once he was out of the Dutch environment, Romario arguably developed into the best footballer in the world.

De kruik gaat net zo lang naar te water, tot zij barst, say the Dutch. The water jug goes so often to the well that it finally breaks. And then you are in trouble. You can try and preserve *gezelligheid* to the very last moment, but you cannot achieve the impossible. The contact is broken. You find yourself on the street. You go to a bar and stare at the wall. Across the road, on the other corner, there's another bar. One drink follows another. The barman puts them in front of you with a curt *Alstublieft.* It is sometimes not easy to be in Holland. What use is it then being a prince in your own square metre?

A hopeless prospect? Not necessarily: in the Netherlands, houses like this can soon be demolished to make way for new homes.

6

A land that is ticking like a time-bomb?
The Dutch and their ethnic minorities

Growing ethnic diversity. The empire and the collective guilty conscience. Increasing racial tension. The Netherlands as a haven for immigrants. Integration versus adaptation.

In 1995 the Postbank, part of the powerful ING concern, had a song written for a television commercial that was intended to show how much the company loved the Netherlands. The song became the dream of every commercial maker by becoming an instant hit. It is still played regularly on the radio and anyone making an optimistic speech about the state of the country likes to quote from it. This was how lyricist Eric Martin described the Netherlands in the final days of the twentieth century.

> *Land van 1000 meningen*
> *Het land van nuchterheid*
> *Met z'n allen op het strand*
> *Beschuit bij het ontbijt*
> *Het land waar niemand zich laat gaan*
> *Behalve als we winnen*
> *Dan breekt acuut de passie los*
> *Dan blijft geen mens meer binnen*
> *Het land wars van betutteling*
> *Geen uniform is heilig*
> *Een zoon die noemt z'n vader Piet*
> *Een fiets staat nergens veilig*
>
> *15 Miljoen mensen*
> *Op dat hele kleine stukje aarde*
> *Die schrijf je niet de wetten voor*
> *Die laat je in hun waarde*
> *15 Miljoen mensen*

Op dat hele kleine stukje aarde
Die moeten niet 't keurslijf in
Die laat je in hun waarde

Het land vol groepen van protest
Geen chef die echt de baas is
Gordijnen altijd open zijn
Lunch een broodje kaas is
Het land vol van verdraagzaamheid
Alleen niet voor de buurman
De grote vraag die blijft altijd
Waar betaalt 'ie nou z'n huur van

't Land dat zorgt voor iedereen
Geen hond die van een goot weet
Met nassiballen in de muur
En niemand die droog brood eet

A country of a thousand different thoughts
A country of common sense
Altogether on the beach
Breakfast of rusks and jam
A country where no one lets themselves go
Unless of course, we're winning
Then suddenly the passion breaks out
And no one's left indoors
A country where no one's petty
And no uniform is sacred
A son who calls his father Piet
And your bike isn't safe anywhere

Fifteen million people
On a very small piece of land
They don't tell you what to do
Each one to his own
Fifteen million people
On a very small piece of land
They won't wear a straitjacket
Each one to his own

A country full of protest groups
No boss who's really in charge
Curtains open all the time

A roll with cheese for lunch
A country full of tolerance
Except of course your neighbour
You always really want to know
How he manages to pay his rent

A country that cares for everyone
No one's left in the gutter
Nasi snacks from a machine in the wall
And no one has to eat dry bread

At that time, the Netherlands was experiencing a full-blown economic boom. It was time when journalists from around the world came to the country to tell their readers and viewers about the renowned 'poldermodel', the consensus model of government that gave everyone their own place under the Dutch sun, which then at least was rarely hidden behind the grey clouds of the low sky. I know exactly how long that sunny period lasted. It came to an end on 11 September 2001.

Every Dutch person knows exactly what he or she was doing when the airplanes flew into the World Trade Centre in New York. In the Netherlands it was late afternoon. I was in my office, when I heard someone say: 'Something strange has happened in New York. An airplane has flown into a skyscraper.' I tried to look at the CNN site but it was not accessible. The BBC site too could not handle the flood of concerned surfers. So I decided to do it the old-fashioned way and switched on the radio. The Radio 1 news channel reported that there had been an attack of some kind on the USA and that two planes had now flown into the Twin Towers of the World Trade Centre. It looked like a suicide attack and there was an unknown number of fatalities. I sent an email to my colleagues telling them the news and saying that I would switch on the television in our meeting room.

No one did any more work that day. Slowly but surely people came from all corners of the building to the meeting room. We all watched the television in silence. 'This is Pearl Harbour', someone said. It seemed clear to us all from the first moment that Arab or Islamic groups must have been behind the attack, although that was by no means certain in that first hour after the drama.

Why were we all so quiet in the meeting room? Partly of course because the catastrophe was so unimaginable, but also because we all understood that, from now on, everything would be different. The fall of the Berlin Wall and the demise of the Soviet Union had given the West a false sense of security for ten years. Now we knew that there were still enemies. And what was worse, there were enemies who did not even bother to engage in a war of words. Osama bin Laden and his followers restricted themselves to war and violence. Their message was intended only for the *umma*, the community of Muslims. Their frame of reference was alien to the Christian, agnostic and hedonistic majority of the populations. The terrorists of the 1970s, the Rote Armee Fraktion or the homegrown RaRa group fought from the view point of distorted Marxism. Their ideology was familiar and you might not empathize with their aims, but you could at least understand their arguments. But it was impossible also to understand these new terrorists from the Islamic world. In their messages to their fellow Muslims, they used sources like the Koran, the Hadith or the interpretations of old Koran scholars. They used concepts that were unknown to Westerners, but which obviously meant enough to them to justify mass murder.

In the last quarter of the twentieth century, the Netherlands had also not been spared terrorist attacks. Moluccan activist who fought for independence for their homeland, a group of islands in Indonesia, hijacked trains. The Dutch action group RaRa set fire to branches of the Makro wholesale chain in protest against apartheid in South Africa. In the early 1990s, they also blew up the house of state secretary for alien affairs Aad Kosto, because they were offended by his admission policy for aliens. Public opinion responded with indignation, while these days most people shrug their shoulders at such excesses.

But the attack on the Twin Towers was different. A wave of fear swept across the Netherlands, mixed with unadulterated rage. There were two reasons for that. First, there was the literal 'strangeness' of this new enemy. Perhaps this was the start of what Samuel Huntington had called the 'clash of cultures' in his contro-versial book at the end of the twentieth century. Second, many people in the Netherlands made a direct link between the attacks in New York and the radical demographic changes that had taken place in the past 40 years. The Netherlands now had a large immigrant population. In the 1960s, there was a severe shortage of labour in the productive sector. That had largely been filled by workers from Turkey and Morocco, but people from other countries also came here in search of a better future. One of the consequences was that the Netherlands now had a vital Islamic community with hundreds of thousands of members who lived mostly in the larger cities. Slowly but surely, they had learned to organize themselves. A network of Islamic schools emerged which, like its Christian counterparts, was subsidized by the government. The old garages and warehouses in which the faithful met to worship were replaced by new mosques, built along the lines of their counterparts in the Middle East. Nearly every town of any size now had at least a Turkish mosque with a dome and minarets, just like those in the suburbs of Istanbul, Ankara or Alanya. Sometimes the building was funded by rich Muslims from the Middle East. In Rotterdam, for example, this resulted in a mega-mosque with minarets 45 metres high which has become one of the landmarks of the city. This meant that a lot of (ex-)Christian Rotterdammers, who in recent decades had become accustomed to a hedonistic lifestyle, no longer felt at home in the city in which they had been born and bred.

The followers of Islam not only made their presence felt by building mosques. There was a sort of religious revival under way in the global Islamic community that seemed to have much in common with the Christian Reformation of the sixteenth century: 'born again' Muslims rejected many of the changes that had

The Mevlana mosque in Rotterdam: mosques are now a familiar sight in the Netherlands since Islam became the country's second-largest religion after Christianity.

taken place in their faith over the centuries as frivolous and lax and advocated a pure Islam, based on a 'literal' interpretation of the Koran and the Hadith, the accounts of Mohammed's fellow defenders of the faith. They saw this as the only way to adhere to the letter of God's word.

The preachers of this radical neo-Islam fought fiercely among themselves. Yet their doctrines were very similar. They all prescribed a devout way of life, with little room for pleasure. For outsiders, the most visible manifestation of this strict faith was the way in which women in particular were expected to dress. They had to protect themselves from the shameless gaze of strange men by wearing chaste clothing. That entailed at least a headscarf, but stricter preachers also insisted on loose black dresses and a niqaab, a veil that covers almost the entire face. Some women were even seen wearing burqas.

In the 1990s, more and more Islamic women chose to wear a headscarf. This identified them as Muslims. It became quite normal to see women in headscarves on market squares and in the centre of the major cities. Non-Muslims had a tendency to associate such clothing with the repression of women, even though those who wore it insisted that was not the case. Either way, Islam had become very visible in Dutch streets and squares. To the outside world, all those head-scarves were a reminder of repressive, Islam-based regimes like Saudi Arabia and Iran and made them wonder whether, if it came to it, they would prove loyal to the Netherlands? Did they also aim to turn the Netherlands into a theocratic totalitarian state along Iranian lines? Did they secretly support the attacks of 11 September? Had they established themselves in our naïve country as a fifth column? Homosexuals in the large cities complained that they were increasingly the victim of discrimination by aggressive hooligans of Moroccan origin. These young men were also strongly anti-Semitic, supporting their fellow Muslims in Palestine against Israel.

This presented the Dutch Muslims with an enormous PR problem. The image of their faith had been hijacked by terrorists, repressive theocratic regimes and extreme fundamentalists. Public opinion responded accordingly. President Bush may have visited a mosque the day after the attack on the Twin Towers, and Dutch political leaders may have drawn a sharp distinction between terrorists and followers of Islam, but for many people in the Netherlands none of this made any difference. Their worst suspicions had been confirmed, because the immigrants had never been popular.

During a survey carried out by the Social and Cultural Planning Office in 1993, 50% of those asked said that 'too many people of other nationalities lived in the Netherlands'. On the question of whether they would like to live next door to people of other nationalities, the participants in the survey were split roughly down the middle. Two years previously, 43% of Dutch people thought that there were too many foreigners living in the country. Other figures confirmed this trend of decreasing tolerance. In 1985, 20% of people said that Dutch families – however you may define 'Dutch' – should be given priority in the allocation of municipal housing.

So when populist politician Pim Fortuyn turned his attention to the Islamic threat shortly after 9/11, he could count on many willing ears. Fortuyn accused the establishment in the Netherlands of covering up all social problems in the Netherlands under a blanket of benevolence. He said that one of those problems was integration. Newcomers – and by that he primarily meant Muslims – had not been sufficiently integrated. He called for an immediate halt to immigration and a more resolute policy of assimilation for those already here: they should not only master the Dutch language but also our norms and values, as laid down in the Constitution. Fortuyn did not shrink from calling Islam a danger to democracy and traditional freedoms in the Netherlands. He even published a book in which he argued that radical Muslims could put a stop to the free-thinking practices that had become commonplace in the Netherlands since the 1960s. At the same time, however, he developed a broad political programme which had much in common with other political mavericks like the American Ross Perot. His scorn was largely aimed at bureaucracy, excessive regulation and the associated waste of money. He declared that the Netherlands should be run by entrepreneurs. The message was not new, but he presented it in very flamboyant fashion. In the spring of 2002, more and more Dutch voters took Pim Fortuyn into their hearts – he was the champion of the Netherlands as depicted in the song 15 miljoen mensen. And that friendly little country was now under threat. Finally, they said, someone had come along who was prepared to say out loud what they were thinking and who refused to be silenced.

Anyone in the Netherlands who identifies specific groups as the source and cause of social problems soon invokes memories of the Second World War. Then, the Nazis had accused te Jews of being responsible for just about all the evil in the world and Dutch society had allowed them to be taken away with very little effective protest. That must never happen again. In the media, established opinion-leaders therefore soon linked Fortuyn's ideas to fascist – or even worse, neo-Nazi - beliefs. In the late 1990 Frits Bolkestein, who was then leader of the liberal vvd, had already questioned the success of integrating newcomers in the Netherlands, especially those from Turkey and Morocco. That generated a lot of support and possibly also votes for his party, but politicians from other parties accused him of playing on people's onderbuikgevoelens, their primal fears and instincts. Since the vvd was a member of the governing coalition, Bolkestein was unable to push his ideas too far. Fortuyn however presented himself as the only alternative to the political establishment. He had to answer to no one. He refused to be seen as a neo-Nazi and accused those who accused him of such as 'demonizing' him. In doing so he made Huntington's ideas of a society under threat from alien cultures socially acceptable. From then on, anyone who had anything against foreigners could recoil in horror at any suggestion of onderbuikgevoelens or extreme-right leanings. They simply refused to be demonized. They had freed themselves from left-wing tyranny. They could speak openly and freely, and they no longer had to be politically correct.

Political correctness is a term used by conservative academics in the United States to describe the anti-discrimination policy at universities, which is their eyes has gone too far. Fortuyn and his sympathizers eagerly picked up on the concept, but changed its meaning. For them, political correctness meant closing your eyes to interracial differences and the threat of Islam. It means refusing to accept unpleasant facts and continuing to believe stubbornly in the fairy tale of the multicultural paradise. Political correctness is the same as political naivety. It would be a rude awakening for the politically correct among us when – sooner than you might think – the green flag of Islam was flying above the Binnenhof, the home of the Dutch government.

Attitudes like this have become a part of regular political discourse in the Netherlands since the turn of the century. They are aired on the opinion pages of the serious newspapers. They can be heard in parliament. In 2006 integration and immigration minister Rita Verdonk was the most popular politician in the country, because of her image as the person who had closed the country's borders to new-comers.

This runs entirely contrary to the free-thinking reputation that the Netherlands has enjoyed throughout the world in the past 40 years. When the Dutch Constitution was revised in the 1970s, it was given a new Article 1: 'All persons in the Netherlands shall be treated equally in equal circumstances. Discrimination on the grounds of religion, belief, political opinion, race or sex or on any other grounds shall not be permitted.' That was not intended as a new start, but as the end point of a desired process: everyone in the Netherlands must be allowed to be themselves as long as they did not disrupt others in their exercise of the same freedom. There are now serious proposals to replace this article with a text based on 'Judeao-Christian-humanist principles'.

It would be too superficial to blame the trauma of 9/11 for this. The Dutch used to call their colonies in Asia and Latin America 'the Tropical Netherlands'. They were different, strange and faraway. Now they encounter people from other cultures and with different lifestyles on the corner of the street. That takes a lotr of getting used to. Anyone who wants to understand the issue of immigration and integration as it is today in the Netherlands, the deep-seated and conflicting emotions that debate, must start at the beginning, with the Dutch empire, on which the sun never set and where, in the words of the seventeenth century governor-general Jan Pieterszoon Coen, 'something great was being achieved'.

The empire has left us with more than just Chinese-Indonesian restaurants

In the 1930s King Abdul Aziz, the creator of Saudi Arabia, asked his Dutch counterpart Queen Wilhelmina for advice, because he considered her the ruler of the most important Muslim kingdom in the world. After all, she was also the sovereign of the fifty-million Indonesians, shiploads of whom made the pilgrimage to Mecca every year.

The collective memory of the tropical Netherlands of the colonies is still with us at all levels. It helps to determine the way in which the Dutch respond to foreigners, ethnic minorities, immigrants, non-Dutch nationals or whatever other name is given to them. No one consciously makes the connection, but for unprejudiced outsiders, it is clearly visible. The empire has left us with more than just a Chinese-Indonesian restaurant in every village.

The use of the word 'empire' is not an exaggeration. Until 1945, the Netherlands was the world's third colonial power, after Britain and France. This was due to its possession of the Dutch East Indies, now Indonesia, a group of islands in South-East Asia that cover a surface area larger than the entire continent of Europe. The Netherlands also ruled six small islands in the Caribbean and Suriname (formerly also known as Dutch Guyana), a large country to the north of Brazil but which had

Dutch soldiers land on the coast of Indonesia.

a population of only a few hundred thousand. But it was the East Indies, with its population of 50 million (it is now four times that) that made the Netherlands a large colonial power. Possession of the Dutch East Indies was a source of great national pride. The majority of Dutch people believed that their fellow countrymen out there in *Insulinde* (Multatuli's name for the colony) or the *Gordel van Smaragd*, the Emerald Band, were doing a good job. They protected the people against the tyranny of the local chiefs and brought progress and civilization. There was a general assumption that the local population were grateful for the Dutch rule over their land. The Javan, it was commonly said, was the most kind-hearted being on the face of the earth. Reports of independence movements and nationalist leaders were therefore taken with a pinch of salt. They were rejected as isolated pockets of unrest which had not yet fully understood the beneficial nature of Dutch rule. They were completely isolated and of no significance whatsoever.

All good intentions ended in disaster

It was not so surprising that the Dutch public interpreted the situation so incorrectly. There were never more than 80,000 Dutch people in the colony at any one time. As a consequence of the development of mass tourism, more Dutch people have set foot in Indonesia since 1980 than in all the centuries before. Previous generations had to rely on hearsay and information filtered through the colonial sieve. The severing of the ties between the two countries was therefore an extremely traumatic experience. It created wounds that have still not healed 60 years later. Relations with Suriname, which became independent in 1975, are equally traumatic. Consequently, most people believe that the Dutch did not handle the process of decolonization at all well. All good intentions ended in disaster.

The basis for the Dutch colonial empire was laid in the Golden Age by the United East India and the West India Companies. As we have seen, they were trading companies whose main purpose was to ship foreign goods of all kinds to Europe. They tried to acquire an import monopoly, and did not flinch from the use of weapons to achieve this aim. The East India Company, for example, occupied the entire coastal area of Ceylon (now Sri Lanka) effectively cutting off access to the sea for the island's ruling monarchy and thereby ensuring its monopoly position. A minority group known as the 'Dutch Burghers' still lives in this coastal region and their Dutch surnames bear witness to the fact that their ancestors were company employees who married local girls. (Racism did not exist at this time. It only developed later when the Europeans realized that military superiority alone did not justify the subjugation of other races and began to believe that they were also morally and intellectually superior.)

Batavia (now Jakarta), where the East India Company had its headquarters, was also a multiracial city and the colonial elite were very much an integral part of the community. Local rulers were not particularly enthusiastic about the trade monopoly that the East India Company imposed upon them. This frequently led to armed conflicts, which they generally lost. As a consequence of these wars, the territory governed by the Company steadily expanded, even though it was still very small compared to the area covered by present-day Indonesia. Three-quarters of that area was conquered – or, as colonial sources preferred to put it, pacified – only in the last half of the nineteenth century and the first fourteen years of the present century by the KNIL, the Royal Netherlands Indies Army. This was often accompanied by such cruelty, violence and bloodshed that it bears comparison with Vietnam.

The East India Company went bankrupt in 1799, after which the Dutch state took on its debts, possessions and political responsibilities. The West India Company concentrated its activities in North and South America. Initially, it focused on officially sanctioned piracy – known as *kaapvaart*, privateering – against

Spain, with whom the Netherlands was at war until 1648. Every Dutch child learns the song of Piet Hein, who conquered the silver fleet. It has even become a favourite of football supporters. The company was also involved in normal trade, but that demanded greater efforts in the Americas than in Asia. Any reasonably well-advanced civilizations that the company could perhaps have done business with had been completely wiped out in the decades following Columbus' discovery of the continent. The land was suitable in many areas for the cultivation of tropical crops (in the seventeenth and eighteenth centuries, sugar was in great demand) but there was no one there to grow them. The Spaniards and Portuguese had solved this problem by setting up plantations. Initially they enslaved the local population and, later, imported black slaves from West Africa. To take part in the sugar trade, the West India Company therefore had to get its hands on a number of plantations. It competed with the French, British and Danes to occupy a whole array of islands in the Caribbean. It also conquered the northeast of Brazil, driving out the Portuguese, and appointed Prince Maurits van Nassau-Siegen, second cousin to the Stadholder of the time, as governor.

Johan Maurits ruled like a Renaissance prince. He governed as fairly as he was able, became a patron of the arts, aimed to invest in the country and its people and dreamed of a new Netherlands on the Brazilian coast. This was, however, not to the liking of the company directors in Amsterdam, who were concerned more with the pursuit of profit. After seven years, Maurits resigned, an embittered man. In the years that followed, the company's power in the area was destroyed by a popular uprising in favour of the Portuguese. The prince, however, still has a place – as Mauricio – in the Brazilian folk memory and belongs in the nation's pantheon.

Eventually the company achieved permanent access to sugar plantations. Under the provisions of a peace agreement with Britain which brought an end to a trade war between the two countries, Suriname was exchanged for the trading post of New Amsterdam, which had already fallen into the hands of the Duke of York. The Duke decided to underline the new situation by giving the settlement a new name. New Amsterdam became New York.

Supply and demand came together

At the end of the sixteenth century, privateers from Middelburg once returned home with a slave ship. The local people were so shocked that they immediately freed all the slaves. They and their fellow countrymen soon, however, became accustomed to the sight. The West India Company accounted for a considerable share of the slave trade from the very beginning. This meant that outposts had to be set up on the West African coast. Small areas were conquered and forts built on them with large dungeons where the slaves could be imprisoned until the ships arrived. The main settlement was Elmina on the Gold Coast, where families with Dutch surnames live to this day. The deserted fort still rises above the rooftops of

LIJST VAN SLAVEN,
laatst gewerkt hebbende op Plantaadjen,
dewelke op Dingsdag den 29sten Junij 1841 , des nademiddags
om *vier* uren zullen verkocht worden , door den *gequali-*
ficeerden Vendumeester S. A. C. FLU , ten huize van den
Heer L. A. DE MESQUITA , aan de *Saramaccastraat.*

Aankomende den uitlandigen Heer J. J. DE MESQUITA:

N°.			N°.	
1. Guidion ,	1°. Timmerman.		Elissbeth ,	Werkt op Steen.
2. Pieter 1°.,	2°. Idem.		Santje ,	Spelend Kind.
3. Anthony ,	3°. Idem.		Laurens ,	Delver.
4. Cornelis ,	Delver.		15. Martha 2°.,	Veldmeid.
5. William ,	Idem.		Anna ,	Idem.
6. Carol ,	Idem.		Christiaan ,	Werkt op Steen.
7. Hendrik 1°.,	Veldneger.		Adriaan 2°.	Idem.
Montje ,	Werkt op Steen.		Mietje 2°.	Spelend Kind.
Felix ,	Veldneger.		Leentje ,	Idem.
8. Samor ,	Idem.		Carolina 3°.,	Idem.
Jacobus ,	Delver.		16 Patria ,	
9. Petronella ,	Creolen Moeder.		Marietje ,	Veldmeid.
Karnot ,	Delver.		17. Francina ,	Idem.
Lissette ,	Veldmeid.		Constantia ,	Werkt bij Huis.
Carolina 2°.,	Idem.		18. Agatha ,	Veldmeid.
Jeannette ,	Werkt op Steen.		Sergeant ,	Delver.
Arriantje ,	Veldmeid.		19. Juno ,	Veldmeid.
Andries ,	Spelend Kind.		December ,	Delver.
Treintje ,	Veldmeid.		A-law 2°.,	Veldneger.
Silvia ,	Werkt op Steen.		Eva ,	Wasch en Veldmeid.
Frederik 2°.,	Spelend Kind.		Samuel 1°.,	Spelend Kind.
10. Europa ,	Veldmeid.		20. Julia ,	Huismeid.
Guillaume ,	Dresneger.		Susanna ,	Werkt bij Huis.
Carolina 1°.	Veldmeid.		Eduard ,	Leert Timmeran.
Nanoe ,	Idem.		Hendrik 2°. ,	Spelend Kind.
Onrust ,	Werkt op Steen.		Doortje ,	Zuigeling.
Charlotte 1°.,	Veldmeid.		21. Avans 2°.,	Delver.
Marie ,	Spelend Kind.		22. Jan ,	Idem.
11. Anaatje ,	Veldmeid.		23. Prinses ,	Veld neid.
Clarijntje ,	Idem.		24. Astrea ,	Werkt op Steen.
Martina ,	Werkt op Steen.		25. Regina ,	Veldmeid.
Magdaleintje ,	Spelend Kind.		26. Aurora ,	Werkt op Steen.
Gerard ,	Idem.		27. Semire ,	Veldmeid.
12. Finette ,	Veldmeid.		28. Swaantje ,	Idem.
Bebé 2°.,	Huismeid.		29. Kea ,	Idem.
Kaatje ,	Veldmeid.		30. Lucretie 2°.,	Idem.
Sultan ,	Delver.		31 Marjana ,	Werkt op Steen.
Willem 1°.,	Voeteboei.		32. Jansje 2°,	Idem.
Frans 2°.,	Werkt op Steen.		33. Adam 1°.,	Delver en Officier.
13. Louisa ,	Veldmeid.		34. Damon ,	Timmerman.
Pieter 2°.,	Delver.		35. Jetta ,	Veldmeid.
Lucretia ,	Veldmeid.		36. Jonas ,	Veldneger.
Philip ,	Werkt op Steen.		Sibille ,	Veldmeid.
Ami ,	Timmerman.		37. Jacob ,	Veldneger.
Prins ,	Werkt op Steen.		38. Fortuna ,	Huis- en Veldmeid.
Amerika ,	Spelend Kind.		Theodorus ,	Spelend Kind.
Lotje ,	Idem.		Mietje 3°.,	Idem.
14. Maria 2°.,	Veldmeid.		39. Catharina ,	Veldmeid en Kokin.
Johanna ,	Idem.			

Aankomende de Heeren J. J.- en L. A. DE MESQUITA:

1. Kwamie ,	Delver.	
2. Masaera ,	Veldneger.	
3. Domicilia ,	Veldmeid.	
Dirk ,	Spelend Kind.	
Adam ,	Idem.	

A large slave auction is announced for 29 June 1841. Qualified auctioneer Flu wields the hammer at the house of Mr Mesquita in the Saramaccastraat in Paramaribo, the capital of Suriname. It is not clear if Mesquita himself is selling the slaves who, according to the poster, are plantation workers. They are all listed by name and job, e.g. digger or field-maid. Note Santje, a 'playing child' who is therefore too young to work and was therefore probably about three years old.

the town and tourists are still shown the secret staircase between the governor's bedroom and the quarters of the female slaves.

It is difficult to say how many slaves were transported to America on Dutch ships. Nor does it matter. It is sufficient to know that they were stowed in their hundreds in the holds of slow sailing ships; and that the voyage was so harrowing that they needed a couple of months rest on the island of Curaçao (known appropriately as the 'slave plantation') before the company branded them like cattle and put them up for sale on the slave market. The mortality rate during the ocean crossing was considerable - and was taken into account in the selling price, which was about ten times higher than was paid for the unfortunate wretches on the African coast. Despite modern claims to the contrary, the slave trade was not particularly profitable. Slaves on the middle passage were insured, with the insurance companies always applying an own risk of 15%. It was not necessary for the Dutch slave traders to round up their human merchandise themselves. Along the West African coast there were large, well-organized kingdoms, where slavery was already a large-scale phenomenon. Supply and demand therefore came together. The fortress at Elmina, in Ghana, appears now and again on the television in programmes documenting the excesses of the period. The substantial part played by the Netherlands in the slave trade is considered a dark chapter in the country's history. But unlike their competitors for the gains to be made from the 'middle passage', the Dutch slave traders did not have to contend with opposition to their activities at home. In England, a mass anti-slavery movement grew up during the eighteenth century. During its radical period, the French Revolution abolished the entire system. In the Netherlands, no such movements developed and parliament abolished slavery in two steps – in the East Indies in 1859 and in the Caribbean colonies in 1864 – compensating the owners for their 'losses'. Anyone wishing to go into the slave trade now faces a maximum prison sentence of twelve years.

There are, however, signs here and there of a guilty conscience. In the eighteenth century Jacobus Elisa Joannis Capitein, a freedman from what is now Ghana became renowned when he was awarded a doctorate in theology by Leiden University. His thesis argued that slavery and Christian liberty were not contradictory. And one of the last companies in the Netherlands to specialize in the buying and selling of human beings was known by the extremely neutral name of *Middelburgsche Commercie Compagnie*. No one defends the moral acceptability of street lighting. It is only when customs or institutions acquire a moral foundation that they become controversial.

The development of racist ideologies in the nineteenth century had a great deal to do with this phenomenon. White Europeans – including the Dutch – had to reconcile their position as colonial rulers with the fundamental Christian idea that all men are equal before God. Anyone who traded in other peoples or deprived them of their basic human rights in some other way, therefore had to come up with some good arguments. One of these was to 'prove' that they were of an inferior species, or at least different in some way. Consequently, the trade in Africans was frequently justified by reference to the biblical story of Noah, the builder of the Ark and the forefather of all mankind. Noah had cursed his son Ham. Clearly enough, the Africans were the descendants of Ham. For example this was the central thesis of a seventeenth century book with the title *The Christian rudder of the merchantman*. The various pseudo-scientific attempts to link genetic differences between races to greater or lesser intelligence are another example of this kind of reasoning.

There is also a non-racist form of justification for European colonial rule which enjoyed considerable support in the Netherlands. It was closely related to Kipling's famous concept of the 'white man's burden'. The Europeans brought civilization to the world, nurturing and educating barbarian peoples until they achieved a level of development comparable to that of their mentors. Until that level was actually reached, European domination remained a necessary evil. The campaigns of conquest undertaken by the KNIL in the Indonesian islands from 1870 on were in part officially justified as crusades against the slavery practised by uncivilized local rulers. According to the official propaganda, the entire campaign was a war of liberation.

A clear element of structural rape

At the same time, colonialism became an increasingly 'white' affair. This was largely due to the arrival of the spouses. In the days of sailing ships, a journey from Amsterdam to the East Indies and back could take a year and a half. It was considered normal if a third of the crew embarked on their final voyage to eternal life on the way. The death rate in the colonial outposts was also high, because the newcomers were very susceptible to tropical diseases. The Dutch made this problem even worse by settling in places that reminded them of home – marshy river deltas. Batavia looked very much like a Dutch city, complete with canals and bridges, and provided a perfect habitat for malaria-carrying mosquitoes. Immediately after the conquest of North-East Brazil, the Dutch moved the centre of government from the town of Olinda – which, like the African slave forts, has now been declared a monument to mankind by Unesco – to the fishing village of Recife, which was situated lower down on a nearby river estuary. Recife now has a population of millions and is still regularly disrupted by floods.

These were not the kind of places to send women. The United East India Company did experiment with *compagniesdochters*, women recruited from the dregs of Dutch society, but those that survived the journey did nothing to add to the moral element in the far-flung outposts of the empire. Moreover, the colonial masters had little need of 'consolation' from home when there were mistresses aplenty available to them from among the slaves. The colonial system as a whole contained a clear element of structural rape.

The construction of the Suez Canal and the arrival of steam-powered ships made the journey shorter and less hazardous. This made the tropics a safer bet for well-brought-up young women looking for a secure future. The colonial masters – themselves changed now that the greater chances of survival made colonial service more than just a desperate refuge for bankrupts and others who were well advised, for one reason or another, not to show their faces in the known world – wanted to find a nice girl of good stock and get married. The arrival of these fresh young spouses resulted in a powerful 'Europeanization' of the colonies. They fiercely took on their local competitors, the unofficial native wives (known in Indonesia as *njais*) and mistresses of their husbands. They also tried to lay siege to the *sociëteiten*, the gentlemen's clubs where far too much strong liquor was consumed, but with considerably less success.

They had little choice in this – the colonies were still a man's world. European wives ran their households but their status depended entirely on the position and reputation of their husbands. They were wives and mothers, and nothing more. They therefore had to keep their husbands on the straight and narrow as far as possible, at least in the eyes of the outside world.

Bumi Manusia (Earth of Mankind) – written by Indonesian author Pramoedja Ananta Toer tells the story of how a *njai* is robbed of her child after the death of her old-fashioned and therefore not officially married master by his white Dutch family. The novel is a condensation of historical fact and makes a direct link between such incidents and the development of Indonesian nationalism. In this way, an element of racial segregation crept into colonial society.

Ethical politics

In 1899, the liberal politician Conrad van Deventer published an article in the political-cultural monthly magazine *De Gids* that caused great uproar. The article was entitled *Een Eereschuld*, A Debt of Honour, and introduced a new concept of 'ethical politics'.

Van Deventer showed clearly with facts and figures that the Netherlands had always exploited the East Indies, sucking the colony dry. He argued that the Dutch therefore had a debt of honour that current generations were morally bound to repay. One of his suggestions was that, from then on, the colonies should be governed in the interests of the local population, so that, in time they would be ready to rule themselves independently. Much of what he proposed closely resembled what we today call 'development policy'.

Public opinion in the Netherlands had been prepared for this approach to the country's colonial responsibilities by Multatuli – who I already mentioned earlier – and his long-standing bestseller 'Max Havelaar or the Coffee Auctions of the Dutch

The good life in the colonies: planters pose as their staff kneel before them.

Trading Company'. In the novel, through the eyes of Batavus Droogstoppel, Multatuli portrays the Netherlands as a small-minded and hypocritical colonial master, which wishes only to earn as much as it can from its power in the East Indies. Max Havelaar, the noble leading figure, is ruined because he defends the oppressed natives and his superiors simply drop him like a stone. The story is practically identical to what happened to Multatuli himself. It should, however, be noted that the novel is not a plea for emancipation of the native people from the colonial yoke, but for more paternalistic government on the part of the Netherlands. The traditional native chiefs, whom Havelaar – as an official in the colonial service – must keep under control, are held primarily responsible for the exploitation of their people; the colonial bureaucracy is guilty only indirectly.

Yet the advocates of ethical politics were serious and their concern was genuine. In the meantime, the Dutch public had come to believe that they did indeed owe a debt of honour to the colony, and it was gradually prepared for independence. The key word was 'gradually' – even the most progressive supporters of ethical politics believed that this process would take generations. The response to the Indonesian nationalist movement, which fought for Merdeka (independence), was therefore rather contorted. Radical leaders were interned in the Boven-Digoel camp in New Guinea, where the indigenous population still lived in the Stone Age and censorship was imposed to keep a firm grip on the opposition press.

More moderate nationalists argued for a relationship between the Netherlands and Indonesia in which the latter was permitted internal self-rule. The Dutch government rejected this proposal.

The whole house of cards collapsed within three months

After the attack on Pearl Harbour, the Netherlands declared war on Japan. The whole house of cards in the East Indies collapsed within three months. Most of the 80,000 Dutch people in the colony looked on with amazement as the local population, rather than rallying behind the Dutch flag, waited with a certain enthusiasm to see how they would be treated by the new occupiers. When they arrived they gave the budding nationalism a free reign, in as far as the nationalist leaders identified with the Japanese war aims. But at the same time, the occupying armies proved themselves capable of terrible atrocities. They looted the country and terrorized the people. The Dutch colonists were interned, with the men and women in separate camps, where there was severe lack of food and other basic facilities.

When the Japanese capitulated after the bombing of Hiroshima and Nagasaki, their occupation of Indonesia was still intact. The nationalist leaders Sukarno and Hatta took advantage of the power vacuum to declare independence. This came as a great surprise to the inmates of the internment camps, who had assumed they would simply carry on where they left off. They soon discovered that they were safer where they were than outside, because radical nationalists were hunting down their former colonial masters. The government in the Netherlands – where the occupiers had also been driven out – declared that the nationalist leaders, who had after all cooperated with the Japanese, were just as much traitors as those at home who had collaborated with the Nazis. They sent in an expeditionary force to restore order. This led to an extra four years of war in the region. Under great pressure from the international community, the Netherlands entered into negotiations with the new republic, but little progress was made. On two occasions the expeditionary force was ordered to conduct an offensive, known euphemistically as 'police actions'. It was a bloody affair, in which the Dutch also proved capable of cruel reprisals. Eventually the United Nations as good as forced the Netherlands to cast Indonesia loose.

Sukarno had to agree to New Guinea staying in Dutch hands. Formally it was a trust territory of the United Nations. The new Indonesian president pursued a policy of confrontation to bring the region under his power and finally succeeded in 1963 when the UN once again made it clear that it would no longer support any further obstinacy on the part of the Netherlands.

The dismantling of the East Indies provided the Netherlands with its first minority groups

The dismantling of the East Indies provided the Netherlands with its first two genuine minority groups. A large part – about 250,000 – of the *Indo's*, people of mixed Dutch-Indonesian descent, fled to the Netherlands. They had developed a complete identity of their own – particularly in and around Batavia – complete with a unique version of the Dutch language and, with a few exceptions, had remained loyal to the colonial regime. Afraid of reprisals, they now sought refuge in what they considered their fatherland.

Once in the Netherlands, the Indos did their best to accentuate the Dutch side of their identity. In fact, they had little choice. They were initially housed in camps and boarding houses where social workers gave them a rather harsh introduction to Dutch norms and values. Many of their instructors, for example, tried to persuade them to abandon their rice-based diet and those who served up traditional Dutch potatoes with the evening meal were given priority in the allocation of houses. The Indos tolerated this because they had chosen to live in the Netherlands and tried to bring their children up to be as Dutch as possible. In spite of this, the entire community has suffered to this day from a debilitating homesickness for what has become an idealized image of their home country. This is known in Malay as *tempoe doeloe*, the 'olden days'.

In every large town or city in the Netherlands, you will regularly see posters announcing a *pasar malam* (evening market) or a *pasar dalam* (covered market). The venue is usually a local sports centre and the markets offer a broad cultural programme, so that the *tempoe doeloe* can be created for a short time, within the restrictions imposed upon it by Dutch society and the cold maritime climate. The younger generations are in the process of rediscovering their Indonesian roots. They are very critical of the way their parents and grandparents were received in the 1950s and seek to develop new ties with Indonesia.

The Moluccans felt betrayed and used by the Dutch

Around the same time as the Indos, the Moluccans also arrived in the country. The Christian community on the minute island of Ambon had traditionally made a sizable contribution to the colonial army. The loyalty of the Moluccan soldiers to their Dutch masters was, if anything, stronger than that of the Indos and Indonesian independence held little promise for them. They came to the Netherlands not out of choice, but because they had obeyed the orders of their military superiors to do so. On arriving on Dutch soil, they were immediately demobilized, much to their surprise and anger. On Ambon itself, there was a separatist movement, which did not make the situation any easier. Hence, the orders to embark for the Netherlands and the subsequent demobilization. On Ambon itself, a Republic of the South Moluccas had been declared, but this was very short-lived.

The Dutch government was unequivocal in its rejection of this ideal, and generally continued to pursue a policy of integration. This led to occasional conflict with the exiled community and, in the 1960s, the Dutch looked on in amazement as the Moluccans consistently refused to exchange their now leaky barrack homes in the camps for nice houses outside, because it could be seen as accepting that they would be staying in the Netherlands for good.

In the 1970s, a new generation of Moluccans emerged that employed completely different weapons. Inspired by the liberation movements of the sixties and organizations like the PLO, radical splinter groups adopted terrorist tactics. It started with the taking of hostages in the Indonesian Embassy. Later, they hijacked trains full of passengers and, on one occasion, a children's day-care centre. The first fatalities occurred. The Dutch government responded invariably by setting up a crisis centre, complete with psychologists and psychiatrists, and holding consultations with the terrorists which, in one case, lasted three weeks. This wore the terrorists down and enabled them to be overpowered by elite commando units from the Dutch army.

The Moluccans failed to recruit support for their ideal outside their own community but, on the other hand, the terrorist attacks did not provoke anti-Moluccan sentiments of any consequence among wider Dutch society. The Moluccans themselves disappeared from public view. Statistics show that the newer generations have been reasonably successful in finding a place for themselves in society without entirely losing their identity. In the 1970s, the communities that grew up when the moderate elements moved out of the camps suffered from typical 'ghetto-related' problems, such as drug abuse and unemployment, but these have now become less acute. The old soldiers – now old men – who still refused to accept their enforced demobilization, allowed the last of the barracks to be renovated in the 1990s, from which the conclusion could be drawn that they were no longer seen as temporary accommodation.

The Netherlands' colonial past in Indonesia can still evoke strong emotions from time to time. When Lou de Jong, the author of the official history of the Netherlands, wrote the sections on the war with the Japanese and the subsequent Indonesian fight for independence, he was overwhelmed with criticism. For the first and only time, he found himself pressurized from outside to change the text. He had to tone down references to Dutch war crimes during the period, using less controversial terms like 'excesses'.

The history of decolonization in the Caribbean is no more edifying. The colonial authorities had learned their lesson from Indonesia – they would not make the same mistakes again. Dutch colonial possessions in the region were modest – Curaçao, Aruba and Bonaire, three small islands off the coast of Venezuela with a total of less than two hundred thousand inhabitants; Sint Eustatius, Saba and half of Sint Maarten, three minute islands to the south of the Dominican Republic and Puerto Rico. These together constituted the Netherlands Antilles. Lastly, on the coast of Guyana, was Suriname, a region of wild jungle with an urban enclave in Paramaribo, which was surrounded by agricultural land.

The Netherlands, as a modern country, felt a little ashamed

After the Second World War, the Netherlands did in the Caribbean what it had intended to do in Indonesia – it gave the colonies self-rule. This was laid down in the Charter for the Kingdom, which divided the country into three parts. The Netherlands itself was responsible for foreign affairs and defence for all three. The other two parts, Suriname and the Antilles, sent a minister to represent their interests in the Dutch cabinet but, other than that, had complete freedom to go their own way.

The reformers of the 1960s derived great inspiration from colonial liberation movements. The younger generation, kicking against the conservatism of their parents, identified more with nation-builders such as Julius Nyerere, Kenneth Kaunda and Nelson Mandela – who was already world-renowned – than with the ethicists of the colonial period. And the General Assembly of the United Nations – full of representatives of recently decolonized countries – was keen on reminding the Dutch delegation that the tricolour with the horizontal red, white and blue stripes was still flying in the Caribbean. And the Netherlands, as a modern country, felt a little ashamed.

Events in Curaçao reinforced this feeling. Anti-government demonstrations in 1969 ended in a riot in which the business district was looted. The government in The Hague – with the support of the social democratic opposition – ordered Dutch

Marines to be sent in to restore order. This was met with a great deal of criticism at home and abroad. The use of Dutch troops to call a bunch of poor and desperate wretches to heel was inconsistent with the country's image of itself as a modern democratic society. And particularly at the end of the 1960s, when so many young people in Europe had a poster of Che Guevara hanging over their beds. Joop den Uyl, the social democratic leader, realized more clearly than ever that Dutch colonial possessions had to be relinquished as soon as possible. He vowed that, if he were to become prime minister, he would at least guarantee the independence of Suriname. Shortly after, he became prime minister.

The 'umbrella structure' of the Kingdom had its advantages

In Suriname and the Antilles, however, the response to the Charter was generally favourable. If the Queen visited the overseas territories, she was greeted by enthusiastic crowds. In the Surinamese parliament, independence was demanded only by a small splinter party, consisting of intellectuals who had studied in the Netherlands and had been introduced to nationalism and modern theories on the Third World. The riots in Willemstad were directed against government corruption and low salaries, not against the Dutch flag.

Cycling along the canal with the baby. This picture comes from Suriname, in South America. Even in the field of spatial planning, the Netherlands has left its mark in almost all of the world's continents.

Suriname has been independent since 1975, but a young Queen Wilhelmina still looks out across the Suriname River.

The 'umbrella structure' of the Kingdom had its advantages. The Netherlands repaid its debt of honour by making sizable contributions to the former colonies, where the standard of living was significantly lower. On the other hand, the government in The Hague made little effort to monitor how these funds were allocated. It was assumed that this would occur according to Dutch norms. And, what is more, they had abandoned the paternalism of their predecessors, who had the debacle of Indonesia on their consciences.

The Antilles and Suriname are essentially Caribbean societies. An exemplary democratic constitution conceals a system of nepotism and corruption, where electoral support is provided in exchange for favours and tangible benefits. Politicians who do not take part in this system, lose their power. This offers considerable scope for corrupt practices.

By clever negotiation, the elites in the Antilles successfully resisted attempts by the government in The Hague to give the territories greater independence, until the Dutch politicians finally gave up. Aruba managed to negotiate itself a separate status in the Kingdom, apart from the Antilles. Since 1990, The Hague has accepted that the Caribbean territories are a permanent part of the Kingdom.

Suriname was promised a bonus of several billions if it took the step

The elite in Suriname did permit themselves to be talked into independence, partly on the basis of the pledge that the country would receive a bonus of several billions if it took the step. The Surinamese parliament accepted the offer by a majority of one and a referendum was effectively ruled out.

Suriname is a multiracial society. After the black slaves were given their freedom, they exchanged forced labour on the plantations for a usually poverty-stricken existence in Paramaribo. To replace them the government recruited contract workers, first in India and then, when the British authorities imposed a ban on this, in Java. The plantations finally folded because these imported workers did not renew their contracts. Consequently, the population became a mixture of an approximately equal number of Creoles of African ancestry and Hindus, together with a smaller group of Javans. There were also even smaller groups of Chinese, native Indians and 'maroons', the descendants of black slaves who had escaped into the jungle. The various groups lived closely together and the political parties generally followed the same lines. The government, however, was a multiracial coalition. The system bore great similarities to the Dutch 'pillar' structure, with the pillars representing racial rather than religious groups.

Bimre – a new city of miracles

The divisions in this society were so sharp that many people feared they would erupt into violence if the Netherlands withdrew. When it became clear in 1975 that independence was inevitable, half of the people 'voted with their feet' – they bought tickets to Schiphol before they had to exchange their Dutch passports for Surinamese ones. The Creoles in particular headed for a new city of miracles whose fame had spread across the Atlantic Ocean – *Bimre*, where they knew that a golden future awaited them.

Bimre is a distortion of *Bijlmermeer*, a polder to the southeast of Amsterdam, on which apartment blocks were built shoulder-to-shoulder at the end of the 1960s. Parks were laid out between the blocks and there was a strict separation of motorized and pedestrian traffic. Gigantic parking garages were built to accommodate the cars of Amsterdammers who would use their increased prosperity to rent one of these attractive and roomy flats. But the people of the city found the Bijlmer too impersonal and too far away. It became a second choice for them. People who wanted to settle in Amsterdam were often given a flat in the Bijlmer, but generally considered it a temporary solution. For most Dutch residents, the flats were a first step towards finding something better closer to the city centre. When the Surinamese immigrants started to arrive in their thousands, they therefore had little trouble in obtaining a flat and Bimre soon became Suriname's second largest city.

The Hindus preferred The Hague, far from the Creoles. Many Creoles also settled in the *Oud-West* district of Rotterdam, where it was also easy to find a place to live because the housing was run-down and badly in need of renovation – and therefore no longer met the requirements of the increasingly prosperous local population. Consequently whole areas grew up within the major cities with an overwhelmingly immigrant population. The 'foreign' atmosphere of these districts was intensified by the fact that the local authorities followed the example of their predecessors in the colonies and made no concerted effort to impose their culture and language on the minorities under their jurisdiction. This is not surprising for a society founded on the basic principle of 'sovereignty in one's own domain'.

The new arrivals had to find themselves a place on the labour market

The new arrivals had to find themselves a place on the labour market. They thought that this would not be too much of a problem because there was work for everyone – more than the Dutch themselves could handle.

The labour market had indeed come under pressure during the boom of the 1960s. Salaries had increased considerably, and with them the purchasing power of the less prosperous groups in society. Yet it remained difficult for employers to recruit personnel, especially for unskilled work. Drastic salary increases may have solved the problem, or the involvement of women in the labour market on a large scale – which had been tried successfully in Finland. Dutch employers, however, chose a different option. In cooperation with the government, they began recruiting in the Middle East and North Africa, in particular in Morocco and Turkey. In doing so, they were following in the footsteps of their German counterparts, who were also faced with labour shortages.

In Morocco and Turkey, on the other hand, there was high unemployment. The Netherlands set up recruitment agencies in the two countries, agreeing with Germany that they should not get in each other's way. Since Germany had already been recruiting in the larger cities, the Netherlands focused on the rural areas. Consequently, there was an influx of Berbers from Morocco and people from Eastern Turkey, most of whom intended to save as much as they could in a couple of years and start their own businesses back at home. This new wave of immigrants came directly from their traditional rural communities to the world of the large Western European city.

Most guest workers eventually brought their families over

These immigrants were known as *gastarbeiders*, guest workers. They were given lodgings in boarding houses and quickly learned a painful lesson – although the wages were far higher than at home, so were the prices. This thwarted their plans to save. Furthermore, life in a completely strange culture, far from their homes and families, proved more difficult than they had imagined. This was exacerbated by the fact that they were more or less stuck in their new environment. Most guest workers eventually brought their families over. The Dutch government could hardly object to this; the preservation of family values has always been one of the battle cries of Christian politicians, and social democrats – considering their ideological beliefs – could hardly object to workers wishing to be reunited with their families. This led to the development of relatively permanent Turkish and Moroccan communities, even though surveys have shown that the dream of returning to their home countries has never faded. They have increasingly come to accept, however, that it will never be anything more than a dream.

When it comes down to it, most employers prefer to take on Dutch employees

The ability of minority groups to compete for jobs has proved limited. When it comes down to it, most employers prefer to take on Dutch employees. Article 1 of the Constitution forbids discrimination of this nature, but prospective employers always have sufficient other reasons for rejecting a candidate. Furthermore, although discrimination plays a role in this situation, it is not the whole story. Many members of minority groups do not have the qualifications required to find employment in an economy which demands an increasingly high level of education and training from its workers. This is often one reason for their being rejected for jobs. The same applies to their children, even though most of the younger generation have grown up in the Netherlands.

Anyone who studies education statistics will be put in mind of the Third World. A growing, but still too small, number of people from the minority groups are successful in pushing their way through to the higher levels of Dutch society. They complete a university education with honours and become absorbed in the middle classes. But below them, there is a great gap. Very few members of immigrant groups study vocational subjects at intermediate level, and the drop-out rate is high. It would appear that only the most intelligent are able to survive the Dutch education system. The large majority seem to come up against an insurmountable hurdle at some point.

This hurdle is related to Dutch culture and traditions. Immigrant groups find themselves in a society based on *overleg*, where each group is left to its own devices and help is given only to those who ask for it. This is not the way things

The 1960s: the first Moroccan guest workers in their shared accommodation.

are done in Turkey or Morocco. Generally speaking, the minority groups from the Islamic countries have a strong patriarchal culture, with great respect for parental authority, where having one's own opinions is often seen as a form of contradiction. The Hindus also have a strong family structure.

This is less true of the Creoles and the Antilleans. The slaveowners did not permit close family ties to develop on the plantations, since they could pose a threat to their absolute power. Consequently, a culture of rapidly changing relationships developed, and children were the responsibility of the mother.

Creole and Antillean families are still frequently headed by very strong women, who are responsible not only for the household but also for the income. Survival in Suriname is a matter of being able to improvise and acquire small personal advantages wherever possible. This requires forming continually changing alliances with others. In the political sector, it is a matter of 'I'll support you and you find me a job in the bureaucracy'.

It is therefore difficult for these groups to operate effectively in a society dominated by Dutch values. This is compounded if you do not speak the language very well and so miss many of the subtleties of what is said. It can lead to a great deal of misunderstanding if you are talking to someone who is seeking a compromise which is satisfactory to everyone concerned, while you are trying to extract a favour or make a deal.

Children from minority groups were surprised when they first went to a Dutch school. The lessons often started with a group discussion, in which the teacher acted almost as their equal. He or she seemed interested in what the pupils had to say, rather than simply teaching them what was in the books. The teaching methods included a lot of working on their own or in groups, and searching for solutions together. It was not the intention that the pupils should purely reproduce the truth as it was written in the school books. Teachers had a tendency to assess children on the basis of their creativity and ability to think for themselves. This was a stark contrast to their own cultures, where the children mainly had to imitate what they were taught as well as they could; where there was a strong belief that an opinion of one's own could only be developed from a great experience of life; and where children were expected to keep quiet and show respect for their elders. And if you do not understand the language, because you still speak Turkish, Berber or Sranan Tongo at home, it is even more difficult to adapt.

It was not in the Dutch character to demand that minority groups adapt their own customs and traditions. The Ministry of Education and Science responded initially by providing teaching in their own language and culture, recruiting teachers from their home countries. This was partly induced by some vague idea of sovereignty in one's own domain; but it was also a response to the desire to return home. The generations that grew up in the Netherlands would also have to be able to survive if the dream ever came true.

In addition, the government encouraged the minorities to form their own organizations, and developed an extensive system of grants. As a result all kinds of bodies were set up to represent minority interests, staffed by the happy few who had had a good education. They projected themselves as representatives of what the Dutch government considered as their particular group, whether they had actually gained a reasonable level of support among their own people or not.

For good or for bad, these leaders defended the interests of their 'grassroots members'. They tackled real and imagined discrimination and were fierce defenders of their language and culture. They demanded affirmative action and a policy of preference to put an end to the disadvantaged position of their people on the labour market. In this, they were following closely in the footsteps of the feminists, who had had relative success with similar tactics.

Their efforts met with a favourable response from the official channels in the Netherlands. After all, discrimination and distinction according to race or ethnic origin were to be deplored. It was laid down in Article 1 of the Constitution, and with good reason. And, of course, the Netherlands had clearly and publicly broken with its own colonial past.

This was not enough for immigrants

For immigrants, there are many ways of making a situation like this bearable on a personal level. But there are two extremes: you can withdraw as far as possible into your own traditions and become isolated from society at large, or you can throw caution to the wind and rid yourself of all inhibition. Most immigrants choose a solution somewhere in the middle of this spectrum, making them, in principle, 'invisible'. But those who choose one or other of the extremes become extremely conspicuous.

For many Turks and Moroccans, the traditional Islamic beliefs from home give them something safe to hold on to. They reject Dutch society – with its mini-skirts and sex programmes on tv, its drink and drugs – as a 'den of iniquity'.

The same applies to those who throw off all their inhibitions. At first glance, it may appear that 'anything goes' in Dutch society. Women in sexy clothes are looking for sex. You need have no respect for public property. Ticket inspectors in the tram are few and far between, so you can travel free. And if you do get caught breaking any rules, the punishment will be light. No one expects an outward show of respect – and they treat you like dirt anyway, because there are no jobs to be found. Terrible conflicts arise at home, particularly in patriarchal households, because children continually have to switch between a home life in which parental rule is absolute and the outside world where they are expected to have their own opinions and show initiative. The fathers' authority is not supported by society, at least not in the way to which they are accustomed. This can often lead to serious crises, which makes the younger generations of immigrants susceptible to the temptations of the wild life, of drugs and the world of crime of which they are a part. Anyone who chooses this path is also very visible. A stoned Antillean playing with a knife on the number 3 tram is soon seen by his fellow passengers as representative of his whole community. The same applies to the bent little women with their headscarves and their faded raincoats. This is a difference that strikes fear in the hearts of 'normal' citizens. One of the Netherlands best known cabaret performers, Wim Kan, wrote a song in the early 1980s – 20 years before 9/11 – to describe this fear. He called it *Khomeini op het behang*, 'Khomeini on the wallpaper'.

A whole anthology of urban myths has grown up around the ethnic minorities

Since the 1970s a whole anthology of urban myths has grown up around the ethnic minorities. They are based on an incomplete knowledge of their customs, but they never give specific dates and times. One of the most tenacious of these myths is that 'they' slaughter sheep in their homes. The next-door neighbour has a friend who has blood dripping over her balcony or even through the ceiling because the Moroccans in the flat above are slaughtering sheep. And there are plenty more where that came from. The other neighbour has a brother whose children can't get jobs because the 'foreigners' always get first choice. It's no use asking the local council for a house, because the foreigners (or, more often these days, the asylum-seekers) are given priority. More and more of them are arriving and the council doesn't want to discriminate. Or there is the one about a cousin or some other distant relative who was told by a policeman that there was no point in reporting a crime committed by a foreigner because 'even if we arrest him, he'll be walking around as free as a bird within the hour'. The same is often said about junkies – in spite of the fact that the police insist that all crimes are reported. And, of course, the old favourite – foreigners live like kings from the social security. They get child benefits for ten children, all of whom live back in Morocco.

The tenacity of these urban myths bears testimony to the tension that exists between the various groups that comprise present-day Dutch society. The official policy of tolerance had, also in the twentieth century, little or no parallel in society at large. There is much fear and suspicion and no one knows how best to respond, or just how deep it really goes, because statements that may be interpreted as racist are strictly taboo. They are often preceded with such disclaimers as 'I don't want to discriminate, but...' People who protest about the building of a mosque at the end of their street tend to base their arguments on the lack of parking space or the extra noise. They will even claim that the mosque will lead to a concentration of Muslims in one area, providing fertile feeding ground for racism and discrimination, which they themselves – of course – abhor.

This undercurrent of racism was long ignored by officialdom. The comparison was quickly made with Nazism and you simply didn't communicate with fascists. There was no place for racism in Dutch society.

Bimre's night of tragedy

In the early 1990s, fifteen years after the first mass migration from Suriname, opinions on the Bijlmermeer were sharply divided. Many people were frightened of Bimre. Junkies hung around the graffiti-ridden metro stations that connected it to the city. Bimre's design provided excellent opportunities for anti-social behaviour. The architecture made social control difficult. People had to walk down long corridors, sometimes hundreds of metres long, to get to their flats. The windows offered a poor view of the small parks between the enormous complexes. A single drunk could easily terrorize a whole block by, for example, destroying lifts or kicking in doors. The public areas consequently became run-down and neglected. Reports drawn up on the situation offered little hope. The housing associations that owned the apartment blocks decided that the Bijlmer had been a terrible mistake in planning. They carried out improvement schemes, demolishing a number of the blocks. This was one face of Bimre. But at the same time, the town had a number of other, more hopeful facets. Despite all appearances to the contrary, a complete social network had developed that was unseen by the authorities and the official welfare bodies. Bimre's pride was the gigantic Kwakoe Festival, which had started as a tournament for Surinamese football teams and now attracted hundreds of thousands of visitors every year. On Sundays, swinging music and joyful singing could be heard coming from many of the local meeting places. It was the sound not of raucous parties, but of church services. Bimre had

Tragedy in the Bijlmer: the El-Al cargo plane has just crashed onto De Kruitberg.

developed into a very religious town, but the churches had little in common with official Calvinism. They more closely resembled Pentecostal communities, which do exist in the Netherlands but, compared to the congregations in Bimre, practice their faith with considerable reserve. It also became a centre for followers of the Afro-Surinamese *winti* religion. Mediums even made contact with Dutch winti spirits, including those of Jews gassed by the Nazis who had originally lived in Amsterdam-Zuid, which is adjacent to the Bijlmer. In this way, Bimre acquired its own understanding of the drama of Mokum.

On 4 October 1992, an El Al Boeing cargo plane experienced problems while approaching Schiphol. The pilot flew in wide circles above Amsterdam in search of a free runway. Twice, the plane roared across the city centre. There was clearly something seriously wrong, serious enough to be mentioned on the radio news. The pilot was apparently having trouble lining the plane up with the runway. At the third attempt the Boeing lost height rapidly. It bore down on Bimre at enormous speed and crashed through one of the apartment blocks, De Kruitberg. It was a Sunday evening, around seven o'clock. Prime time. The whole country was watching Studio Sport. CNN brought news of the crash a little before the Dutch NOS. That Sunday evening, the whole country watched the drama unfold in front of their eyes. The flames rose high in the air above De Kruitberg, which had been partially demolished. Frightened people from the whole of Bimre rushed to the scene of the crash. No one would be able to survive this inferno, hundreds must have died. The television showed the whole thing live – the flames, the fire brigade working frantically to get it under control, the desperate family members and the hastily set up crisis centre, the police trying to keep onlookers at a distance and the shocked mayor of the city. Eye witnesses were interviewed. It soon became clear that the people living in De Kruitberg were largely Surinamese or Ghanian. But no one knew how many there were. The reporters said that, in addition to the official residents, there could have been a lot of other people living there, illegal immigrants who had gone underground and earned a living in the informal sector, the 'black' economy. There were soon rumours of a thousand dead, most of whom were not registered anywhere.

It took several days to recover all the bodies. After a week or so had passed, the authorities said that the death toll had been at least 250. A wave of emotion and sympathy swept through the country. For that first week, Bimre's night of tragedy was headline news. The television broadcast a moving memorial service, where the speakers included not only the prime minister but also the leaders of all the minority groups in Bimre. At the end of the service, the Mayor of Amsterdam led a procession of 20,000 people to De Kruitberg to lay flowers at the scene of the tragedy. It was accompanied by effusive expressions of grief and religious faith from the various ethnic groups, while television reporters explained the various ways in which the different cultures expressed their sorrow. The tragedy had left a great impression on everyone and the nation was united around the victims. It actually made you feel good to be a part of it. The Netherlands was proud of this display of mass solidarity and grief.

The authorities pledged their full support for the victims, including, of course, those living in the immediate vicinity of De Kruitberg who had been psychologically traumatized by the disaster. They also promised residence permits to all illegal immigrants living in the destroyed blocks. The people concerned were told to report to the Aliens Police. It had, by this time, become clear that the final death toll of the crash had been a little more than 60. The Aliens Police were, however, overwhelmed by nearly 2,000 people who claimed to have been living in De Kruitberg. It was a multifarious and, as time wore on, increasingly aggressive crowd. Reporters discovered that many had come from as far as Paris in busloads to take advantage of this 'chance of a lifetime'. It took a long time for the crowds to be dispersed. Eventually, about 50 people who had lived in De Kruitberg were given residence permits.

This incident, however, reversed the sympathetic mood of the nation. It confirmed all the prejudices that the emotional pictures of the crash had covered with a veneer of sentiment. The image of Bimre as full of good people, people who shared the suffering of their fellow residents, evaporated overnight.

Where did all these people come from? As most of the other members of the European Union, the Netherlands had become more of a haven for immigrants than ever. Development experts had a very clear explanation for this – if the wealth will not go to the people, the people will come to the wealth. A global process of migration was under way towards places that could offer work and economic security and the Netherlands was one of the favoured destinations.

Like most rich countries, however, the Netherlands had closed its borders to foreigners without money. They were not given residence permits or allowed to take up paid employment. Exceptions were made for people who were persecuted by the authorities in their own countries for political reasons and who could prove that their lives would be in danger if they returned. These people were granted political asylum, which in effect gave them the same status as Dutch citizens, with the exception of the right to vote. In practice, however, political asylum is very rarely granted. The other alternative is to go underground, a feasible option in a democracy with reasonably open borders.

The channels for receiving asylum-seekers were soon more or less clogged up.

In the 1990s vvd leader Frits Bolkestein was the first politician to genuinely concern himself with what was already the favourite topic of conversation in so many bars and cafés across the country. The Netherlands was not a haven for immigrants, he insisted. He demanded that the borders be closed and – in the same breath – that foreigners already in the country should learn to adapt to Dutch society. He claimed that the policy pursued up until then had been too soft and it was time to adopt a harder line. His arguments received an immediate response. The social democratic state secretary for justice Aad Kosto did what he could to close all the loopholes in the immigration legislation, resulting in a series of very tough measures. His successor Job Cohen – also from the Labour Party – introduced even stricter measures, which were later implemented by Rita Verdonk of the vvd.

Another loophole that was closed up was the 'love connection'. Anyone wishing to start a relationship with a Dutch national had to apply for a permit from the Dutch Embassy in their own country. The Dutch partner also had to meet certain requirements. They had to have decent accommodation and a gross personal income of at least 1800 euros a month. This is well above the minimum wage and the level of social security benefits. The measures were designed to put an end to marriages of convenience.

After the turn of the century, people began to see another reason for restricting the influx of immigrants: if Turkish and Moroccan men were permitted to choose partners from their home countries and bring them to the Netherlands the backwardness and maladjustment of these cultures would be imported again with each generation. It would also give strict Islamic men the opportunity to avoid marrying women who had grown up in the Netherlands and who might therefore be more emancipated. It therefore became government policy to place as many obstacles in the way of such marriages as possible. Since 2006, potential partners of Dutch citizens who come from a number of non-eu countries must first do a language and integration examination at the Dutch embassy. They pay a fee of a few hundred euros. Then they take the exam on the computer. Once they get to the Netherlands, they then have to take a compulsory integration course that costs thousands of euros. These measures did indeed affect the intended target groups, but also tens of thousands more Dutch people who met the partner of their dreams while travelling abroad or on holiday and who now found it very difficult to bring them to the Netherlands. Politicians had little sympathy for such sad love stories. If you wanted so much to live with your chosen partner, you should go and live in their country, was their response.

The media also became less and less cautious about linking social problems to the composition of the population. They laid heavy emphasis on the fact that these young people had not become criminals because of their ethnic backgrounds but because they did no know how to make a life for themselves in a culture so different from their own. But generally, the blame was seen as laying not with society but with the people themselves. This reflected a new hardness that was also manifesting itself in other areas of social life, such as the extensive cutbacks in the system of social security benefits. People had to solve their problems themselves as best they could and – you might think – the large majority of those in minority groups were living quiet lives and not causing any difficulties at all.

In government circles, a new school of thought developed that was a radical departure from the established practice. The minorities had been 'smothered to death' and now found themselves in a position of dependency.

That was more or less the situation as Pim Fortuyn found it when he allowed himself to be put forward as the leader of the new party *Leefbaar Nederland*

In the first few months after the assassination of Pim Fortuyn, his home in Rotterdam was a place of pilgrimage. The sign says: 'Pim, you were right!'

(Habitable Netherlands). It was actually a merger of local political groupings who shared the idea that, at municipal level, it was unnecessary to have ideological affiliations to work for the common good.

Fortuyn immediately provided this party with its own ideology. He called for referenda and elected mayors. He railed at the bureaucracy, especially in the health-care sector. But, above all, he called for an immediate halt to immigration, otherwise the country would fall prey to Islam and all the libertine achievement of the previous decades would be lost. But the Leefbaar Nederland executive thought that this last appeal smacked of racism and Fortuyn was expelled from the party. He decided to go it alone, so that he could make his anti-Islam case even more forcefully than ever. Politicians from the established parties knew exactly what this meant: Fortuyn was a racist. He breathed new life into National-Socialist ideas. Fortuyn responded angrily to these allegations, claiming that he was being falsely accused and demonized. That was decisive. In the polls preceding the 2002 elections, the *Lijst Pim Fortuyn*, as his party was called for lack of a better name, achieved unprecedented popularity. Fortuyn behaved like a celebrity and his rising stare was reflected in votes. He made no secret of the fact that he saw himself as the next prime minister of the Netherlands.

Then – on 6 May 2002, a little after 6 in the evening – Pim Fortuyn was shot dead in the car park of the national broadcasting centre in Hilversum. His killer was caught almost immediately. His name was Volkert van der Graaf and he was a radical environmental activist. He considered Fortuyn a danger to the Netherlands who had to be stopped at all costs. He never gave a clear motive for his deed, not even when the judges gave him ample opportunity during his trial.

In the Dutch collective memory, the murder of Pim Fortuyn has a comparable status to 9/11. Fortuyn was the first politician to be assassinated in the Netherlands since William of Orange in 1584. Everyone in the country can tell you where they were and what they were doing at the moment they heard of the shooting. I was at home when the news came on the television. I immediately sent an email (again!) to all my associates telling them to switch on the television. Like most Dutch people, I spent the whole evening glued to the screen.

The third date on which an unforgettable tragedy occurred was 2 November 2004. On the morning of that day, film-maker Theo van Gogh was shot by Islamic activist Mohammed Bouyeri while he was on his bicycle. Van Gogh cried for mercy, but Bouyeri cut his throat with a butcher's knife. After that he used another knife to stick a letter to Van Gogh's chest. The letter was for member of parliament Ayaan Hirsi Ali. He then intended to die in a shoot-out with the police, but survived and was later sentenced to life imprisonment. Bouyeri stated that he had killed Van Gogh because of his religious beliefs and held no personal resentment against the film-maker. Van Gogh, he said, was condemned to die because he had insulted Allah.

Theo van Gogh was an avid supporter of Pim Fortuyn. He too feared a takeover by radical Muslims, who he referred to in his columns and on his website as

Ayaan Hirsi Ali gives instructions to the actress who plays in the documentary 'Submission', for which she wrote the script and which was directed by Theo van Gogh. In the film, the girl complains about abuse by her husband and family, while texts from the Koran are projected onto her near naked body. Since the film appeared, Hirsi Ali has been forced to live under permanent heavy security. Van Gogh was murdered by a Muslim fanatic.

geiteneukers (goatfuckers). But it was not that cost him his life. Bouyeri assassinated him because he had directed a short film entitled 'Submission'. He had made it at the request of Ayaan Hirsi Ali, who had provided the scenario: it was the lament of a woman who had been abused and oppressed on the basis of the Koran. She was shown half naked, with texts from the Koran on her bare skin.

The murder confirmed the worst fears of those who no longer trusted Islam and Muslims. Bouyeri proved to be a member of a network of radical and very young strict Muslims, some of whom had firearms. They discussed not only matters of faith, but possible terrorist activities, including the murders of Hirsi Ali and another parliamentarian, Geert Wilders, who also voiced fierce anti-Islamic opinions. A few days after the murder of Theo van Gogh, after siege of several hours, the police removed a number of supporters of Bouyeri from a house in The Hague. One officer was wounded when one of the suspects threw a grenade. In 2006 the members of this network went on trial. The secret service called the network the 'Hofstad Group' because it appeared to be based in The Hague, the *Hofstad* (Seat of the Royal Family). The members were given – in some cases, long – prison sentences.

Fortuyn openly and repeatedly called Islam a 'backward religion'. He said that the Koran and its rules were in opposition to Dutch norms and values. What those norms and values exactly were, he and his supporters were unable to say. But the call for respect for norms and values reflected a strong desire to return to the 1950s, when life was safe, there was still sufficient social control and, above all, there was as yet no multicultural society. The assassination of Fortuyn, and even more of Theo van Gogh, made it clear that you could not say exactly what you wanted in the Netherlands and get away with it. After Van Gogh was murdered, Ayaan Hirsi Ali and Geert Wilders were surrounded with a system of personal security that was comparable to the protection afforded to Salman Rushdie after the ayatollahs had declared a fatwa against him. The government has felt the need to maintain this level of security for years since both members of parliament are allegedly on the death list of extreme Muslim organizations. They cannot go anywhere without their guards, and can do nothing without careful planning in advance.

Ayaan Hirsi Ali is the daughter of a Somali clan-leader. She fled to the Netherlands in the early 1990s, partly to avoid an arranged marriage. She studied political science, and joined the Labour Party. When the VVD offered her a seat in parliament, she switched her allegiances.

In the meantime, she renounced her Islamic faith. She is now an avid atheist who criticizes Islam in all its forms. In her eyes, religion is an obstacle to progress and scientific development. In her eyes, Islam is also hostile to women. She has made her position on all of these issues very clear, including in 'Submission'.

She is not the only newcomer to experience such a transformation. Leiden lawyer Professor Afshan Elian, who was born and bred in Iran, shares Hirsi Ali's ideas. Both continually warn against the dangers of Islam. A third kindred spirit is Sylvain Ephimenco, the Dutch correspondent for the Parisian newspaper *Libération* and a controversial columnist in the Dutch daily *Trouw*. Ephimenco grew up in Algeria. Their remedies are radical and do not always fit in with the Dutch tradition. They advocate, for example, scrapping government support for special schools as this also opens the door to Islamic schools. But suggestions like this rudely step on the toes of many sacrosanct aspects of the pillarized society and the typically Dutch compromises they have produced. Do they, in doing so, exclude themselves from any serious discussion? Only very marginally: opinions like those of Hirsi Ali, Elian and Ephimenco are taken seriously. The same applies to their view of citizenship: in their eyes, integration means assimilating the Dutch lifestyle, complete with the contemporary spirit of libertinism and hedonism. Such views are very popular at the base of society. And many segments of the political establishment have been converted to the assimilation model in the hope of laying claim to Fortuyn's legacy. It has therefore become fashionable for many people in the Netherlands to claim that they are freethinkers and have distanced themselves from all that political correctness. They then declare the multicultural society bankrupt. It was a pipedream of the political leaders of the 'purple', centre-left governments of the 1990s, but a nightmare for normal people. They are confronted with a clash of cultures outside their front doors. It is time to stop giving minorities all that special treatment. They should go to work. They should learn Dutch. If they feel the need to walk around in a burqa, then they would perhaps be better off migrating to Iraq or Afghanistan. In the old days, these people add, they thought all these new cultures were wonderful, and they even voted for the green-left party GroenLinks. But reality has caught up with them. As far as it was still necessary, Pim Fortuyn open their eyes.

This is bad news for those who wish to combat racism or who do not share Huntington's ideas on the clash of cultures. The long-standing undercurrent of mistrusting immigrants – especially immigrants with an Islamic background – has risen to the surface and become part of the official discourse of media and politicians.

Ayaan Hirsi Ali felt impelled to leave the Netherlands. The neighbours in the apartment building in which she lived felt unsafe because she was a possible target for Islamic terrorists. She lost a lawsuit against those who wanted to force her to sell her apartment. It then appeared that, when she entered the Netherlands she had not told the truth about her flight from Somalia and had given a false name. Under a new and stricter law on Dutch citizenship, the government was entitled to withdraw her Dutch passport. Meanwhile Ayaan Hirsi Ali found a new job with a think tank in the United States and announced her intention to leave the post-Fortuyn Netherlands.

Anyone giving a false name when applying for naturalization is considered under the law of the land never to have acquired Dutch citizenship. Immigration minister Rita Verdonk, an ardent opponent of the policy of tolerance, applied the law without discrimination. She stated that Hirsi Ali had effectively disqualified herself from Dutch citizenship. Parliament was enraged and demanded that she rescind her decision and come up with a solution which would allow Hirsi Ali to retain her Dutch citizenship, preferably without others who had given false names being able to benefit from it too. She was, after all, a special case because she had to be permanently protected from Islamic terrorists.

Some weeks later Verdonk found an emergency solution, in which the 'name law' in the non-existent state of Somalia was an important factor. She demanded, however, that Hirsi Ali sign a letter in which she accepted blame for the entire affair. The former parliamentarian did so, but declared later the same day that she had signed under pressure.

That led to coalition party D66 withdrawing its support in minister Verdonk and the entire government. As a consequence, a new government was formed without D66, but with Verdonk, and the elections originally due in 2007 were brought forward to the autumn of 2006. Not much more was heard of Hirsi Ali – she was busy preparing her emigration to the USA.

The whole affair was like a tragic-comedy with strong satirical elements which showed that reality can sometimes be much stranger than the most bizarre imaginary scenarios: a minister wants to take away the citizenship of a member of parliament from her own party, while the latter is a symbol of the cultural assimilation she advocates so strongly. It was as though the Netherlands no longer knew which way to turn.

In 2005 rappers Lange Frans and Baas B. – strong supporters of the establishment and respected by the authorities and the upholders of law and order – a song about this new Netherlands, clearly inspired by *Vijftien miljoen mensen.*

> *Kom uit het land van Pim Fortuyn en Volkert van de G.*
> *Het land van Theo van Gogh en Mohammed B*
> *Kom uit het land van kroketten, frikadellen*
> *Die je tot aan de Spaanse kust kunt bestellen*
> *Kom uit het land waar Air Max nooit uit de mode raken*
> *Waar ze je kraken op het moment dat je het groot gaat maken*
> *Kom uit het land van rood-wit-blauw en de gouden leeuw*
> *Plunderen de wereld, noemen het de gouden eeuw*
> *Kom uit het land van wietplantages en fietsvierdaagses*
> *Het land waar je een junkie om een fiets kan vragen*
> *Het land dat kampioen werd in '88*
> *Het land van haring happen, dijken en grachten*
> *Kom uit het land van, het land van Lange Fransie*
> *Dit is het land waar ik thuis kom na vakantie*
>
> *Kom uit het land waar ik in 1982 geboren ben*
> *Waar ik me guldens aan de euro verloren ben*
> *Het land dat meedoet aan de oorlog in Irak*
> *Want ome Bush heeft Balkenende in zijn zak*
> *Het land van gierig zijn, een rondje geven is te duur*
> *De vette hap van de Febo trek je uit de muur*
> *Het land van rellen tussen Ajax en Feyenoord*
> *Maar wanneer Oranje speelt iedereen er bij hoort*
> *Het land van Johan Cruyff en Abe Lenstra*
> *Het legioen laat de leeuw niet in zijn hemd staan*
> *Het land waar we elke dag hopen op wat beter weer*
> *Die Piet Paulusma vertrouw ik voor geen meter meer*
> *Het land dat vrij is sinds '45*
> *Het land waar ik blijf, 'k vind het er heerlijk*
> *Eerlijk*
>
> *Ik kom uit het land waar je door heen rijdt in 3 uurtjes*
> *Met een ander dialect elke 10 minuutjes*
> *Kom uit het land waar op papier een plek voor iedereen is*
> *En xtc export nummer 1 is*
> *Kom uit het land waar Andre Hazes*
> *Over 100 jaar in elk café nog steeds de baas is*

Kom uit het land waar Peter, Gert-Jan, Raymond en Jutten
Frans, Bart en Ali de game runnen
Kom uit het land waar hiphop een kind van 30 is
En je mag zelf weer gaan vullen hoe vet dat is
Het land waar als je rijk wordt je zoveel inlevert
Dat je bij jezelf denkt, hoeveel zin heeft het?
Het land waar prostitutie en blowen mag
Het land van sinterklaas en Koninginnedag
Dit is het land waar ik verloren heb, bedrogen ben
Kom uit het land waar ik geboren en getogen ben
Kom uit het land met de meeste culturen per vierkante meter
Maar men is bang om bij de buren te gaan eten
En integratie is een schitterend woord
Maar shit is fucking bitter wanneer niemand het hoort
Ik deel mijn land met Turken en Marokkanen,
Antilianen, Molukkers en Surinamers
Het land waar we samen veels te veel opkroppen
En wereldwijd gerepresent zijn door Harry Potter
Het land waar apartheid, internationaal
het meest bekende woord is uit de Nederlandse taal
Kom uit het land wat tikt als een tijdbom
Het land dat eet om zes uur en ook nog eens op tijd komt
Dit is het land waar ik zal overwinnen aan het einde
Totdat je deze meezingt aan de ArenA-lijnen
En tot die tijd zal ik schijnen ik heb mijn hart verpand
Dit is voor Nederland, Baas B, Lange Frans

I come from the land of Pim Fortuyn and Volkert van der G.[5]
The land of Theo van Gogh[6] and of Mohammed B.[7]
The land of croquettes and frikadellen.
Which you can order right down to the Spanish coast.
I come from the land where Air Max is always in fashion.
Where they cut you back just as you're about to hit the big time
I come from the land of red-white-blue and the golden lion.
Which looted the world and called it the golden age
I come from the land of weed plantations and cycling marathons
The land where you can ask a junkie for a bike
The land that was European champion in 1988
The land of herring, dikes and canals
I come from the land, the land of Lange Fransie.
The land I come home to when I come back from holiday

I come from the land where I was born in 1982
Where I lost my guilders to the euro
The land that's taking part in the war in Iraq
Cause Uncle George has Balkenende[8] in his pocket
The land where everyone's far too stingy
To buy drinks all round when they're in the bar
Where you pull snacks out of the wall at the Febo[9]
The land of street fights between Feyenoord and Ajax
But where we're all best mates when Holland is playing
The land of Johan Cruyff and Abe Lenstra[10]
 Where the orange army makes sure the lion doesn't stand alone
The land where we hope for better weather every day
I don't trust that Piet Paulusma[11] anymore.
The land that's been free since 1945
The land where I'll stay, because I love it
I really do

I come from the land you can drive through in three hours
With a different dialect every 10 minutes
Where on paper there's a place for everyone
And xtc is the number one export
I come from the land where Andre Hazes[12]
Will still be the boss in every bar in a 100 years time
From the land where Peter, Gert-Jan, Raymond and Jutten
Frans, Bart and Ali B run the game

5 The radical environmental activist Volkert van der Graaf assassinated Pim Fortuyn in 2002, because he considered him a threat to the Netherlands. He was sentenced to 20 years in prison.

6 Film and televison-maker, opinion-maker and journalist. Called radical Islam a danger to democracy, made the short film 'Submission' on the basis of a scenario by Ayaan Hirsi Ali. Many Muslims considered the film blasphemous.

7 Mohammed Bouyeri, born and bred in Amsterdam and a devout fundamentalist Muslim of Moroccan (Berber) origin. He killed Theo van Gogh because of his film 'Submission' and used a knife to pin a letter on his chest containing threats to Hirsi Ali. Refused to be defended in court and stated that he would do the same thing again because those who insulted Islam deserved to die. He is now serving a life sentence, after being found guilty on the grounds of the deed and the motive.

8 Professor Jan Peter Balkenende, professor of Christian social thought at the *Vrije Universiteit. Amsterdam*, CDA politician, and prime minister in coalition governments with the libeal VVD.

9 A chain of snack bars famed for the quality of its croquettes.

10 The Johan Cruyff of the 1950s, an equally great footballer.

11 Well-known television weatherman.

12 Singer of sentimental Dutch songs, died in 2004 of the consequences of an unhealthy lifestyle. His 'Zij gelooft in mij' (She believes in me) and 'Kleine jongen' (Little boy) are unforgettable.

From the land where hip hop is a child of 30
And you can feel for yourself how cool that is
The land where, once you're rich you have to give so much away
That you ask yourself what the point is
The land where prostitution and smoking dope is allowed
The land of *Sinterklaas* and *Koninginnendag*
This is the land where I was lost and deceived
The land where I was born and bred
I come from the land with the most cultures per square metre
But where people are afraid to have dinner with their neighbours
And integration is beautiful word
I share my land with Turks and Moroccans
Antilleans, Moluccans and Surinamese
The land where we bottle things op too much
And are represented worldwide by Harry Potter[13]
The land where apartheid
Is the best known Dutch word around the world
I come from the land that is ticking like a time-bomb
The land that eats at six o'clock and gets everywhere on time
This is the land where I will win in the end
Until you'll be singing this song in the Arena
Until that time, I'll keep on shining
I've given my heart
This is for my land, Baas B, Lange Frans

This rap may portray the sharper side of life in the new century, the problems and challenges that are facing my country, but it is by no means all gloom and doom. On one Saturday every summer, the Coolsingel in Rotterdam is transformed into a tropical boulevard. The weather usually enters into the spirit of things and the temperature rises way above the twenty degree mark. An enormous crowd stands expectantly along the side of the road. They are waiting for the Antillean carnival. Traditionally, the high point of the festivities takes place in front of the city hall. The mayor stands up on the balcony, his chain of office around his neck, ready to declare the parade officially open.

The parade varies – it is different every year – between one and a half and two kilometres long. An enormous convoy of NedLloyd trucks carries the cream of Dutch salsa, merengue and kaseko bands through the streets of the city. In between the trucks, dance groups give sparkling performances, usually exotic dances from their home countries, far away across the sea. There are also a lot of traditional carnival floats – most with a theme and some of them with a beauty queen waving to the crowd. In recent years, African groups have also taken part in the procession.

---

13 Nickname for prime minister Balkenende. Funny the first couple of times you hear it.

The multicultural dream becomes a reality once a year on the last Saturday of July: the Antillean Summer Carnival in Rotterdam.

The Rotterdam Summer Carnival is held on the last Saturday in July. No one knows how they do it, but the sun always shines. Low sky or not. And on that day, I see a Netherlands that I am proud to call mine.

The Rotterdam Summer Carnival and the Netherlands of Lange Frans are two sides of the same coin. So what are we to think? Perhaps the best answer to that question was provided by a poet from Brabant. He wrote the following words as long ago as 1560, but they are still meaningful today:

> *Half ghoet/half quaet*
> *Half vlas/half draet*
> *Half dicht/half leck*
> *Half wijs/half geck*
> *Half eer/half schande*
> *Is de Manier van den lande*

> Half good and half evil
> Half flax and half thread,
> Half closed and half agape
> Half wise and half bemused
> Half in honour and half in disgrace
> That is the Way of the Land.

6th revised edition: November 2006

Han van der Horst is a historian and publicist.
He is a staff member of the Department for International Marketing & Communication of the Nuffic, the Netherlands Organization for International Cooperation in Higher Education.

Translation: Andy Brown
Graphic design: Manifesta Rotterdam (Ad van der Kouwe)
Photography: ANP, Freek van Arkel, Ben Deiman, Tineke Dijkstra,
Fotoarchief Spaarnestad, Marco de Nood, Karel Tomeï, Thijs Tuurenhout
Photography cover: Tineke Dijkstra
Print: Hoontetijl, Utrecht

www.scriptum.nl
www.hollandbooks.nl
www.xpat.nl

ISBN 978-905594-405-7